English Idioms

English Idioms

Jennifer Seidl
W. McMordie

A fifth edition of
English Idioms and How to Use Them

Oxford University Press

Oxford University Press,
Walton Street, Oxford OX2 6DP

Oxford New York
Athens Auckland Bangkok Bombay
Calcutta Cape Town Dar es Salaam Delhi
Florence Hong Kong Istanbul Karachi
Kuala Lumpur Madras Madrid Melbourne
Mexico City Nairobi Paris Singapore
Taipei Tokyo Toronto

and associated companies in
Berlin Ibadan

Oxford and *Oxford English* are
trade marks of Oxford University Press.

ISBN 0 19 432775 2 (paperback)
ISBN 0 19 432774 4 (hardback)

First Oxford edition by W. McMordie 1909
Second edition 1913 (reprinted 21 times)
Third edition revised by R.C. Goffin 1954
(reprinted 17 times)
Fourth edition by Jennifer Seidl 1978 (reprinted 10 times)
Fifth edition 1988
Eighth impression 1996

© Oxford University Press 1978, 1988

Phototypeset in 9½/10½pt Ehrhardt
by Tradespools Ltd, Frome, Somerset
Printed in Hong Kong

Contents

Introduction

About this book

Since its first publication by Oxford University Press in 1909 *English Idioms* has proved its usefulness through four editions. This new fifth edition includes important changes which have taken place in the English language in recent years. It is a modern, up-dated survey of idioms in wide current use in Britain. It also includes a number of idioms of American origin which have been adopted by British speakers. Idioms marked (US) or (mainly US) are not generally used in Britain. Idioms marked (GB) are used in British English only.

Level

The book is intended primarily for advanced foreign learners of English, but upper intermediate students should benefit too. Teachers of English will also find it useful.

Organization

The book is divided into ten chapters. Each chapter deals with various key words (e.g. high-frequency adjectives or nouns, numbers, colours) or with a key structure (e.g. noun phrases, phrasal verbs, phrases with prepositions). The contents of each chapter are arranged alphabetically for easy reference. The contents list shows in detail where the various types of idiom are to be found and a full index makes the book particularly user-friendly.

How to use the book

The book can be used as a reference book for finding out the meaning of an idiom. More important, it can be used for systematic learning of groups of idioms both in and out of the classroom. This is a unique feature of *English Idioms*. Almost all idioms are accompanied by examples of typical use. Where two examples are given they are separated by this symbol □.

When looking for an idiom, see if it contains one of the key words (e.g. **bad, end, all, black, two, arm, day**, etc.). All the key words are listed separately in the contents list and are indexed at the back of the book. If the idiom contains two key words, e.g. the **end** of the **line**, you will find it under the first key word, i.e. under **end**. If there is no key word in the idiom, look at its structure. For example, **a raw deal** or **a wet blanket** are listed under the structure *Adjective + noun* in chapter 3; **do someone out of something, hit on something, put in for something** are listed under *Phrasal verbs* in chapter 6.

Use of the stress mark(')

Most idioms are used in speech just like any other phrase or sentence, i.e. the word with the main stress is the last noun (not pronoun), verb (not auxiliary), adjective or adverb. For example, in the idioms **a rough ride, take the biscuit** and **run for it**, the words **ride, biscuit** and **run** are stressed. Idioms which have an unusual or unpredictable stress are marked with the stress mark(').

Use of / and ( )

The slant mark / is used to show alternative possibilities in idioms. For example, **break fresh/new ground** can be used in either of the forms **break fresh ground, break new ground.**

The brackets ( ) are used to show optional words. For example, in **(all) at sea** both the forms **all at sea** and **at sea** can be used.

Sometimes an idiom is given with both a slant and brackets. For example, **not (so/too) bad** means that any of the forms **not bad, not so bad, not too bad** can be used.

Exercises

English Idioms: Exercises on Idioms, which is a revised edition of *Idioms in Practice* (1982), contains exercises on all the types of idioms presented in this reference volume. A second book of exercises, *English Idioms: Exercises on Phrasal Verbs*, which deals very fully with phrasal verbs alone, is also available. Both books may be used alongside *English Idioms* or on their own.

1 Idioms in perspective

We often read the phrase 'language is a living thing', but most of us do not stop to think what it really means. Living things grow and change, so does language. This chapter takes a look at *how* and *why*.

Since the general tendencies of present-day English are towards more idiomatic usage, it is important that this book on idioms should show the learner how the language is developing. Idioms are not a *separate* part of the language, which one can choose either to use or to omit; they form an *essential* part of the vocabulary of English. A description of how the vocabulary of the language is growing and changing will help to place idioms in perspective.

Growth and change in English vocabulary

The vocabulary of a language grows continually with new developments in knowledge. New ideas need new labels to name them. Without new labels, communication of these new ideas would be impossible. Many new words come from the English of special subjects such as computer sciences, sociology, advertising, politics and economics.

Computer technology has given birth to *software, diskette, high-tech, on-line, printout, modem, computer-literate, to format, to interface, to log on,* to mention only a few. The technology of nuclear power has given us interesting noun compounds such as *meltdown* or *reactor spent-fuel reprocessing plant.* From economics we have *wage-freeze, price-freeze, stagflation* (see also below). The field of advertising has given us *soft sell* and *hard sell* (subtle and aggressive sales techniques), *hype* (intensive, exaggerated sales promotion/publicity/marketing) and the corresponding verb *to hype.*

Words which already exist can take on an additional meaning in a special context. For example, the field of industrial relations has given new meaning to the verbs *to walk out, to lock out, to sit in, to go slow.* The noun forms *walk-out, lock-out, sit-in* and *go-slow* are used almost exclusively in this context. The words *leak, spill* and *waste* are typically used in the context of the technology of nuclear power, as well as in everyday contexts. In computer jargon, the verb *to hack* and the nouns *memory, drive* and *hardware* have taken on new meanings. The word *hard* as used for example in *hard copy* has taken on the specialized meaning 'readable by the eye', i.e. not only machine-readable output as on magnetic tape.

American English is particularly flexible and creates new words by changing a word's grammatical function, e.g. verb to noun, as in *a set-up, a buy-out, a screw-up, a trade-off, a work-out, a phone-in, a shoot-out.* Nouns are made into verbs, as in *to access, to window* (computer jargon), *to microwave, to rubber-stamp, to scapegoat, to colour-match, to air-freight, to headline.* Adjectives are made into verbs, as in *to soundproof, to streamline, to skidproof, to net* (i.e. to bring in a net profit), *to temp* (i.e. to do temporary work). British English quickly absorbs such American forms. All these changes are short cuts in language, as they make the form of words shorter and more direct, and for that reason are becoming increasingly popular.

Another popular short cut joins words together to form one adjective instead of a long phrase. Here are a few typical ones: *a round-the-clock service*, instead of 'a service which is offered around the clock (i.e. for 24 hours a day)', *a same-day service, on-the-job training, low-income groups, a non-profit-making organization.*

New words are made by adding endings such as *-ize, -ization* to adjectives or nouns. This indicates a process: *to decimalize, to containerize, to computerize, to departmentalize; computerization* etc.

Prefixes such as *mini-, maxi-, super-, micro-, mega-, hyper-* indicate the quantity or quality of something in the shortest possible way. Here are some well-established examples: *mini-diskette, superchip, micro-teaching, micro-surgery, megastar, megachip, hypermarket, hypersonic.*

New words are made by combining parts of two existing words: *smog* (smoke + fog), *newscast* (news + broadcast), *flexitime* (flexible + time), *stagflation* (stagnant + inflation). Here are some typical combinations from American English, which uses more than British English:
brunch (breakfast + lunch), *motel* (motorist + hotel),
laundromat (laundry + automat), *medicare* (medical + care),
cablegram (cable + telegram), *workaholic* (work + alcoholic),
gasohol (gasoline + alcohol).

Changing attitudes to language

Educated usage has become much more flexible and tolerant about what is considered to be correct or acceptable. Such changes of attitude can be observed in several parts of grammar, including case, number and tense.

The attitude of users towards style has also become more flexible. Several words which were considered to be *slang* in the past have gradually been up-graded in status and are now often considered *informal* or *colloquial*. Much of what was labelled *informal* in the past is now considered *neutral* in style. This is partly due to the spread in the use of *taboo words* by educated speakers. Several such words give much less offence than in the past and are widely used in both American and British television productions.

Different aspects of the idiom

1 *What is an idiom?*

It is important to realize that idioms are not only colloquial expressions, as many people believe. They appear in formal style and in slang, in poetry, in the language of Shakespeare and the Bible. What then is an idiom? An idiom can be defined as a number of words which, when taken together, have a different meaning from the individual meanings of each word.

2 *Kinds of idioms*

Idioms take many different forms or structures. An idiom can have a regular structure, an irregular or even a grammatically incorrect structure. The clarity of meaning is not dependent on the 'grammatical correctness'. A few examples will illustrate this:

1 Form irregular, meaning clear, as in *give someone to understand, do someone proud, do the dirty on someone.*
2 Form regular, meaning unclear, as in *have a bee in one's bonnet, cut no ice, bring the house down.*
3 Form irregular, meaning unclear, as in *be at large, go great guns, be at daggers drawn.*

We find, in fact, that most idioms belong to the second group, where the form is regular but the meaning unclear. However, even in this group some idioms are clearer than others. For example, the meaning of *to give someone the green light* can be guessed as 'to give someone permission to start'. Others are too difficult to guess because they have no association with the original meaning of the individual words. Such examples are: *to tell someone where to get off, to carry the can, to drop a brick, to call the shots.*

Several *fixed idioms* cannot be changed in any part (except the tense of the verb). For example, *to paint the town red, to fight shy of something, to get down to business.* Others allow a different number of variants. For example, *to know one's onions/stuff, a hard/tough nut to crack, to take/have/enjoy forty winks, to come to a bad/nasty/sticky/no good/untimely end.*

Where and when to use idioms

One of the main difficulties for learners is knowing in which situations it is correct to use an idiom, i.e. the level of style. The book gives help with labels such as *informal, slang, taboo* and *US.* Unmarked idioms are neutral and may be used in most situations. Informal idioms are used in everyday spoken English and in personal letters. Learners are advised to avoid using slang and taboo expressions until their mastery of the language is complete. Several examples are, however, included for reference purposes.

A further difficulty is knowing whether an idiom is natural or appropriate in a certain situation. Examples of typical use in particular situations, such as in business contexts, are given and these should be studied carefully.

Another difficulty is that of fixed idioms and idioms with variants. It is most important to be exact in one's use of fixed idioms, as an inaccurate idiom may mean nothing to a native speaker. Above all, remember that it is extremely unwise to translate idioms into or from one's native language. One may be lucky that the two languages have the same form and vocabulary, but in most cases the result will be utterly bewildering to the English native speaker – and possibly highly amusing.

2 Key words with idiomatic uses

Adjectives and adverbs

bad

bad blood unfriendliness or enmity between two people or families. *There's been bad blood between the two brothers ever since their father's death. He left more to one son than to the other.*

bad language swear words or taboo words. *No bad language in the classroom! If you must swear, save it until you're outside!*

a bad lot (informal) a person with bad personal qualities, someone who is dishonest etc. *I'm so glad that Jerry has stopped going about with Mike Parsons. I heard that he had been in prison for stealing. In my opinion, he's a bad lot.*

bad news a person, often with criminal tendencies, who brings trouble to others. *Take care, Lucy! That young man is bad news.*

bad news travels fast (saying) bad news is spread more quickly than good news. *'My son flew to Cairo last week and I haven't heard from him yet.' 'He'll be fine, because bad news travels fast.'*

a bad patch a period of difficulty or unhappiness; problems. *All right, I admit that our marriage is going through a bad patch, but it isn't the first time, and we're still together.*

a bad workman always blames his tools (saying) an unskilled, inefficient person puts the blame for his mistakes on the materials, tools, machine etc. he is using. *'This knife isn't sharp enough to carve the meat properly.' 'It's not the knife that's the problem – a bad workman always blames his tools.'*

be in someone's bad books be out of favour with someone. *If you don't get the essay finished by tomorrow, you'll be in your teacher's bad books again.*

come to a bad end become a criminal, have to go to prison, suffer disgrace. Said of someone who leads a wild life and perhaps has criminal tendencies. *Harry was expelled from school for stealing and now he's been sacked from his very first job. He'll come to a bad end if he's not careful.*

give someone/have a bad/hard time treat someone badly or unfairly, make someone suffer/be treated badly or unfairly, suffer. *In my first job I had a very difficult boss who gave me a really bad time.*

give something up as a bad job stop trying to do something because it seems very unlikely to succeed. *Jonathan started learning German three times, but he didn't make much progress. So now he's given it up as a bad job.*

go from bad to worse deteriorate still further. *Business is going from bad to worse – we may have to close down.*

in a bad way (informal) in a poor condition/state of mental or physical health. *'How's your father after his heart attack?' 'In a bad way, actually. Making very little progress.'*

(it's/that's) too bad it's a pity/unfortunate. *It's too bad that you can't come to Peter's twenty-first birthday party. We'll miss you.*

make the best of a bad job do the best one can in a difficult or unfortunate position, regard a problem optimistically. *Andrew didn't get a place at university, so he can't study maths after all. He's decided to make the best of a bad job and go into banking.*

not (so/too) bad (informal) relatively good, satisfactory. *'Hello, Sue! How was the exam?' 'Oh, not too bad, thanks.'*

big

be/get into/hit the 'big time (informal) be making a lot of money in business, often in the entertainment business; become famous. *Liz is into the big time now – her latest album's been a great success in the States.*

a/the big cheese (informal) the most important person of a group; someone who thinks he is the most important. *Just because Dad's been promoted and is a big cheese at work, he seems to think he can boss us around at home, too.*

big deal! (informal) terrific! great! (ironical). Said when one is not impressed/pleased etc. by something. *'I got the job! I got the job!' 'Big deal! You were the only applicant, weren't you?'*

a big fish in a little/small pond someone who is important only in a small unit, group, community, company etc. *Bob prefers to be a big fish in a little pond, so he works for a small company with only fifty employees.*

a big hit something/someone very popular with others. *By the way, your new flat is a big hit with your parents. They think it's perfect for you.*

big league (informal) something to be taken seriously because it's important, dangerous, involves a lot of money etc. *You mustn't get involved in that, David. It's big league. Those men are criminals.*

a 'big mouth (informal) someone who boasts, exaggerates, makes promises he doesn't keep etc. *'Graham says he has an uncle with a villa in Cannes and he'll take me there one day.' 'Well, don't believe it. He's just a big mouth.'* Note also: **have ~**.

a 'big noise/shot (informal) an important person with influence (implies arrogance, self-importance). *There's some big noise coming up from headquarters tomorrow, so we'll have to get things tidied up in here.*

big of someone (informal) generous or kind of someone. (Often said ironically because one thinks the opposite.) *'Uncle Harold sent me fifty pounds for my birthday.' 'That's big of him – considering he's a millionaire.'*

big talk/words boastful, empty talk. *I heard Mark telling Alex that he couldn't decide whether to buy a Jaguar or a Mercedes – all big talk, I'm sure. He'll keep his Ford Fiesta, I bet.*

in a big way on a large scale. *Carol and Tony have invited over a hundred guests to their silver wedding party. They always do things in a big way.*

give someone a big hand applaud someone with enthusiasm. *George acted very well in the drama group's performance of An Inspector Calls. He was given a big hand every night.*

make it big (slang) be very successful, usually in business. Make a name for oneself, money etc. *His dream was to make it big in television – but it's still just a dream.*

too big for one's boots conceited, arrogant, feeling and acting in a superior way. *Since Douglas got his novel published he's been altogether too big for his boots. It's time someone taught him a lesson.*

dead

be dead a'gainst something/someone be completely opposed to something/someone. *I am dead against camping holidays. I can never sleep comfortably in a tent.*

come to a dead halt come to a complete stop (e.g. a vehicle). *The lorry came to a dead halt just in front of the fallen child.* Note also: **stop dead.** *We almost had an accident this morning. A big van pulled out in front of our car and stopped dead without giving a signal.*

cut someone dead ignore someone completely, treat someone as though one does not know him. *What's wrong with Linda? She cut me dead in the bank this morning.*

dead ahead/in front in a position exactly ahead. *We came out of the wood and found the village we were looking for dead ahead of us.*

dead and buried/gone long forgotten, of the past. *No one ever talks about Uncle Joe's prison sentence any more. That's all dead and buried now.*

dead beat/tired (informal) physically exhausted after hard work. *You ought to have an early night – you look dead beat!*

a dead cert (slang)/**certainty** something that is very sure, will certainly happen; someone who will certainly achieve a target, win etc. *'Who do you think will win the Cup?' 'Leeds United – it's a dead cert.'*

dead drunk extremely drunk. *I've never seen Simon in such a state. He was dead drunk.*

dead easy very easy. *I expected the maths test to be dead easy, but I couldn't do a single question.*

a dead end 1 a road that does not lead anywhere. *We took the first turning after the church, but the road was unfortunately a dead end that only led to a field.* 2 a point or stage where no further progress can be made. Note: **a dead end job** is a job without prospects or opportunities for the future. *Peter feels that he's in a dead end job with his present firm. He's thinking of making a fresh start as a freelance journalist.*

a dead heat result of a race or competition in which two competitors finish at the same time or with the same score. *In the European Song Contest there was a dead heat for first place, so there were two winners this year.*

a dead loss (informal) someone/something that is of no use/help to anyone in a certain matter or with a certain job etc. *It's no use asking Jack. He's a dead loss at maths.*

dead on time   exactly on time, punctual. *The train arrived dead on time, so we didn't have to wait long on the platform.*

deadpan   expressionless, dull, showing no emotion (e.g. on one's face.) *Marsden's face is always so deadpan. I never know whether he's in a good mood or a bad one.*

dead right   (informal) exactly right. *Remember you told me that John was friendly with Alison Miller and I didn't believe you? Well, you were dead right – I saw them together yesterday.*

a dead silence   a total, unbroken silence. *There was a dead silence in the room as the solicitor opened the envelope and prepared to read Uncle John's last will and testament.*

dead slow   hardly moving, almost stopped. *Unfortunately, I got stuck on the inside lane of the motorway and the traffic was dead slow for about fifteen miles.*

dead to the world   in a deep sleep. *'I'll whisper. I don't want to wake the children.' 'Oh, that's okay. They've been dead to the world for over an hour.'*

a dead weight   very heavy. *I can't possibly carry this suitcase. It's a dead weight.*

'dead wood   someone/something that is no longer needed or useful or is out of date. *It's time we brought these files up to date. We'll start by throwing out all the dead wood.*

flog a dead horse   (informal) waste one's time/efforts. *I've been showing the new clerk how to use the computer but it's like flogging a dead horse. He simply can't remember which keys to press.*

make a dead set at someone   try deliberately to attack someone (with words, angry looks etc.); make an obvious attempt to interest someone of the opposite sex. *Robert met a girl at Joe's party and made a dead set at her – without much luck, according to Joe.*

over my dead body!   (informal) used to state that the speaker is very much against something, will not agree to/allow something, that something will not happen if he can prevent it. *'I'm going on holiday with three other boys this year, Dad.' 'Over my dead body! You're coming on holiday with us.'*

wouldn't be seen dead (doing something etc.)   (informal) would not do something because one considers it unacceptable. (Used to express strong dislike.) *What a terrible colour! I wouldn't be seen dead in it.* □ *Liz won't accept Barry's invitation to the disco. She doesn't like him – says she wouldn't be seen dead with him.*

flat

... and that's flat!   (informal) and that is my last word on the matter. (Used to end an argument or after giving an order.) *You will go to Aunt Maud's with us for the weekend – and that's flat!*

fall flat   (a plan/project etc.) not materialize, fail to develop. *We had plans to go to Canada to visit friends, but they fell flat when father had to go into hospital.*

a flat battery a battery that must be re-charged. *There's no wonder the engine won't start. You've got a flat battery.*

a flat denial/refusal etc. an absolute, definite denial etc. *We made him a good offer, but he gave us a flat refusal.*

flat out with all one's powers or energy; as much or as quickly as possible (with **go/run/race/work** etc.). *I've been working flat out all day trying to get the last chapter of the book finished.*

a flat tyre a tyre with no air in it, or not enough. *Sorry we're late. We had a flat tyre on the way here.*

in two minutes etc. flat (informal) in no more than two minutes etc. (Expresses surprise at the short time needed or emphasizes that little time will be needed.) *When I told the children we were going to the park, they were ready in ten seconds flat.*

knock someone flat 1 knock someone off his feet with a blow. *This man started making trouble in the pub. Joe was very patient at first, but when he insulted Joe's wife, Joe stood up and knocked him flat.* 2 shock/stun someone with a mental blow. *The dreadful news knocked us flat.*

tell someone flat tell someone in a very positive and definite manner. *She told him flat that she had no intention of lending him any money.*

good

a good deal often, a lot. *He travelled in India a good deal when he was young.*

a good few/many (+ plural noun) quite a lot, several. *There were a good few people at the concert last night, more than we had expected.*

a good way quite a long way. *'How far is Wells from here?' 'Well, it's a good way, actually. It'll take you two hours.'*

as good as almost certain(ly), for all practical purposes. *Mike as good as knows that he has passed his exam. He saw his professor and he gave him a broad smile and a wink.*

as good as gold said of a well-behaved child. *Mary is as good as gold most of the time.*

as good as one's word true to one's promise, absolutely reliable. *Steve is as good as his word. If he said he'd help you, then he will.*

be (all) to the good be an additional advantage. *'I'm considering taking a secretarial course after my degree.' 'I think you're very wise. It would be all to the good.'*

be for one's own good be for one's own advantage or benefit. *We bring our son up rather strictly, I suppose, and he doesn't always see that it's for his own good.*

be good for (+ noun) have the necessary qualities, energy, ability etc. to provide something or to survive. *'Is your old car still running?' 'Oh, yes. It's good for another ten thousand miles yet.'*

be in good company be in the same situation as someone else/others. (Said to encourage, comfort or agree about something.) *'I failed my driving test yesterday.' 'Oh well, you're in good company – so did I last week.'*

be in someone's good books be in favour with someone. *Joanna has been in her teacher's good books since she started taking school more seriously and working hard.*

be on to a good thing (informal) have found a pleasant, financially advantageous occupation. *Mrs Bellamy pays Frank generously for the few jobs he does in her garden. Frank knows when he's on to a good thing.*

do someone good help/be good for someone's health, state of mind etc. *Why don't you take a short holiday? It would do you good.*

do someone a good turn do someone a favour in order to help him. *I like Henry. Just after the war he did me a really good turn and I've never forgotten it.*

for good forever, permanently. *Rosalind's gone to Canada – for good. She's not coming back.*

give (someone) as good as one gets retaliate, fight back, act towards someone in the same way as he acted towards you. *Sheila said a woman in the accounts department is always rude to her, but knowing Sheila I'm sure she gives her as good as she gets.*

give someone a good 'talking-to/telling-'off criticize someone vigorously. *A customer complained about one of the waiters, so the manageress came and gave him a good talking-to.*

good for nothing (a person) having no good qualities; lazy, unreliable, worthless etc. Note also: **a 'good for nothing.** *I've never liked Charles. He's a good for nothing.*

good God! a strong expression of surprise (often unpleasant), shock or amazement. *Good God! He's dead.*

good gracious/heavens/Lord! an expression of surprise. *Good heavens! It's John. He's two days early.*

good grief! an expression of dismay or displeasure. *Good grief! You'll never pass any exams if you can't do better work than this.*

good riddance! (informal) said to show relief when one gets rid of an unpleasant person or something unwanted, or when one completes a tiresome job of work etc. *Thank goodness that's finished – and good riddance! I've never had such a tricky report to write.*

have a good time enjoy oneself. *I wasn't looking forward to the staff outing, but we all had a really good time.*

have had a good innings have lived a long time; have enjoyed something pleasant for a long period, e.g. influence, success, fame. *If Paul isn't re-elected Chairman, he can't complain. After twelve years he's had a good innings.*

hold good continue to be true or valid (e.g. a promise, an offer). *If your invitation still holds good, I'd like to visit you this summer with my family.*

in good time early, with plenty of time to spare. *We got to the theatre in good time, so we were able to have a sandwich before the play began.*

it's a good job (that...) it is lucky, it is a good thing that... *It's a good job that the flight was an hour late or we would have missed it.*

it's no/not much good doing something there is no use/value in doing something. *It's no good phoning Peter. He's in Spain.*

make good do well; be successful in getting a good job, securing one's future etc. *Martin is a very ambitious young man. He's determined to make good, and I'm sure he will.*

make good time (usually in a vehicle) progress with a journey faster than expected. *It was pretty quiet on the motorway, so we made good time and arrived an hour early.*

throw good money after bad lose more money in an attempt to compensate for a loss. *Douglas lost money on some foreign investments, so I suggested a good investment scheme in this country. But he said that he wasn't prepared to throw good money after bad.*

while the going's good as long as the situation is favourable. Said when the speaker expects the situation to be unfavourable in the future. *I haven't got a lot of work to do at the moment, so I'm taking a few days' holiday while the going's good.*

hard

be hard hit be severely affected by something unpleasant. *The universities have been hard hit by the government cuts in spending.*

be hard on someone treat someone in a strict, harsh manner. *I think Bill is being unnecessarily hard on his son. He won't allow him any of the freedoms and pleasures that other boys of his age have.*

be hard pressed (to do something) have difficulty doing something. *'Could you name all the states of the USA?' 'Well, I'd be hard pressed to do it without preparation.'*

be hard to please said of a person who is critical or who sets unusually high standards. *Our new teacher sets terrifically high standards and is very hard to please.*

be hard 'up be short of money. *Come on, John. If you're hard up again, I'll pay for lunch.*

(do something) the hard way by the most difficult or most unpleasant method. *Nicole has a French mother, so she's bilingual. I learnt French the hard way – years of irregular verbs at school!*

drive a hard bargain be tough in business dealings and consider only one's own advantages, profits etc., often unfairly. *'I think I can persuade Hawkins to accept our terms.' 'Don't be too sure. He drives a very hard bargain.'*

a hard and fast rule a rule that applies without exception. *Is the addition of '-s' in the third person singular present tense a hard and fast rule?*

hard cash notes and coins, not a cheque or credit card. *I've heard that Palmer pays all his bills in hard cash, even if they're for thousands of pounds.*

hard of hearing partly deaf. *You'll have to speak up. Father's rather hard of hearing.*

a hard 'luck story an unhappy story (judged to be untrue) told by someone who wants money, sympathy or help. *A man came to the door*

*wanting money. He said he was out of work and his wife and children were ill.
A real hard luck story.*

a hard/tough nut to crack a difficult problem to overcome; a difficult
person to deal with. *Is it a design fault that we can correct or not? Whatever is
wrong, it's going to be a hard nut to crack.*

the 'hard stuff (informal) a drink high in alcoholic content, e.g. vodka.
Just a glass of white wine for me, please. No spirits – I can't take the hard stuff.

have a hard 'time (of it) experience a difficult or unpleasant time. *Many
families had a hard time of it during the war.*

play hard to 'get pretend to be less interested in someone/something
than one really is. *'David hasn't said definitely whether he'll let us show his
paintings at the exhibition.' 'Oh, playing hard to get, is he?'*

take a hard 'line be uncompromising, not give in. *The government has
taken a very hard line against strikers over the past few years.*

high

be for the 'high jump (informal) be liable to be punished, criticized etc.
severely. *I shall be for the high jump if I make a mess of these export order
forms again.*

be/get high (on something) be/get high spirited as a result of the
influence of alcohol, drugs etc. *Grandad won't drink Coke. He seems to
think he'll get high on it.*

be in high spirits be in a lively, cheerful mood. *'You're in high spirits
today.' 'Yes, I've just had some very good news.'*

be/get on one's high horse behave in an arrogant manner. *Patrick's been
on his high horse ever since he won a scholarship to Oxford.*

be riding high be very successful in one's career, especially in the eyes of
others. *Diana's riding high at the moment. She's just been promoted and is
expected to be made head of department within the year.*

high and dry abandoned, ignored, isolated. *The car broke down, miles away
from anywhere. A van took Barry to the next village to get help, so I was left
high and dry until he got back.*

a high flyer a person who is very ambitious in his career wishes/plans.
*Rosemary is trying for a job in the diplomatic service – but then she always was
a high flyer.*

high and low everywhere possible (with **look, search**). *Where on earth can
the keys be? I've searched high and low for them!*

high and mighty behaving in a superior, arrogant manner. *Why is Roger
so arrogant these days? What's he got to be so high and mighty about?*

in high places (friends, people) in top-level positions in government and
administration; people of influence and power. *'I hear Charles is in a spot
of trouble with a drunken driving charge.' 'Yes, but he'll be all right. He has
friends in high places.'*

it's high time (one did something) said when something must be done
without more delay. *If the examination's next week, it's high time you started
doing some work.*

with a high hand, in a high-handed fashion/manner in an arrogant fashion, without consideration for the wishes or opinions of others. *Jan deals with everyone's complaints with a very high hand. Some customers have complained about her.*

hot

be (all) hot and bothered (informal) be in a state of worry and upset, often because of lack of time in which to finish something. *Don't disturb Mum. Her train leaves in an hour and she's still packing, so she's all hot and bothered.*

be hot on something (informal) be very well informed, knowledgeable and good at something. *Sarah was never too hot on science in school. She was better at languages.*

be in/get into hot water be in/get into serious trouble. *You'll be in hot water when your father finds out what you've done to his car!*

blow hot and cold (informal) be undecided, wanting something and then not wanting it alternately. *'Have you decided whether or not to move house?' 'Not yet. We're still blowing hot and cold.'*

a hot line a direct, secret telephone link between two important people, e.g. heads of government. *Throughout the entire crisis there was a hot line between the two heads of state.*

a hot potato (informal) an issue that is dangerous, highly controversial or embarrassing to deal with. *If this is a government cover-up, then it's a real hot potato and Fleet Street won't touch it!* Note also: **drop someone like a hot potato** break off contact with someone abruptly. *When you are no longer useful to Ken, he'll drop you like a hot potato.*

the 'hot seat an important position in which one is open to criticism and attack and has to face difficult questions etc. *As managing director of a chemical concern, I'm continually in the hot seat now that everyone is so worried about the environment.*

a 'hot spot an area of political unrest or danger. *I don't think I'd like to be a journalist, being sent around the globe to all the political hot spots.*

hot under the collar annoyed and irritated. *The editor has just been told to cut her budget so she's rather hot under the collar this morning.*

make it hot for someone (informal) make things unpleasant or difficult for someone. *If I were you, I would treat Kenneth Marsden with a little more respect. If he doesn't like you, he's in a position to make it hot for you.*

piping hot (food) served very hot, suggesting that it has just been freshly cooked. *When the weather's cold I like to have piping hot soup for lunch.*

strike while the iron is hot (saying) take advantage of something while the situation/time is favourable; make the most of present opportunities. *If your father has offered to pay for your holiday, strike while the iron's hot! If you say no, he may not offer again.*

long

at long last finally, after a long wait. (Expresses relief.) *I've been expecting a parcel to arrive from the States for over three weeks. At long last it has arrived.*

be as broad as it's long the result/situation is the same whatever one decides to do. *It's as broad as it's long. Taking your car to Spain is just as expensive as flying and renting a car when you're there.*

go a long way be successful, make a career for oneself. Said of a person who shows promise when young or at the start of his working life. *The new assistant manager seems to be a very bright young man. He should go a long way.*

go a 'long way towards (doing) something be a great help. *The money we won will go a long way towards paying for the new car.*

have come a long way have matured in one's views and outlook, have learnt a lot about life, gained in personal or professional experience etc. *Margaret has come a long way since her divorce. She used to be very timid and reserved, but now she's confident and resolute.*

in the 'long run over a long period of time. *We've had to put a lot of work into the improvements on the house, but we're hoping that it will pay off in the long run.*

in the long term in planning for the distant future. *Make sure that you fulfil the contract. It's important for our credibility in the long term.*

long drawn 'out (talks, negotiations) taking too much time, too slow or lengthy. *'What did you think of the headmaster's speech?' 'Not bad, but too long drawn out.'*

a 'long shot a hopeful guess, an attempt that will probably fail because of lack of information etc. *Mary's disappeared. I know it's a long shot, but could she have gone to visit her cousin in Cornwall?*

not by a 'long chalk (informal) not at all, in no way. (The phrase refers to a previous statement.) *'Trade has been very brisk today. We've never had such a good day.' 'You're right. We haven't. Not by a long chalk.'*

the long and the short of it the essential facts of a matter/event/ situation. *Brian has offered us three good reasons why we shouldn't transfer him to York, but the long and the short of it is that he just doesn't want to go.*

old

a chip off/of the old block a son or daughter who is very much like his or her father in character or temperament. *'Young Ben is just as stubborn and short-sighted as his father.' 'Oh, yes, he's certainly a chip off the old block.'*

for old 'times' sake for sentimental reasons related to pleasant memories from the past. *I spent my childhood in Worcester. I'd like to go back there one day – for old times' sake.*

an old flame someone of the opposite sex to whom one was strongly attracted at some time in the past. *David met Linda by chance in a restaurant yesterday. She's an old flame of his from their student days at Cambridge.*

an old fogey an elderly, narrow-minded person who is out of touch with modern thinking. *You can call me an old fogey if you want, but I think that young people today are totally misguided.*

an old hand (at something) someone with a lot of experience and practice at (doing) something. *'I need someone to help me fix these shelves'. 'Well, ask Larry. He's an old hand at that sort of thing.'*

old hat out of date, no longer original, topical or fashionable. *'What did you think of the guest speaker's lecture?' 'Well, quite honestly, most of it was old hat!'*

the old man (informal) a term used for a father or a man in authority over a group of employees etc.; e.g. a firm's director, a headmaster. *Oh, by the way, I just saw the old man. He wants to see you in his office immediately.*

the old school traditional thinking/standards/code of behaviour as in former times, as opposed to modern thinking etc. *Our history professor is one of the old school. He expects us to be the same as students in his day.*

short

a short cut a quicker or easier way of going somewhere or doing something. *Don't take the main road, it's too far. There's a short cut behind the church and through the woods. □ There are no short cuts to success in becoming a good doctor, just a lot of hard work and experience.*

at short notice with little warning, shortly before something has to be done etc. *You can't expect me to translate ten pages of a difficult contract at such short notice.*

be short with someone be abrupt, unfriendly. *Have I done something wrong? Mrs Bellamy was very short with me.*

be/run short (of something) not have enough of something, e.g. time, money, food, writing-paper. *We're running rather short of time, so we had better discuss the last two points on the agenda next week.*

be taken short have to make a hurried visit to a lavatory. *How embarrassing to be taken short in the middle of a speech!*

cut something short bring something to an end before the expected time. *We got an emergency call to say that there had been an accident in the factory, so we had to cut the meeting short.*

fall short of one's hopes/expectations be inadequate, disappointing, not as much/as good as one had hoped or expected. *The interview went very well, but the salary they offered me fell short of my expectations.*

for short as an abbreviation. *His name's Konrad Jackson, but everybody calls him 'Kojak' for short.*

have a short temper become angry easily, frequently or quickly. *Father had a short temper, so I was seldom really naughty as a child.*

in short briefly, in a few words, in summary. *The weather was good, the hotel was first-rate, and we had lots of fun. In short, the holiday was most enjoyable.*

in short supply scarce, not enough available. *Hard workers seem to be in short supply in this department. Almost everyone's taking a coffee break again.*

little/nothing short of... little/nothing less than... *What you are suggesting we do is little short of blackmail.*

make short work of something deal with something quickly. *'Are there many letters to answer?' 'Only three, so we'll make short work of them.'*

pull something/someone up short 1 stop a vehicle suddenly. *This car pulled up short in front of me, so I had to swerve and almost fell off my bicycle!* 2 interrupt someone when speaking, often in order to correct. *The boss noticed immediately that I was quoting the wrong figures and pulled me up short.*

short and to the point (a speech, order, letter etc.) short, direct and clear, possibly abrupt. *Don't make the speech too long. Keep it short and to the point.□ What she had to say was short and to the point: she was not standing again for election.*

short of something/doing something except, apart from. *They say he's capable of anything short of murder.□ Short of throwing me out, he tried everything to get me to leave.*

thick

as thick as thieves (two people) very friendly, sharing the same (often profitable) interests. *Les and Larry have been as thick as thieves for years. They both have a large share in the industrial redevelopment project.*

as thick as two short planks (informal) very stupid. *If Gloria doesn't see through Jim's little scheme, she must be as thick as two short planks.*

have/grow a thick skin be/become insensitive to criticism, rebuke, reproach; not be hurt by these. *As a politician in the public eye, you quickly learn to grow a thick skin.* Note also: **be thick-'skinned.**

in the thick of it/of doing something right in the middle of some activity, at the busiest part or time of something. *We were in the thick of decorating the living-room – buckets of paint and paste everywhere – when our visitors from Chicago arrived, a week early!*

lay/pile it on thick (informal) exaggerate, especially when praising or criticizing. *John gave a good talk at the conference, but Dawson was piling it on thick when he spoke of 'an unforgettable experience'.*

thick and fast in large numbers/quantity and quickly. *Our advertising campaign has been a great success. Orders for the new product are coming in thick and fast.*

thick on the ground numerous, in great supply/quantity. *If I were you, I would take the job. Such good opportunities are not thick on the ground.*

through thick and thin through good times and difficult times, under all conditions. *Jack and Bert went through thick and thin together in the war, and they've been great friends ever since.*

thin

as thin as a rake (a person) extremely thin. *Some people can eat as many fatty foods and sweet things as they like, and still be as thin as a rake.*

be skating on thin ice be in an uncertain, risky situation. *Be careful, Bob. If you make any promises, you're skating on thin ice. We don't know yet whether we can guarantee these prices.*

disappear/vanish into thin air disappear without trace. *Wherever can my blue notebook be? It can't have vanished into thin air.*

out of thin air from nowhere. *The story I told you about Roger didn't just come out of thin air, you know. There's some truth in it, whether you want to believe it or not.*

a thin audience not many spectators. *The local drama group gave a really good performance of 'Private Lives'. What a pity that there was such a thin audience on the first night.*

the thin end of the wedge just the beginning of something that will develop into a much greater event, problem, scandal etc. *I have the feeling that this one incident at the factory is only the thin end of the wedge. The dissatisfaction among the workers is likely to lead to a major strike.*

a thin excuse an unconvincing excuse. *So you couldn't find your pen. Isn't that a rather thin excuse for not doing your homework?*

thin on top not having much hair, becoming bald. *I'm a bit thin on top already. I expect I'll be bald by the time I'm 35.*

a thin time a period of unpleasantness, poor health, lack of money etc. *When Jack came out of prison, he had a pretty thin time. His wife had left him, he couldn't get work and nobody was willing to help him.*

Nouns

end

at the end of one's tether in a position where one has no more patience, hope etc. left. *Children ill, husband out of work, mother in hospital – poor Annie's at the end of her tether.*

at the end of the day when one has considered everything. *I know Chris has his faults, but at the end of the day he's the only man who can do the job properly.*

at a loose end having nothing to do, having time to waste. *Judy feels at a loose end, now that the term is over.*

be the end (informal) the worst, the most exasperating etc. *I know some people talk a lot, but Marilyn is the end. She never stops!*

(not) be the end of the world (for someone) (informal) (not) be a total disaster. *If I didn't get the job, it wouldn't be the end of the world. I've got another offer.*

get hold of the wrong end of the stick misunderstand the meaning, intention, situation totally. *No, no, I said exactly the opposite! It's just like Iris to get hold of the wrong end of the stick.*

go off (at) the 'deep end (informal) lose control and become angry. *When father heard that I'd given up physics, he went off at the deep end.*

in the end finally, at last, after other things have happened. *Ruth didn't want to chair the committee, but in the end we were able to persuade her.*

keep one's end up continue to be in good spirits even when one is sad, disappointed etc. *Bad luck, Steve, but keep your end up, there will be other opportunities.*

light at the end of the tunnel promise of better things (e.g. success, happiness) after a long time of difficulty, hardship etc. *After months of hard work and no income, there was light at the end of the tunnel. A small publisher had agreed to publish his first novel.*

never hear the end of it (informal) hear a matter talked about again and again. *My husband was so angry when I threw away his old gardening trousers. I'll never hear the end of it!*

no end of ... very many/much. *Jeremy has no end of books on football.*
  □ *There was no end of argument at the meeting last night.*

on end continuously. *Bill studies for hours on end.*

the end justifies the means (saying). If the aim is good, it may be achieved by any method, fair or unfair. *I know I exaggerated about my past job experience at the interview, but I got the job, and after all, the end justifies the means.*

the end of the line/road the point at which some activity or situation must stop (e.g. a relationship) because no further progress is possible or because it has no future etc. *When Stephanie discovered that Dan was seeing another woman, she knew that it would mean the end of the line for their relationship.*

to no end in vain, for nothing. *He tried to convince his father that he was telling the truth, but it was all to no end. He didn't believe him.*

make (both) ends meet manage with the money one earns or has. *How can anyone make ends meet on £40 a week?*

tie/clear up loose ends complete small matters/jobs; attend to matters, questions etc. that are still to be decided. *I still have quite a few loose ends to tie up at the office before I go on holiday.*

line

all along/right down the line at every point/stage, in every way/aspect, in all matters. *Since he started paying more attention to his appearance, he's been a success right down the line – got himself a good job and made lots of friends.* □ *Jim needs our support. Tell him that we're with him all along the line.*

be (next) in line for something be the next person due for something. *Who's next in line for promotion in your department?*

be in one's line be to someone's taste, what someone likes doing etc. *I'm sorry, but discos aren't exactly in my line.*

be off/on line (a machine) 1 be out of operation/in operation. *Attention! Printer not on line!* 2 not computer-controlled/computer-controlled. 3 (a person) (informal) not working/functioning as normal. *Barry has just had six weeks' vacation, but he'll soon be back on line when he's had two or three days of office stress and routine.*

be/do something in/out of line (with something) be/act in agreement/disagreement. *Your suggestions are out of line with my former proposals.* □ *The Minister was clearly not acting in line with party policy.*

be/get/step out of line act in a way that is offensive to others, say something to someone that is unfair, incorrect, insulting, hurtful etc. *Cliff, you are way out of line! That's both selfish and unreasonable. I think you owe Diane an apology.*

the bottom line the essential result/outcome/conclusion of a matter; the sum of money that has to be paid etc. *No explanations, please, just give me the bottom line. How much did we lose on the deal?*

bring someone/something into line persuade someone to conform, make something fit, match, suit. *At first he didn't agree with my way of organizing the business, but I managed to bring him into line.* □ *She must bring her speech fully into line with company policy.*

choose/follow/take the line of least resistance choose etc. the easiest, least unpleasant way of achieving something. *After the scandal, Joe took the line of least resistance and simply left the country.*

come/fall into line with someone/something agree with someone; accept a plan or procedure. *I'm sure Damien will fall into line with us on the matter when he realizes how serious it is.*

draw the line at something/somewhere set a limit/standard for one's behaviour or for the behaviour of others, put a stop to something. *I'll lend you another fifty pounds and no more. I have to draw the line somewhere.*

drop someone a line write an informal letter or note to someone. *Be sure to drop us a line and let us know your new address.*

get a line on someone/something find out information about someone/something. *Can you get a line on Walker's whereabouts? He hasn't reported to headquarters for two weeks.*

give someone a line on someone/something give someone information about someone/something. *Get Trevor to give you a line on Daniels. He used to work with him in Scotland.*

in the line of fire in a position between two opposing sides, groups etc. and therefore likely to get hurt by their attacks on each other. *As both Joe's sister and Bill's wife, she was right in the line of fire whenever the two men quarrelled.*

lay it on the line (informal) state something with force, e.g. an order, threat, opinion. *The team manager was very dissatisfied with the discipline in the team. Then when two of us missed training, boy, did he lay it on the line!*

lay something on the line (informal) put something at risk. *Two years ago I laid my reputation on the line for him – and this is how he repays me.*

sign on the dotted line agree to do something unconditionally (as if one had signed one's name to it). *The boss needs volunteers for our branch in Glasgow, but so far no one has signed on the dotted line.*

somewhere along the line at some stage/point in the process or development. *The progress of a new project is rarely rapid. There's always a hitch somewhere along the line.*

take a firm/hard/strong line (with someone) (on/over something) deal firmly or decisively with. *Some of the employees have produced bad work. The management will be taking a firmer line with them in future.*

along/on the lines of something in the style/fashion of, similar to. *The book is written along the lines of his first novel, which is set in the Far East.*

get one's lines/wires crossed be mistaken about/misunderstand what another person means/intends/wants etc. *No, that's not what I meant at all. I think we've got our lines crossed somewhere. I'll explain again.*

read between the lines understand or sense more than the actual words say; have insight into a situation. *She didn't tell me directly, but reading between the lines I think she intends to settle in Geneva.*

matter

a matter of concern something to worry about. *Our son's behaviour at school has been a matter of concern to us for some time now.*

a matter of life and/or death something vitally important/urgent. *Maureen has been working furiously to finish the designs all day – as if they were a matter of life or death.*

a matter of opinion a subject on which people have different opinions. *Whether or not video games are bad for children is a matter of opinion.*

a matter of time something which is certain to happen sooner or later. *It's only a matter of time before John's old car falls to pieces altogether. It's twenty years old.*

(as) a matter of course in accordance with what happens naturally or with what usually happens. *Most young married couples start a family as a matter of course.* □ *To most young married couples, starting a family is a matter of course.*

be the matter be wrong, not be in order. *Patrick looked pale and tired. I knew something was the matter.*

for 'that matter also, as well. *France makes over three million cars a year – so, for that matter, does West Germany.*

no laughing matter nothing to laugh about, something very serious. *Being out of work these days is no laughing matter.*

no matter what/who/where/which etc. it is not important what etc. *No matter who phones, I'm not at home, okay?* □ *I must speak to her, so ask her to phone me, no matter how late it is.*

mind

at the back of one's/someone's mind a secret/hidden intention/idea/worry in a person's thoughts only, not told to others. *John's worried about the stomach pains he often gets. I know what's at the back of his mind. He's afraid he has a serious illness.*

be (all) in the mind in one's imagination, not fact or reality. *'But I'm sure that man's following us.' 'People often say that. It's all in the mind.'*

be of one/of the same mind be in agreement with someone about something. *My wife and I are of one mind about the education of children. We both believe they learn more at home than at school.*

be out of one's mind be mad, crazy. *Frazer must be out of his mind to cancel the contract!*

call/bring something to mind recall something to one's memory. *The name sounds familiar to me, but I just can't call her face to mind.*

change one's mind (about something/someone) make a different decision or choice. *Frances wanted to go to Italy for a holiday, but now she's changed her mind and is going to Spain instead.*

cross someone's mind (a thought, idea) occur to someone. *'Perhaps Sandra would like to go to the art exhibition with us. Shall we ask her?' 'Yes, the thought had crossed my mind as well.'*

drive someone out of his mind make someone very nervous or angry. *For the last time, turn that music down! It's driving me out of my mind.*

give/put/set one's mind to something give one's attention or mental energy to solving or finishing something. *If you really put your mind to it, you could have the letter written in no time.*

give someone a piece of one's mind reprimand someone; tell someone exactly what one thinks about his behaviour etc. *I'm tired of Jack's excuses. The next time he says he hasn't got time to help, I shall give him a piece of my mind.*

have half a mind to do something be inclined to do something but not sure that one will do it. *I've half a mind to tell Tim's mother about his bad behaviour – but then I don't really want him to be punished.*

have a good mind to do something want to do something and be almost sure that one will do it, especially if one is angry. *I've a good mind to call the waiter and send this food back to the kitchen. It's almost cold.*

have a mind of one's own have a strong and independent will, not be easily influenced by others. *You won't succeed in telling Roger what he ought or ought not to do – he has a mind of his own.*

have something/a lot/enough etc. on one's mind be worried, troubled; have many things to think about. *Janice is very quiet these days. She must have something on her mind.*

in one's/the mind's eye in one's/the imagination. *In my mind's eye I can still picture the house by the river where I spent my early childhood.*

keep/bear someone/something in mind remember. *I'll keep you in mind when I want to sell my car.* □ *Please bear in mind that I'd like to have your decision by tomorrow.*

keep one's mind on something concentrate on something. *The class is very restless because of the heat. The children can't keep their minds on their work.*

know one's (own) mind know exactly what one wants, what one's aims are etc. *Dick's always changing jobs. I don't think he knows his own mind.*

a load/weight off one's/someone's mind a great relief, the end of a worrying or anxious time. *Tom has just heard from the doctor that there will be no permanent damage to his leg from the accident. That's a great load off our minds.*

make up one's mind take a decision. *Has Sally made up her mind which universities to apply to?*

mind over matter overcoming a physical weakness or inconvenience by means of willpower. *The last stage of any mountain climb is always a question of mind over matter.*

slip one's mind be forgotten. *Maggie said she would give me her new address, but it must have slipped her mind.*

speak one's mind say openly what one thinks or feels. *I know you don't want to hurt anyone, but I think in this case you ought to speak your mind.*

take one's/someone's mind off someone/something divert one's own or another person's attention from someone/something unpleasant. *Let's go to town and see a film. It will help to take your mind off your troubles.*

out of sight, out of mind (saying) people or things who are far away, or whom we do not see often, are soon forgotten. *Janet promised to write from Kuwait, but I've heard nothing. A case of out of sight, out of mind, I suppose.*

to 'my mind in my opinion, the way I see it. *Look, to my mind the question's quite simple – either he improves the offer or you refuse it.*

point

be beside the point not be relevant to the matter being discussed. *I'm sure Helen will like the present. I don't think she deserves it – but then, that's beside the point.*

be on the point of doing something be about to do something. *I was just on the point of picking up the phone to ring him when he walked in.*

a case in point an illustrative case, an example for the subject of discussion. *'It's hard to believe that anyone would invest his entire savings in such a risky enterprise.' 'Well, Jake Harding is a case in point. He did.'*

come/get to/reach the point come to the most important thing that one wants to say. *That's all very interesting, I'm sure, but I do wish he'd get to the point.*

get the/someone's point understand what someone wishes to express; understand someone's purpose in saying something. *Would you say that again please? I didn't quite get your point.*

get/wander off the point become vague; lose the main argument/ direction of the discussion. *James stated some interesting facts at first, but later he got off the point completely.*

have (got) a point have an idea/argument/reason etc. that others accept as true, good etc. *You've got a point there, Ken. It really would be better to do the easy bits first and leave the difficult bits until last.*

in point of fact in fact, in reality. *Chris may have told you that he has paid all his debts, but in point of fact he still owes me four hundred pounds.*

make one's point state or explain clearly one's argument or idea. *All right, Sharon, you've made your point. Now it's Mark's turn to tell us what he thinks.*

make a point of doing something make sure of doing something because one thinks it is important. *I always make a point of remembering my friends' birthdays.*

not to put 'too fine a point on it speaking openly and bluntly. *Not to put too fine a point on it, we think it's time you stopped being preoccupied with private problems and devoted more time to company matters.*

the point of no return the point at which it is impossible to turn back because the consequences of doing so would be worse than those of continuing. *We can't reverse our decision now or we'll lose the contract. We reached the point of no return when we offered an unconditional guarantee.*

see the point (of/in doing something) understand the purpose or use (of something). *I really don't see the point of going by train when it's just as cheap to fly.*

a sore point (with someone) a matter which irritates or upsets someone when mentioned. *When Sally comes, don't mention Roger. He went on holiday to Las Palmas on his own and it's a sore point with her.*

stretch a point go beyond what is usual or do more than is usual. *When it came to the salary increases, I had hoped the boss would stretch a point in my favour but he didn't. I got the same as everyone else.*

the 'sticking point the absolute limit beyond which one cannot or will not go. *At the auction, don't go higher than ten thousand if you can avoid it, and remember that eleven is the sticking point.*

one's strong/weak point the thing one can do best, knows most about, one's best quality/something one cannot do well etc. *If there's a word you can't spell, ask Jeff. Spelling is his strong point.*

take someone's point understand and appreciate someone's argument or attitude. (Also: **point taken.**) *I take your point about not wanting to risk further money on such a doubtful undertaking.* □ *'I'm not willing to risk further money on the undertaking.' 'Point taken, Fred. Neither am I.'*

that's the (whole) point the essence; the most important thing one is trying to say. *Yes, that's the whole point! If you cancel the holiday at short notice, you have to pay 50%!*

what's the point? there is little use/purpose. *You can speak to the bank manager again, but what's the point? He's already said that they won't extend the loan.*

(what is) 'more to the point (what is) more important or relevant. *Jane's idea is very good, and, what's more to the point, we can put it into practice without extra cost.*

thing

a close/near thing almost an accident, failure or misfortune; a narrow escape. *'Look out! The cyclist!' 'Hell, that was a close thing! I didn't see him.'*

do one's (own) thing (informal) do what one wants to do without being influenced by other people or by rules; act freely. *The new assistant will have to learn that he can't just do his own thing here. There are regulations to comply with.*

first things first (saying) do things in the necessary or correct order. (Often said as a slight warning or reminder). *First things first! Wait until you've got your degree before you talk about a career in banking.*

for 'one thing one good reason/argument is . . . (Often introduces an explanation.) *I really don't think Lloyd is the right man for the job. For one thing, he's got no specialized knowledge of the problem, and for another he can't speak German.*

have (got) a thing about something/someone have a strong liking or dislike for something/someone. *Marjorie has a thing about Chinese food – she eats nothing else.* □ *We were never allowed to have a cat as children. Mother had a thing about them.*

just one of those things (saying) something (usually unpleasant or regrettable) that is unavoidable and must be accepted. *Leaving school and not being able to get a job is unfortunately just one of those things these days.*

just the thing exactly the thing that is needed. *'How about a nice hot cup of tea to warm you up?' 'Oh, yes! That would be just the thing.'*

not quite the thing not what is socially acceptable. *You'd better hurry up and change your clothes, Fred. It wouldn't be quite the thing to arrive at Sarah's wedding wearing your gardening trousers.*

one thing leads to another (saying) one small event starts a whole sequence of events. *Debbie met Roger at a launderette. He asked her out, one thing led to another, and now they're engaged.*

show/teach/tell someone a thing or two show etc. someone something useful or important which they do not know. *Linda thinks she knows all about computers, but I bet I could teach her a thing or two.*

sure thing! (informal) certainly, of course. *'Could you give me a lift to the library?' 'Sure thing! Hop in!'*

a thing of the past something/someone no longer in demand or of topical interest etc. *'Is Carolyn still seeing Howard?' 'Goodness, no. That's been a thing of the past for months now.'*

what with 'one thing and another (saying) because so many jobs, tasks, difficulties etc. came together. (Often used as an excuse or explanation for something left undone.) *I'm sorry about Joe's birthday, but what with one thing and another, I've been so busy that I completely forgot about it.*

way

be/get something under way be/get something going/working; make progress with something. *If there's going to be a June election, we'll have to get the election campaign under way by early May.*

by the way Used to introduce an extra comment or question that is not necessarily related to the topic of conversation. *Oh, by the way, Jack wants you to give him the sales figures for the last quarter.*

by way of something 1 through; via a certain route. *The drugs are being smuggled into Britain by way of London Airport.* 2 as a kind of; for. *What shall we do by way of a surprise for Mother's birthday?*

get/have one's own way get what one wants in spite of opposition from others. *Gerald says he's strict with his children, but they always seem to get their own way.*

give way 1 break, fall down/in etc. *The bridge doesn't look safe. If you walk on it it will give way, I'm sure.* 2 yield to someone's wishes, demands etc. *You shouldn't give way to all the child's wishes. You'll spoil him.*

go one's own way act independently, even if it is against the advice of others. *It's a waste of time giving Peter advice. He'll always go his own way in the end.*

go out of one's way to do something do everything possible to help, even if it is inconvenient. *Our neighbours went out of their way to help us when we moved into the new house.*

have a way with one have something charming or pleasant in one's character which is attractive to others. *Julia isn't really pretty, but she has a way with her which is most appealing.*

have a way with someone/something have a talent for/skill in dealing with someone/something. *Susan has a way with children. They love her.* □ *Father has a way with flowers. Everyone admires his garden.*

in a way/in some ways in a sense, to a certain extent. *I know it was Ben's own fault that he didn't win, but I feel sorry for him in a way.*

in any way at all, in any respect. *Can I help you in any way?*

in the way causing an obstruction. *I can't pull out of the drive. There's a big lorry in the way.*

in the way of something as regards something. *There won't be much in the way of traffic if you take the country roads.*

no way! (exclamation) under no circumstances, certainly not. *'Can I borrow your car over the weekend?' 'No way!'*

not know which way to turn be in a state of worry and confusion, be in a hopeless situation. *He's lost his job and can't pay the bills. On top of that his wife's left him. He simply doesn't know which way to turn any more.*

on the way 'out going out of fashion, not in demand any more. *Tape recorders have been on the way out for years. Most people buy cassette recorders.*

that's the way the cookie crumbles/that's the way it goes (saying) that is the situation and no one can change it. *Sorry to hear you didn't get into the finals, Ken. But that's the way the cookie crumbles.*

way ahead/behind/above/below etc. far ahead etc. *Temperatures are way above average for the time of the year.*

way out (informal) unconventional because very modern; ahead of its time (clothing, music, art, someone's life-style etc.) *She's an artist – really way out, believe me! She makes sculpture out of bits of old cars.*

where there's a will there's a way (saying) if a person wants (to do) something very much, he will find a way of doing or getting it. *'Paul wants to go to India, but he hasn't got enough money.' 'Well, I'm sure he'll get enough somehow. Where there's a will there's a way.'*

it cuts both ways (saying) the same also applies to the other person. *Jack refused to lend me the money. But it cuts both ways. I won't ever lend him money again, either.*

have it both ways have advantages from two opposing things at the same time. *Miranda wants to have a child and carry on working as a journalist at the same time. I've told her that she just can't have it both ways.*

mend one's ways improve one's attitudes, habits, behaviour etc. *Brian will have to mend his ways if he wants to run a successful business. He's too careless and irresponsible at the moment.*

set in one's ways not willing to change fixed habits, opinions etc. *Aunt Lilian and Uncle Herbert go to Brighton every year on holiday. They are so set in their ways that they won't even consider going anywhere else.*

ways and means methods (often unofficial) of doing something successfully. *You're only allowed in here if you're a club member. Mary isn't one, of course, but she's got her ways and means.*

word

by word of mouth in a spoken, not written, form. *Most old legends were handed down by word of mouth.*

from the word go from the beginning. *Neil and Gilbert both joined the company in 1977 and were rivals for a directorship from the word go.*

give someone one's word make a promise to someone. *I give you my word that I won't tell anyone.*

go back on one's word break a promise. *Steven said he would lend me the money, but he went back on his word.*

have the last word make the last statement in an argument etc. to which no one can make a reply or objection. *Father always likes to have the last word in any discussion.*

have a word with someone speak or discuss privately with someone. *I'll have a word with my wife, and I'll tell you our decision tomorrow.*

a household word a person, company, product etc. in the public eye whose name is known by everybody. *Surely you've heard of Terry Wogan and his talk show! His name's a household word with British television viewers.*

in a word briefly. *'What did she say? Will she ever forgive me?' 'Well, in a word, no.'*

keep one's word do what one has promised. *Melissa said she would try to get me a job with the agency. I hope she keeps her word.*

a man/woman of his/her word a person who keeps a promise. *You can rely on Frank completely. He's a man of his word.*

mum's the word! don't tell anyone, it's a secret! *Now remember, mum's the word, or it won't be a surprise!*

not a word don't speak about it. *Remember now, not a word of this to your mother – it's going to be a surprise.*

not another word! don't speak about it any more! *That's enough, now. Not another word!*

one's last word one's final statement, warning, offer, advice. *I'll give you three hundred pounds and that's my last word. Take it or leave it.*

put in a good word for someone speak in a complimentary way in order to help, support, defend someone. *I put in a good word for you with the manageress. She's going to give you a second chance.*

take someone at his word act on the belief that someone will do what he says. *When Henry said he was going to sell his car, I took him at his word and found him a buyer for it.*

take someone's word for it believe someone when there is no proof that what he says is true. *Penny says she's already paid me back. I can't remember whether she did or not, so I'll have to take her word for it.*

that's not the word for it! an exclamation that something is understated. *'It's cold in here.' 'Cold! That's not the word for it! It's freezing!'*

the last word (in something) the most up-to-date, the best kind, the latest style or fashion. *The dress is a Marcello model – he's the last word in Italian fashion at the moment.*

word for word exactly, literally, using all the words. *You can't translate word for word. It won't make sense.* □ *He copied my essay word for word.*

word perfect knowing perfectly a text one has learnt, e.g. a poem, a part in a play. *The children have worked hard to learn their parts in the play. Most of them are already word perfect.*

actions speak louder than words (saying) what one does is more important than what one says. *Don't just tell Jane that you miss her. Actions speak louder than words, so go and visit her!*

have words (with someone) have a quarrel or disagreement. *Pat's in a bad mood. She had words with her boyfriend again.*

mark my words! listen to me! note what I say! (used as a warning). *The man has neither drive nor ambition. If you employ him as a sales representative, you'll regret it. Mark my words!*

mince (one's) words not speak freely and directly. *Stop mincing your words and just tell me straight what you think of my idea.*

not in so many words not exactly expressed or stated, only hinted at. *'Did Sue invite you to her party?' 'Well, not in so many words. But she did tell me that it's on Saturday.'*

words fail me! an expression of shock, surprise, anger. *Words fail me! I wasn't expecting such a wonderful birthday surprise!*

world

carry the world on one's shoulders carry a lot of responsibility. *The boss looks as if he's carrying the world on his shoulders again this morning.*

come 'down in the world lose one's social or financial position. *The Hammonds have certainly come down in the world since his company went bankrupt. The Jaguar's gone and the children aren't at a private school any more.*

do someone a world of good be very good for someone. *You need some fresh air and exercise. It would do you a world of good!*

get 'on in the world be successful in one's job, improve one's financial or social standing. *Deborah is chief consultant with an American high-tech company. She's really got on in the world.*

go 'up in the world rise to a higher social or financial position, not necessarily through one's own success or abilities. *Since Sarah married that rich industrialist, she's certainly gone up in the world.*

(it's a) small world! expression of surprise when one meets an acquaintance somewhere unexpectedly. *Just imagine, I met Paul Hill in a taxi queue at Kennedy Airport. Small world, isn't it?*

a man/woman of the world experienced, with a cosmopolitan background. *Simon's a man of the world. He'll know whether or not this is a case for a lawyer.*

not for the world under no circumstances. *I wouldn't leave you on your own for the world, so don't be afraid.*

on top of the world in a very happy mood because of success, good health etc. *Alan's feeling on top of the world. He's just heard that he's won a prize for the most outstanding journalist of the year.*

out of this world wonderful. *He's a brilliant designer. His designs are really out of this world!*

the world 'over all over the world, everywhere. *People are the same the world over – good, bad and indifferent.*

worlds apart very different from each other. *You wouldn't believe how different Jane is from her sister. They are worlds apart.*

Miscellaneous

all

after all 1 contrary to what one thinks, supposes or expects to happen (with this meaning it usually stands at the end of a statement). *I took my umbrella, but it didn't rain after all.* □ *Roger said he wouldn't be able to attend the meeting, but he managed to come after all.* 2 in spite of everything. *Don't be so harsh on Timmy. He's only a child, after all.* 3 **after 'all** (Often used to introduce an argument or reason that the listener should consider, therefore usually at the beginning of a statement. Note also the usual stress pattern with this meaning.) one mustn't forget . . ., it is important to realize . . . *I think we should agree to lend John the money he needs. After* all, he did help us two years ago with a small loan. □ *You really shouldn't worry so much about your daughter. After all, she is nineteen and not a child any more.*

all a'long all the time, from the start until now. *I said all along that you shouldn't invest all your money in only one scheme, but you wouldn't listen to me.* □ *You're telling me nothing new. I've known all along!*

all and sundry everybody, all kinds of people. *Don't talk so loudly. There's no need for all and sundry to hear our business.*

all being well if nothing unexpected or unfortunate happens. *Good! So all being well we'll expect you on Sunday.*

'all but very nearly, almost. *He was very curt and rather rude. He all but asked me to leave.* □ *I've all but finished five chapters, so there isn't much more to do.*

the all 'clear (usually **get/give someone ~**) 1 a signal that a danger/threat/something unpleasant is past. *When the doorbell rang, Barbara ran into the next room, as she didn't want Tony to find her here. As soon as he had left, I gave her the all clear to come out.* 2 permission to start or continue. *We can start on the project as soon as we get the all clear from headquarters.*

'all day and 'every day without a break or change; continuously. *Steve is working hard to finish his novel. He's been sitting at his typewriter all day and every day for five weeks now.*

'all hours at all times whether very early or very late. *I've been working all hours recently to get my new novel finished.*

all 'in 1 everything included. *The staff outing will cost £6.50 per person, all in.* 2 (informal) exhausted from physical work or exertion. *After travelling two days and two nights, he was all in.*

all in all considering everything. *We didn't agree on every point, but all in all, we had a successful meeting.* □ *All in all, and not forgetting that he's a beginner, he speaks English very well.*

(it's) all in a/the day's work (saying) it is part of the normal routine expected and accepted as part of one's duties/work, even if it is unpleasant, tiresome, difficult etc. *When you work as an air hostess, irritating and complaining passengers are all in a day's work.*

all in good time when the time is right; at a suitable opportunity. *'I'm very anxious to hear what advice Jerry's lawyer gave him.' 'Well, I expect he'll tell us all in good time.'*

'all of at least (used to emphasize a number or amount). *It must be all of 200 miles from here to Colchester.* □ *The new house must have cost the Johnsons all of a hundred thousand pounds!* □ *Martha must be all of sixty-five, but she certainly doesn't look her age.*

all 'over the place/shop/show everywhere, in every possible place, (used for emphasis). *What a mess! There were cartons piled up to the ceiling and books and papers all over the place.* □ *So there you are! I've been looking for you all over the shop!*

all the rage very popular, arousing much interest and enthusiasm. *Surely you've heard of the pop-group Kings and Queens. They're all the rage!*

all the same nevertheless, in any case. *I expect the specifications will be accurate, but I'll check them myself all the same.* □ *I'm sure she'll say yes, but I should ask her first all the same.*

all told including all things/persons, having counted and included all. *'How many names have we got on the list?' 'Five hundred and sixty, all told.'*

all well and good all right, acceptable (expresses approval of a certain situation). *If he offers to help us, all well and good, but don't ask him.* □ *She spends weeks away from home, travelling. That's all well and good if you haven't got children to look after.*

'all's well that 'ends well (saying) if the final result/outcome is good, nothing that happened before really matters. *Icy roads, traffic hold-ups, and then the accident – I thought we would never get here. But here we are and all's well that ends well.*

and all in addition, as well. *The thieves stole money, jewellery, paintings, silver, fur coat and all!*

at/till/until 'all hours very late; from night well into the morning. *There was a big party somewhere close by last night. Car doors were banging until all hours.*

one's/the 'be-all and 'end-all the most important aim, interest, thing etc. in someone's thoughts, life etc. *If research work really interests you, take the job, even though it's not well-paid. Money isn't the be-all and end-all in life.* □ *Golf is Jack's be-all and end-all. It's all he ever talks about.*

be all 'for something/all for 'doing something be very enthusiastic about/very much in favour of something. *'Did the boss approve your plan?' 'Oh, yes! She's all for it!'* □ *Whatever you do with the old car is your decision, but I'm all for keeping it.*

be all go (activities, a situation involving people) be very active, hectic, busy, eventful. *We're expecting an important trade delegation from China tomorrow, so it was all go at the office today.*

be all 'Greek to someone be unintelligible, be too difficult to understand, e.g. legal/technical details, terminology etc. *The lawyer quoted a lot of clauses and paragraphs, but I'm afraid that most of the information was all Greek to me.*

be all 'over someone (informal) flatter; fuss over someone in an exaggerated manner. *When Jack realized that Mrs Winters would be responsible for casting the main parts in the new play, he was all over her.*

be all 'right with someone suit someone, be acceptable or agreeable to someone. *'Would you like to come to supper tonight?' ' Well, yes, if it's all right with your wife.'*

be all the 'same to someone not matter, not be important, make no difference to someone. *'Which date suits you better, the thirteenth or the fifteenth?' 'It's all the same to me. Either.'*

be someone all 'over (informal) be typical/characteristic of someone, be the way one would expect a person to behave. *'Everyone paid for a round of drinks except Tom.' 'I'm not surprised. That's Tom all over. He never gives anything away.'*

for 'all + noun in spite of. *For all his money, he's not really happy.*
□ *I wouldn't like to be in her position, for all her wealth.*

for all 'I etc. care expresses indifference, i.e. I etc. do not care. *Jack's coming back from the States next week. Bob says for all he cares Jack can stay there a few months longer.*

for all 'I etc. know expresses ignorance and indifference. *'Where's Jane?' 'At home, for all I know.'*

for all one is worth with the greatest physical effort, with great energy. *When he saw the bull coming, he ran across the field for all he was worth and jumped over the gate.*

go all out (to do something) try one's hardest, be very determined. *Jane's going all out to win a prize in the annual piano-playing competition. She's never practised so much!*

in all in total. *'How many coins have you got in your collection?' 'Three thousand two hundred in all.'*

it's all 'up with someone someone's career/position/success has come to an abrupt end. *It's all up with Walters. The managing director has found out that he gave a rival firm confidential information.*

(it's/they're) all yours etc. 1 you etc. can have something because someone has finished with it. *'Do you need these dictionaries any more?' 'No, no! They're all yours.'* 2 you etc. can have something because I etc. do not want it (usually something unpleasant or difficult). *I don't want to be club treasurer any more, so if Ted wants the job, it's all his!*

it is 'all someone can do (not) to do something 1 have great difficulty in doing something. *Employing extra staff is out of the question. It's all we can do to keep the shop in business.* 2 (with **not**) someone could hardly stop himself from doing something. *It was all she could do not to laugh, when she saw him in top hat and tails. It just wasn't his style.*

(not) all 'there (informal) 1 mentally alert, clever, not easily deceived. *If you think Barry won't notice what you've done, you're wrong. He's all there!* 2 (with **not**) mentally deficient, lacking in practical intelligence or common sense (also used humorously). *I hadn't been listening, so I gave a rather stupid answer. They must have thought I wasn't all there!*

of 'all the 'fools etc./'foolish etc. things to do! expresses annoyance when someone has done something which one thinks is foolish etc. *'Hugh has sold his paintings to some dealer or other in town, for only three thousand pounds!' 'No! Of all the fools! They were worth at least three times that much!'*

of 'all people/things/places used to express surprise, because a certain person/thing/place etc. was thought to be unlikely, unsuitable etc. *Guess who I met at the Frankfurt Book Fair! Bill Parkinson, of all people!* □ *When I told Maggie that I had got engaged, she said, 'And the best of British luck!' Of all things to say!*

once and for all (used for emphasis) for the only or final time. *I'm telling you once and for all. No, I won't lend you another fifty pounds!*

when all is said and done when all the facts, details, aspects of a matter/ situation have been considered. *You can compare old and new teaching*

methods as much as you want, but when all's said and done, it's the amount of
work and effort put in by the students that really counts.

how

and how! (informal) to a great extent, very much. *'I hear that Billy liked the*
present I sent him.' 'Oh, and how!'

'**any old how** in a careless, bad manner. *Johnny doesn't care what his*
homework looks like. He does it any old how. □ *Don't go to the hairdresser's in*
Church Street. He'll cut your hair any old how.

'**how about . . . ?** 1 used for making a suggestion or to ask someone's
opinion. *How about a cup of tea?* □ *How about going to the theatre on*
Saturday? □ *If you can't come before lunch, how about 2.30?* 2 used to
remind someone of something. *You say you've never been drunk, but how*
about the time you had to sleep at Fred's because you couldn't walk home after
his party?

'**how come . . . ?** (informal) why? How does/did it happen that . . . ? *How*
come you never told me about George before? □ *How come there was no petrol*
in the tank?

how 'dare you/he/they etc . . . ? expresses shock/annoyance at
someone's impudence, rudeness etc. *How dare you speak to your mother*
like that? □ *How dare he make such arrangements without consulting us first?*

how do you do? a polite greeting exchanged by people being introduced
to each other. Note: no answer is expected or given.

how is it that . . . ? what is the reason that . . . ? (Not really a question but a
comment, an expression of irritability at someone's behaviour.) *How is it*
that whenever I see James, he's always chatting instead of working? □ *How is it*
that Marilyn can never arrive on time?

how on earth . . . ?/how in the world . . . ? used to emphasize
amazement, surprise, bewilderment etc. *How on earth could he have got up*
on to the roof without a ladder? □ *How in the world could she have found out*
about our plans, when only you and I had the details?

how in/the hell . . . ?/how the heck . . . ? (informal) an expression of
annoyance, strong displeasure, anger etc. *How the hell am I supposed to*
know where Julia is? □ *How the heck do you expect me to have all the answers*
to your problems?

how's it going? how are things going? an informal greeting among
friends. Typical answers: *Fine, thanks.* □ *Not too well, I'm afraid.*

how's that? (informal) why? what is the reason for that? Expresses that
the speaker is puzzled. *'Wendy's just sold her car.' 'How's that? She's only*
had it four weeks!'

how's 'that for /how about 'that for . . . + noun? expression of praise
(often of oneself). *How's that for punctuality? I said I'd be here by four, and*
it's four on the dot. □ *How about that for a good move? I'm better at chess than*
you thought, aren't I?

it

There are several fixed idioms which have **it** as subject or as object, although **it** does not logically or grammatically have a reference. **it** is simply a part of the fixed idiomatic verb phrase. This section gives a useful selection of such idioms.

it as subject

it as subject refers to 'the whole general situation' and not to anything specific. The context makes the meaning clear.

as it is as the present/existing situation is. Usually stands at the beginning of a clause. *'How long will he have to stay in bed, doctor?' 'Well, as it is, a week at least, Mrs Thomas.'*

as it was as the past situation was. *George didn't want to sell the house, of course, but as it was, he had no choice.*

as it were one might say, one might describe it this way. *The congress in Cannes was very relaxing, and my wife accompanied me, so it was rather like an extra holiday, as it were.*

it beats me (how, why etc.) (informal) I cannot explain, understand, accept something. *It beats me how anyone can act in such an irresponsible way.* □ *It beats me why Virginia should say one thing and do another.*

it can't be helped it is unfortunate, but no one can change it. Expresses acceptance of an unfortunate fact etc. *'How depressing! Rain every day of our holiday.' 'Well, it can't be helped. We'll just have to make the best of it.'*

it is asking/expecting a 'lot (of someone) a request is a lot to ask/ expect. *I need some help with these documents. I know it's asking a lot, but could you work overtime today and tomorrow?*

it is/was like 'this these are/were the facts, this is/was the position, this is how it happened etc. Introduces an explanation to a situation. *'How did you find out all this information?' 'Well, you see, it was like this. I met Jim Evans accidentally at Heathrow and he let it out that Simons is planning a visit to the German subsidiary in March, and . . .*

it 'isn't/it's not as if it is not the case that . . . *Marion refused to lend me her car. I don't know why, because it isn't as if I'm always wanting to borrow it – it's the first time I've asked.*

it makes no odds (informal) it makes no difference, it does not matter. *It's the same price whether you fly on a weekday or at the weekend, so it makes no odds which day you choose to travel on.*

it's a bargain! agreed! I will do as you wish. I accept your offer. *'If you just peel the potatoes, I'll do all the rest.' 'Fair enough! It's a bargain! Where's the potato knife?'*

it's a bit 'much (informal) you etc. expect too much; it is unfair to expect this. *It's a bit much, Peter, bringing six friends home to tea without asking first.* □ *The headmaster expects me to take an extra class again tomorrow. That's the third time this week. It's a bit much, don't you agree?*

it's a bit 'off (informal) it is not a fair or correct thing to do/way of doing things. Expresses a complaint about someone's behaviour. *Honestly,*

Damien, I do think it's a bit off, pushing all this work onto me while you go off enjoying yourself. □ *It's a bit off to keep someone waiting for two hours. Why didn't you ring and say you would be late?*

it's a wonder (that) it is very surprising (that). *I forgot to lock the car and left it out all night. It's a wonder that it wasn't stolen.*

it's 'anyone's/anybody's guess it is not possible to predict what will happen, one cannot know beforehand what the result will be. *'Who do you think will win the election?' 'At the moment, it's anybody's guess. The candidates all have equal chances.'*

it's back to the 'drawing board I/we etc. must go back to the beginning and start again. Said when plans, designs etc. have failed or for some reason can no longer be used. *The engine test failed, and it was obviously due to a design fault – so I'm afraid it's back to the drawing board.*

it's/it was no joke (doing something) it is a serious matter, it is not funny etc. (Often said when doing something which others think is easy, a light-hearted matter etc.) *It's no joke getting a piano up three flights of stairs, I can tell you!* □ *I had to give a speech in front of fifty people – totally unprepared. It was certainly no joke.*

it serves you etc. 'right it is a just punishment. *'Janet failed her exam yesterday.' 'Well, it serves her right. She never does any work.'*

so it 'seems that seems to be the case/position etc. *'It's three minutes past two. The guest speaker is late.' 'Yes, so it seems.'*

this is 'it this is the critical part, crucial point/time/event etc. Said just before something important happens, is done etc. *Well, this is it. The race is due to start in a few minutes. So wish me luck!*

it as object

and did I 'know about it! expresses that one is very conscious of something one did, usually because it had unpleasant consequences. *I decided to dig up the garden yesterday. It took me hours – and did I know about it in the evening! I ached all over.*

and don't I 'know it! expresses that one is very conscious of some fact (which may be unfortunate or unpleasant). Also used humorously. *'I hear your department is being reorganized.' 'Yes, it is – and don't I know it! I can't find anything any more!'* □ *'Your teenage son is very popular with the girls, I hear.' 'And don't I know it! The telephone never stops ringing!'*

as 'I see it in my opinion. *Well, as I see it, it would be best to talk to Clive before you come to a final decision.*

be 'asking for it provoke trouble and punishment. *You're asking for it if you leave your car unlocked all night in this area.* □ *I don't like to punish a child, but young Tommy has been asking for it for some time now. So it's no television for a week!*

be 'at it 1 be highly active, be busy working. *Mother's been at it all day. I wish she would have a rest.* □ *'You're studying hard, I see.' 'Yes, I've been at it for hours. My head's reeling.'* 2 be doing some definite thing for which one has been reprimanded in the past. Expresses the speaker's annoyance. *I've told you to stop biting your fingernails, but you're at it again!*

be/have 'done with it finish something properly, bring something to a complete end. Often used to make a humorous suggestion. *You've only got ten more pages to read. Why not read them now and have done with it?*

beat it! (slang) go away! *I don't want your advice! Just beat it!*

beat someone 'to it be quicker than someone else, be first to do/complete/attain something. *I was just going to take the last piece of chocolate cake, but another boy beat me to it.*

believe it or not it is true whether you believe it or you don't. Used when expressing a surprising fact. *I know I don't play football very well now, but believe it or not, at school I was the best player in the team.*

blast it! (GB, informal) strong expression of annoyance when something goes wrong etc. *Blast it, I've spilled the red paint all over the floor!* □ *I've hit my thumb with the hammer, blast it!*

blow it (informal) make a mess of something, spoil one's chance by managing a situation wrongly etc. *You blew it, didn't you? I told you to wait and not to ask her until the time was right!* □ *I didn't get the Japanese contract, so I've blown it for the moment, I'm afraid.*

blow it! expression of annoyance when something doesn't work, especially when one decides not to continue with it. *I've been trying to repair this toaster, but I can't do it. So blow it! I'll let George have a go.*

(not) buy it (slang) (not) believe or accept something. *I didn't think the customer would accept my excuse about delayed delivery dates, but he bought it!* □ *What you're saying is a lie and I won't buy it!*

call it quits (informal) decide to stop some activity (often an argument) and consider both persons/sides etc. equal. *I don't want to continue the argument, so let's call it quits and change the subject.*

can it! (slang) be quiet! stop talking/quarrelling! *I'm tired of hearing your continual complaints! Just can it, will you?*

catch it (informal) be reprimanded, punished. *You'll catch it when your father sees the mess you've made with his tools.* □ *The boys really caught it from the headmaster for letting the air out of his tyres!*

coin it in/be coining it in (informal) earn a lot of money (usually in small amounts). *Sheila has really been coining it in since she opened up her newspaper stand.*

come 'off it! (informal) stop exaggerating or boasting. *'Come off it, Bruce! You caught five fish, not fifty!'*

cool it (slang, especially US) calm down, do not get so angry/excited. *Cool it, Jim! We don't want any trouble in here.*

curse it! (informal) expression of strong annoyance. *Curse it! Why does the bus always leave early when I'm a bit late?*

cut it fine leave oneself with very little time. *Are you sure you can have the report finished by tomorrow? Isn't that cutting it rather fine?*

cut it out! (informal) stop it! *That's enough, boys, just cut it out before someone gets hurt!*

damn it!/drat it! expressions of annoyance. *Damn it! That's the second time the video recorder hasn't recorded properly. I'll have to get it repaired.*

don't mention it a polite phrase said in reply to 'Thank you'. *'Thanks very much for posting my letters.' 'Oh, don't mention it. It was no trouble.'*

easy/gently 'does it said when something should be done slowly and with care. *Remember, gently does it when you drive off. If you try to accelerate on this ice, the wheels will just spin round.*

fight it out solve a quarrel, fight etc. by arguing until the end. *Don't interfere. Let them fight it out, then perhaps there will be some peace.*

for the 'hell of it (informal) for the excitement, fun or satisfaction that something brings. *'What made you drive so fast on a country road?' 'I just did it for the hell of it, I suppose. It was just unlucky that a policeman caught me.'*

forget it! 1 it's all right, it doesn't matter. Often used after an apology or a 'Thank you'. *'I'm really sorry that I can't help you.' 'Forget it. I'll manage on my own.'* □ *'Thank you again for your time.' 'Forget it. It was nothing.'*
2 expresses annoyance, e.g. because someone is slow to understand. *'What did you say I have to do after I've put in the plug and switched on?' 'Oh, forget it! I'll do it myself!'* 3 expresses that something will not be possible. *You said you wanted to play tennis this afternoon. Well, forget it! It's raining.*

get a'way from it all (informal) go on a short holiday so that one can forget about worries and problems at home. *We've had so much trouble with the business recently. We both feel that we need to get away from it all, so we're driving down to the coast for a few days.*

get it (informal) 1 be reprimanded or punished. *You'll get it from the teacher for not doing your homework again!* 2 understand an explanation; see through a plan, situation etc. *So that's how to do it. Get it?* □ *Ah! So that's what Robert is planning to do! Now I get it!*

get it to'gether (informal) organize one's thoughts and actions in order to do something satisfactorily. *I didn't do very well in the audition. For some reason I just couldn't get it together.*

give it a rest (informal) stop talking about something, stop doing something. *Just give it a rest, Jan. We've heard all about your fantastic holiday now, and there's a lot of work to do.*

'give it to someone (informal) reprimand, criticize severely. *I felt so sorry for the poor waiter who spilled the soup. The head waiter really gave it to him!*

'give/hand it to someone (with **have to/must**) praise/admire someone for something done well. *I must hand it to you, Mary. No one I know plays chess as well as you do.*

'go it (informal) do something with energy and vigour; overdo something, exaggerate. *'Paul really has been going it this week. He's spent over £400 on clothes!' 'I agree! That is going it a bit, isn't it?'*

go it a'lone do something of importance without help or support. *Tom and Peter wanted to open up a business together, but they quarrelled. So now Tom has decided to go it alone.*

hang it (all)! an expression of annoyance and dissatisfaction. *Hang it! I've forgotten to buy milk and now the shops are closed!* □ *You say you haven't even started to read the report. Hang it all, David! It's been on your desk for three weeks now!*

have got it badly (informal) be extremely infatuated/in love with someone. *Jerry met a Welsh girl on holiday and he's really got it badly this time! He visits her every weekend and spends hours on the phone.*

have got it 'made (informal) have got advantages that guarantee success, money, an easy life etc. *Mark is going to marry into a wealthy family, and his father-in-law is giving him voting shares in the company. So he's got it made!*

have got what it takes have the necessary personal qualities, intelligence etc. that a job or task requires. *Martin hasn't got what it takes for a job in management. He's too soft and lacks drive.*

have 'had it (informal) 1 fail to do something or get something that one wants. *I'm afraid you've had it, Andrew. The job you wanted in the personnel department has been given to someone else.* □ *It looks as if we've had it. There are no cakes left.* 2 be no use, have no value any longer. *These shoes have had it, there are holes in the soles.* 3 (a person) be no longer welcome, accepted or tolerated by someone. *Jane has had it as far as I'm concerned. She's lied to me once too often!*

have it 'in for someone (informal) be determined to make trouble for or harm someone, often out of revenge or because of a strong personal dislike. *Michael has had it in for Trevor ever since he deliberately tried to take over Michael's share of the family business.*

have it 'off with someone (slang) have sexual relations with someone. *I heard that Tony is having it off with the girl in the flat below. I wonder if his wife has found out?*

have something/nothing/little/not much etc. to show for it have gained an/no advantage or profit after some effort or work, have made (no) visible progress after investing one's time. *I've been working on the report all afternoon, but it's so difficult that I'm afraid I have little to show for it.*

hit it 'off (with someone) (informal) like/understand someone; enjoy someone's company. *I'm sharing an office with a new man. Thankfully we seem to hit it off quite well.*

hold it! (informal) stop doing something for a moment! Stay as you are! Don't move! *Hold it there, please, and a big smile, everyone! That will be the photo of the year!* □ *Okay, everybody, just hold it! We'll have to shoot this scene again.*

hop it! (informal) go away! *Hey, you kids! Just hop it, will you? Can't you see we're busy?*

I knew it! I was sure that that would be so, would happen etc. Said after receiving confirmation that one was right about something. *You see? I knew it! At first Mike said he would come, but now he has just said that he can't come after all.*

I take it (that) I understand/assume (that) . . . *I take it that you intend to accept the invitation?* □ *May I take it that you will support our campaign?* □ *You are Miss Carter, I take it.*

jump 'to it! (informal) hurry, be quick! *I asked you to pack a bag with what you need for the journey. Now jump to it, or we'll miss the train!*

knock it 'off! (slang) stop it! *That's enough, you kids! Knock it off and help me to clear up the mess in here!*

leave it at 'that not pursue a matter further; not say or do more. *I know you think James behaved very badly, but he did apologize, so why not leave it at that?*

let it go (at 'that) take no further action; dismiss a matter even though it has perhaps not been brought to a satisfactory close. *'I think you should report the theft to the police.' 'No. He paid the money back and apologized, so I'm prepared to let it go at that.'*

like it or lump it (informal) whether you like/accept something/a situation or not (expresses the speaker's indifference). *I know you don't want me to go with you, but I'm going – so you can like it or lump it!*

live it 'up pursue pleasure, live an easy life. *Ted says he had a terrific time when he visited his cousin in Canada. They did nothing but live it up for three weeks.*

lord it (over someone) domineer over someone, behave/speak in a dominating or superior manner. *Whenever we do things in a group, Jerry always tries to take charge. He loves to lord it over everybody.*

make it be successful, achieve one's aim. *The concert starts in half an hour. If we don't leave now, we won't make it on time.* □ *Elaine is hoping to make it to assistant manager within two years.*

make it snappy be quick doing something. *'I have to phone Tom before we leave.' 'Well, make it snappy. We haven't much time.'*

move it! (slang, mainly US) hurry! *Come on, you three! I told you to go to bed an hour ago! Now move it!*

not if 'I etc. can help it not if I etc. can prevent something. *'Gary said he's going to Rome next week – without his wife!' 'I bet he won't. Not if she can help it!'*

now you've 'done it! (informal) now you have done/said something that will cause trouble, have consequences etc. *Now you've done it! Why did you have to mention the party to Moira? Now she'll come with about ten of her weird friends.*

'out with it! say directly what you are trying to say; tell me what you are thinking etc. *Out with it, Bill! I can see there's something you want to talk about.*

pack it 'in! (informal) stop it! *Come on, Joe. Pack it in! We've had enough of your jokes, thank you!*

play it by ear act according to the situation without a definite plan; do what seems best at the time something happens. *'Have you prepared what you're going to say at the interview tomorrow?' 'No, I'll just play it by ear this time.'*

play it cool (informal) handle a situation in a calm manner, not become worried, nervous, excited etc. *When you talk to the boss, don't start apologizing straightaway. Play it cool first and see how she reacts.*

play it safe not risk something which is uncertain, even though the risk may bring advantages. *It would be much cheaper to take the bus to the station,* *but if it's late we'll miss the train. Wouldn't it be better to play it safe and take a taxi?*

rake it in (informal) earn a lot of money quickly. *Bill's coffee shop is a great success. He's raking it in.*

ride it 'out endure a bad or unpleasant situation and wait until it becomes better. *Several small independent oil companies are having to ride it out until oil prices increase again.*

rough it live or sleep in rough or uncomfortable conditions or surroundings. *The boys have only a small tent and no modern camping equipment at all, but they are quite prepared to rough it for a few weeks.*

rub it 'in continue to emphasize something that is unpleasant to someone. *I know what I did was stupid, and I've admitted it. But there's no need to keep rubbing it in. Why can't you forget about it?*

'run for it run suddenly and fast in order to get out of danger, etc. *We got caught in a heavy thunderstorm about ten minutes from home, so we had to run for it.*

see to it that... make sure that... *Don't worry. I'll see to it that the children do their homework.*

shut it! (slang) stop talking! *Just shut it for five minutes, Roy! I can't concentrate!*

skip it! 1 forget about something; it is not necessary to talk about/ mention something (e.g. an apology, a thankyou). *I'm so sorry I didn't pick you up at the arranged time, but I got a phone call and...' 'Oh, skip it! It's all right. I took a bus.'* 2 do not talk about this subject. *Peter, I'm tired of hearing you complain about your work. Just skip it, will you? If you don't like it, look for another job.*

sleep on it delay a decision until the next day so that one has enough time to think about it thoroughly. *We don't need an answer now. Sleep on it and tell us tomorrow.*

snap 'to it! (informal) do it quickly! *I asked you to put the dishes in the dishwasher. Now snap to it!*

snuff it (informal, humorous) die. *The sons were trying to persuade their father to change his will in their favour. But the old chap snuffed it beforehand, so most of his money went to the woman he lived with.*

step on it (informal) walk/drive faster. *It's five o'clock already. We'll have to step on it if we want to be there by six!*

strike it rich find a way of earning a lot of money. *Within six months of opening up her health club, Maxine realized that she had struck it rich.* □ *No one really knows how Uncle Alec became a millionaire. He went out to Australia twenty years ago and somehow he must have struck it rich.*

take it bear/endure stress or pain; tolerate criticism, someone's bad behaviour etc. without adverse effects to one's health or state of mind. *Janet's new job is very hectic with lots of stress and trouble – but she can take it!* □ *Please stop this criticism and nagging. I can't take it much longer!*

take it easy (informal) relax, do something slowly with plenty of time; be calm, not become excited or annoyed. *When Fred came out of hospital, the* *doctor advised him to take it easy for a few weeks.* □ *All right, Ros! Take it easy! I didn't say I wouldn't help you.*

take it from 'me believe what I say, take my advice etc. *Take it from me, the share price will drop before Christmas. You should sell now.*

take it or leave it either accept my offer or not. *Fifty pounds, and that's my last word. Take it or leave it!*

take it 'out of someone make someone extremely tired; strain someone. *Father's been digging in the garden. Now he's asleep. The digging seems to have taken it out of him.*

take it 'out on someone treat someone badly; punish someone unfairly because of one's own anger, dissatisfaction, personal troubles etc. *I know you're furious about the affair at the club, but you shouldn't take it out on your family.*

try it 'on attempt to gain an advantage from someone; cheat. *Two youths tried it on in the supermarket by changing the price label on a bottle of whisky.*

to put it mildly not exaggerating; understating something. *You say Sarah has an annoying manner sometimes. She's a damned nuisance, to put it mildly!*

walk it walk to one's destination (as opposed to driving etc.). *'Shall we take the car?' 'No, it isn't worth it. We can walk it in half an hour.'*

want 'jam on it want extra undeserved or unjustified advantages; want something for nothing. *'He wants £15 an hour for painting the kitchen and all meals included as well.' 'Really! He wants jam on it, doesn't he?'*

watch it! (informal) be careful! *Watch it with those eggs! They don't look very safe on top of your shopping basket.*

watch it with someone beware of someone, be careful in someone's presence. *Now watch it with the butcher. He's known for giving people too little change.*

you name it whatever you want/need, say etc. *The bookshop stocks hundreds of titles. You name it, they've got it!* □ *I'm telling you, he'll do anything you want. You only have to name it.*

you said it! I agree fully! You are right! An expression of agreement with what someone has just said. *'The editor's in a bad mood today.' 'You said it! She's just given me back three articles to rewrite!'*

that

at 'that (informal) 1 in addition to that; as well. *She's a lawyer – and a very successful one at that.* 2 Can also express surprise, that something is contrary to what one might expect. *John always says he has no money, but he's just bought a new car – and quite an expensive one at that!*

at 'that rate if that is so; in that case. *'The train leaves at 12.15, not 13.15!' 'Oh, no! At that rate we are going to miss it!'*

come to 'that when I think of that and other similar facts. (Said when the speaker wishes to add something that has just occurred to him.) *I haven't heard from Brenda for weeks. Come to that, we haven't heard from any of the Walkers for quite some time, have we?*

don't give me 'that! (informal) nonsense! Expresses annoyance and disbelief at what someone has said. *'I couldn't phone you because you were in Bristol.' 'Don't give me that! You could have got the Bristol number from my secretary!'*

that 'does it! (informal) expresses that the speaker has reached the limit of his patience after several annoying incidents, and is now ready to act or show his anger. *That does it! Jack's late again! If he can't be here on time, I'm not offering to drive him to work in my car any more!*

that is (to say) used to further define or make clearer something just said, often as an afterthought. *We're going to Rome next week on holiday. That is to say, I'm going to a congress and my wife's visiting her sister for a few days.*

that will 'do 1 that is enough. *That will do for the moment. If we need more sandwiches, we can make more later.* 2 (as a command/warning) no more! *That will do, you boys! No more fighting in here!*

that would be 'telling used (often teasingly) as an answer to someone's question, when one does not wish to give the information asked for. *'What were you and Janice whispering when you thought I wasn't listening? What's the big secret?' 'Ah, now that would be telling, wouldn't it?'*

that's about 'it that is more or less everything; there's nothing important left to be done, said etc. *Well, I think that's about it. We've discussed all the important points, so now we can take a vote.*

that's 'all (at the end of a statement, with rising intonation) that isn't a problem. Expresses acceptance of a situation because there is no alternative. *If Jack isn't in, we'll have to come home again, that's all.*
□ *If Veronica doesn't pass her driving test, she'll have to take a few more lessons and try again, that's all.*

that's all there is 'to it 1 (after giving an explanation etc.) it's not more difficult than I have told/shown you etc. *So when you've fed in all the data, you store it by pressing this key here, then 'S' for 'store'. That's all there is to it.* 2 (after stating or explaining a situation, matter etc.) that's all that you/we etc. can do; that's what you/we etc. have to do. *Well, if you need a lot of money fast, you'll have to sell the house. That's all there is to it.*

that's 'done/torn it! (informal) that spoils or ruins things! (e.g. plans, wishes). Usually refers to something that goes wrong, a mistake, unfortunate incident, something one should not have said etc.
Oh no! That's done it! I've just dropped the mixer and broken it so I can't make a cake for the visitors. □ *Damn! That's torn it! I have to be in Manchester by lunchtime and I've just missed the train!*

'that's for sure (stands after a statement) that is quite certain. *Once I've passed the exam, I shall never open another book on Latin verbs, that's for sure!*

that's/there's + 'noun for you (informal, often ironic) expression of pleasure/displeasure at the degree of some quality that someone/something shows. *Charles Maxwell? Now there's a gentleman for you from head to toe!* □ *I gave Roy ten pounds and he didn't even say thank you! That's gratitude for you.* □ *The car's going rusty already! That's quality for you!*

that's 'it 1 that's finished. *Now we've put in all the ingredients and mixed them all well, so that's it. The mixture can go into the oven.* 2 (ironic) that's right! (Expresses annoyance that something is not all right, because it is dangerous, stupid, risky etc.) *That's it! Break all the other cups as well! Try to carry them all!* 3 good! that's right! (Expresses encouragement and approval.) *That's it! If you continue like that, you'll soon be able to swim!*

that's 'life (saying) it's something that happens and that we have to accept and live with. Often said about something unfortunate. *I'm very sorry that John has lost his job, but then that's life these days.*

that's more 'like it! expresses encouragement/satisfaction with someone's achievements. *'Yes, that's more like it! You've improved the designs a lot. □ I hear you were top in the maths test. That's more like it! I know you can do it when you try!*

that's 'rich! (informal, ironic) that's ridiculous. *Jeff said he would show me how to put up the shelves.' 'Jeff? That's rich – he's never put up a shelf in his life!'*

(and/so) that's 'that that concludes the matter, that finishes things. *We thought Uncle Stan would invite us to his holiday apartment in Palma, but he didn't. So that's that! □ He promised to be home before midnight, but he wasn't. So we simply forbade him to go out for a whole week, and that was that.*

'that's the ticket! (informal) an expression of satisfaction or encouragement. That is good. That is the right thing to do. *That's the ticket, Paula! You show them all who's the best player! □ 'I'm going to tell Christine just what I think of her behaviour!' 'That's the ticket! Don't let her treat you like that!'*

well, I 'like 'that! (informal) expresses surprise at someone's impudence, annoyance at someone's behaviour etc. *Well, I like that! That man at the fruit stall has put three bad peaches in the bag. I'm going to take them back!*

you 'do that! 1 used encouragingly to support what someone plans to do. *'If the big boy starts trouble again, I shall hit him, even though I'm smaller!' 'That's right, son, you do that!'* 2 used discouragingly as a warning. *'I'm going to sell my roller-skates to a boy in my class.' 'Well, you do that, and I'll never buy you a present again!'*

there

... and there you 'are! and there's the solution, the desired result etc. (added to an instruction of how to do something). *Just put the plug in, turn the knob to 'On', press the start button and there you are! Easy!*

hang (on) 'in there! (informal, mostly US) an expression of encouragement to keep trying when something is difficult. *Come on, Joe! Hang in there! You'll do it!*

so 'there! stands at the end of a statement. Said in a triumphant or defiant tone to emphasize self-satisfaction that one was right, better etc. Often used by children. *I asked the teacher. She said you were wrong and I was right, so there!*

there a'gain additionally, alternatively (used to introduce an additional or alternative thought, idea, statement etc. to what one has just said). *If*

Spain was too hot for you last year, why not go to Italy for a change? But there again, in August it may be just as hot as in Spain.

there and then straight away, on the spot. *I simply asked him whether the company needed any more civil engineers, and he offered me a job there and then!* □ *If you take all the forms and necessary documents with you to the passport office, they can give you a new passport there and then.*

there are no 'buts a'bout it no excuses are acceptable because there is no doubt about something. *You haven't done your homework, so you can't go out to play. There are no buts about it!*

(but) there it 'is that's where the problem lies, that's just how it is, those are the facts. *Yes, there it is, you see. You can't apply for a work permit unless you have a definite job offer, yet a lot of employers want to see your work permit before they offer you a job! □ I can't allow in non-members, I'm afraid. I'm so sorry, but there it is.*

there is (a bit/a lot/much) more to it than 'that it is more complex, involved etc. than that. It is not that simple. *Jack said he had just been lucky in winning the music scholarship, but anybody knows that there is much more to it than that. □ When you want to join the diplomatic service, it's not just a case of applying and going for interview. There's a lot more to it than that.*

there is (much/a lot) 'more to someone than . . . someone is not just . . . *Mandy's a very clever young woman. There's much more to her than she tells you.*

there is no 'knowing/telling what/when/where etc . . . one cannot know/be sure/say what will happen etc. *There's no knowing when Jack will be back at work after his accident. It could take a few months. □ There's no telling what will happen if the opposition wins the next election.*

there is no mistaking someone/something someone/something is easy to recognize. *Yes, of course I'm sure it was Liam on the phone. There's no mistaking his Irish accent.*

there is no question there can be no doubt. *There is no question that Sue could do better at school if she worked harder. She's very bright, but lazy.*

there is no 'stopping/holding someone someone cannot be prevented from doing something. *Once Alf starts telling jokes, there's no stopping him. □ When the children saw the table laden with birthday presents, there was no holding them!*

there is nothing (else) 'for it (informal) there is no other way. Expresses disappointment and resignation, when the speaker has to do something unpleasant. *There's nothing else for it – we'll have to cancel the holiday this year.*

there is nothing 'in it it is not true, it is only a rumour. *'I've heard that the Freemans are moving to Glasgow.' 'So have I, but there's nothing in it, I'm sure.'*

there is nothing like (a) + noun (for doing something/to do something) something is better than everything else. *There's nothing like a comfortable chair and a good book to make you feel relaxed after a hard day at the office.*

there's nothing 'to it it's easy, there is nothing difficult involved. *Working this machine looks very complicated, but there's nothing to it really.*

there is something to be 'said for . . . something has its advantages and can be recommended for certain reasons which may not be immediately apparent. *There's something to be said for an off-season holiday – no traffic jams, no crowds, and cheaper hotel rates.*

there is a time and (a) place for everything (saying) there are certain things which are only appropriate at a certain time or place, i.e. they are often inappropriate and should not be done. *A waiter was flirting with a girl in the restaurant. The manager soon appeared and warned him that there was a time and a place for everything.*

there, there!/'there now! said when comforting or calming someone who is crying etc. *There, there, dear! Drink this hot tea and you'll soon feel much better.*

there you 'are! 1 said when giving something to someone that he wanted. *There you are, Mrs Jones, your butter and your tomatoes. That will be £6.50 altogether.* 2 said triumphantly after hearing one's opinion etc. confirmed. *'The book says Goethe was born in 1749.' 'Well, there you are! I said so all along!'*

'there you go/he goes etc. again! (informal) you are starting to do/say again what you do/say repeatedly (often to the annoyance of others). *There he goes again! All he can talk about is football!* □ *There you go again! You worry about your daughter too much. She'll be fine.*

there's a good 'boy/girl/dog! said to a child or animal in praise of something done well, or as encouragement. *Come on, now, eat up your carrots. There's a good boy!*

you've got me 'there (informal) I don't know the answer to your question, you know more than I do. *'Do you know how many cars Britain produces a year?' 'No, I don't. You've got me there.'*

too

all/only too + 'adjective/adverb very. (As an emphatic assertion or contradiction.) *'Did you have a good time?' 'We had a wonderful evening. It was over all too soon.* □ *No, Jerry won't lend you any money – we know him all too well!* □ *I'd be only too pleased to help you.*

be/prove (a bit) too 'much (for someone) 1 (a person) be better than/ superior to someone e.g. in intelligence, strength. *I tried to beat Charles at chess, but he was simply too much for me.* 2 (a person, a situation) be too difficult to manage/handle. *I won't look after Nicky any more. He's a bit too much. He's cheeky and naughty all the time.* □ *Glynn started doing an Open University course. But with a full-time job as a mechanic at the same time, it soon proved too much for him, so he gave it up.*

have (got) too many 'irons in the fire be involved with too many different things at the same time. *Besides writing books, Oliver does translation work and teaching. He's continually overworked because he simply has too many irons in the fire.*

it's too bad it's unfortunate. An expression of regret. *It's too bad that you couldn't come yesterday. You missed a lot of fun.*

it's too 'bad of someone an expression of displeasure at something someone does. *It's too bad of you to squirt water at the neighbour's cat, Jimmy!*

it's/that's just too 'bad 1 an expression of acceptance that something is unfortunate but cannot be changed. *It's just too bad that it hasn't stopped raining all day. We wanted to play tennis.* □ *It was just too bad that Jim fell ill the week we should have gone on holiday.* 2 (ironic) expresses lack of sympathy for something unfortunate, that one is not really sorry. *If Trevor missed the lecture because he was too busy with his girlfriend, that's just too bad! I'm not going to give him my lecture notes!* □ *If we don't get these letters finished on time, then it's just too bad.*

none too soon etc. certainly not too soon etc., not soon etc. enough. *'They've arrived at last!' 'And none too soon!'*

not/none/never too ... + adjective/adverb (often used in understatement) not very. *It's not too warm in here. In fact, it's freezing!* □ *This chair is none too comfortable.* □ *Hugh is never too punctual. In fact, he nearly always keeps us waiting.*

too big for one's boots (GB)/**breeches** (US) too conceited; behaving in a superior manner. *Since Colin won the local chess championship he's become too big for his boots.*

too close for comfort (often a vehicle) very close, making one nervous or afraid. *The van behind us is too close for comfort. I'd let him overtake if I were you.*

too funny for words (often a situation, a sight etc.) very funny. *So there was poor Tom holding the woman's parcels, with the poodle's lead wrapped round his legs and the poodle pulling in all directions. It was too funny for words!*

too good to be true (of news, a pleasant surprise etc.) so good that one can hardly believe it. *Janice is thrilled about the job offer in Rome. She still thinks it's too good to be true.*

too hot to handle (informal) too dangerous or controversial to deal with, so that it is better not to become involved. *None of the daily newspapers ran the true story about the spy murder. At the time, Fleet Street obviously thought that the truth was too hot to handle.*

too many cooks (spoil the broth) (saying) if too many people try to do/ organize a job etc. it will not be done satisfactorily, as each person will do it differently. *Please tell Debbie that we don't need any more helpers to organize the bus transport. You know what they say about too many cooks ...*

too 'much of a good thing so much of something good that one can no longer appreciate it. *We went to Tunisia for some sunshine, but at 40 degrees in the shade it was almost too much of a good thing.*

too true! completely true/correct! Expresses strong agreement with what someone says. *'The government has made so many changes, but nothing has been done to improve the educational system.' 'Too true! I agree!'*

what

and/or what 'have you (informal) and/or all the rest; and so on. *And I've also got to pay the grocer, the greengrocer, the baker, the newsagent and what have you.*

and 'what not/and I don't know 'what and other things of a similar kind. *There were cakes and biscuits and pastries and what not.* □ *Johnny got so many birthday presents – cars and books and games and toy soldiers and I don't know what.*

and what's 'more moreover, in addition (introduces an additional important statement or thought). *The car is only three years old, and what's more, it's in excellent condition.*

for what it's 'worth although this information/opinion may not be worth much, not be very important, of interest etc. *For what it's worth, I heard today that Cooper may be leaving the company.* □ *'Moira says you have something to tell me?' 'Yes, for what it's worth.'*

guess 'what! (informal) introduces some information which the speaker thinks will surprise the listener. *Guess what! Peter's passed his driving test at last!*

have (got) what it takes have the necessary qualities etc. *I'm telling you, Simon has got what it takes to go right to the top – drive, vision and tenacity.*

I know 'what/I'll tell you 'what (informal) introduces a suggestion. *I know what, we'll pay Mum and Dad an unexpected visit this weekend!* □ *I'll tell you what, June was at the lecture, so perhaps she'll lend you her notes.*

know what's 'what be knowledgeable and experienced. *Ask Jenny. She certainly knows what's what with antique furniture.*

or 'what (informal) short form of what the speaker wants to say, e.g. or what shall I do? (stands at the end of a clause). *He asked me to contact him, but should I write or phone or call in at the main office personally, or what?*

so 'what? (informal) what does it matter? who cares? Expresses indifference. *Let Brian be jealous if he pleases. So what?*

that's what it 'is/was that is/was the reason for someone's behaviour or reaction. *'The waiter looked displeased.' 'Well, you didn't give him a very big tip, did you? That's what it was.'*

(well) what do you 'know? expresses great surprise at something unexpected or improbable. (Note: said as an exclamation, not as a question, i.e. with falling intonation.) *'Mike's just got back from a yachting holiday in the Caribbean.' 'The Caribbean, on his salary? Well, what do you know?'* □ *'Well, what do you know? That was Ruth Barnes on the phone. She hasn't contacted me for years!'*

'what about ...? used to make a suggestion. *What about going to see a film this evening?* □ *What about a drink?* □ *What about Nancy?*

what 'for?/what (...) for? why? for what purpose? (Only in positive questions.) *You gave the man a very black look. What for?* □ *You just threw John's letter away! Now what did you do that for?*

what 'is it? 1 what do you want? (often expresses irritation). *Yes, Jane. What is it? Can't you see I'm busy?* 2 what's the matter? *You look troubled, Ian. What is it? Come on, you can tell me, whatever it is.*

what is it to 'you? why does that interest you? (suggests that it is not someone's concern, that the matter has nothing to do with someone). *Why do you want to know how much Sylvia earns? What is it to you?*

what is someone 'driving at? what is someone trying to say/express? *Fred talks in riddles! What's he driving at?*

what is 'eating someone? what is worrying someone, making someone nervous, irritated or bad tempered etc? *George is snapping at everyone today. What's eating him, I wonder?*

what is someone 'getting at? what is someone indirectly saying/ suggesting/hinting? *What's he getting at? Is he saying that we won't be getting any salary increase after all?* □ *I didn't realize what he was getting at at first, but then it suddenly struck me!*

what is someone 'playing at? (informal) expresses surprise, bewilderment, annoyance at someone's behaviour. *Janet has taken all the dictionaries, and I need them. What does she think she's playing at?* □ *Bob has borrowed money from five people. What's he playing at, I wonder?*

what makes someone/something tick (informal) what makes someone think/live/react the way he does; what is most important to someone; what makes something work. *I don't understand Paul at all. I just can't work out what makes him tick.* □ *You seem to know what makes New York tick – at least in the world of business and finance.*

what 'next? expresses surprise, amazement, annoyance at someone's impudence, at what someone will do/ask etc. next. *No, you can't have your mother's fur coat to dress up in! What next?* □ *So she expects you to pay her bills for her while she's away for three months! What next?*

'what of ...? what about ...? what will/would happen to ...? *Joanne knew that she was safe, but what of Jim, what of the children, what of her parents?*

what 'of it? what does it matter? (often expresses indifference). *'Don't forget that Friday is Uncle Alec's birthday.' 'Well, what of it? I've still got to go to Geneva.'*

what the hell! (informal) exclamation of annoyance/anger expressing that one does not care about something. *I've typed this letter four times! But what the hell! I'm not going to do it again!* □ *Oh, what the hell! I haven't got time to wash the floor, so Aunt Polly will have to see it dirty!*

what the hell/heck/devil ...? (informal) expresses the speaker's anger. *What the hell does Stephen think he's doing? Just look at this mess!* □ *What the devil's all this shouting about? I'm trying to work!*

'what with ... considering, because of. *What with the visitors and all the extra housework and cooking, I've had a very busy week.*

what's all 'this (then)? (informal) what's happening here? Expresses disapproval, a warning to stop some activity. *What's all this then? You can't have your tea break in the boss's office, just because he isn't here today.*

what's the big idea? (informal) criticizes someone's unreasonable behaviour. *I've just put all those books on the shelves and you've taken them* *all down again! What's the big idea?* □ *Mike just told me that you've broken off your engagement with him. What's the big idea, my girl? I couldn't wish for a better son-in-law!*

what's someone's (little) game? (informal) what is someone's secret intention/purpose/scheme? *Max has been behaving very strangely towards me. What's his little game, I wonder?* □ *I know what Robertson's little game is! He's plotting to have me transferred to another department, so that he can take my job here!*

what's the game? (informal) what are you doing? what is going on? Expresses displeasure at what someone is doing. *Hey! What's the game? Those are my private papers!*

what's 'this/something in aid of? (informal) what's the purpose of this? what is this for? *What's all this in aid of? Three packed suitcases? Where are you going?* □ *What are these big boots in aid of? Are you climbing Everest?*

what's 'up? (informal) what is the matter? what is wrong? *What's up now? She's crying again!*

what's yours? what would you like to drink? (used when you wish to buy someone a drink). *What's yours, Harry? Another whisky?*

you know 'what? Used to introduce a (usually serious or important) statement/thought/idea which the speaker wishes the listener to consider. *You know what? I believe Michael is jealous! That would explain his behaviour.* □ *You know what? You ought to sell your dollars, before the exchange rate drops again.*

3 Idioms with nouns and adjectives

Noun phrases

another cup of tea something or someone very different from that which has been discussed/encountered etc. previously. *'I wasn't talking about Jeremy. I meant his brother.' 'Ah, now Rodney's way of doing business is quite another cup of tea.'*

an Aunt Sally 1 a person who is a target for ridicule, criticism etc. *What Rawlings did wasn't really as wrong as the opposition would have people believe. It seems as if they just need an Aunt Sally to take the public's attention away from other unethical dealings.* 2 an idea or suggestion known to be bad, but which is brought up for discussion/criticism with the object of producing constructive thought, good ideas etc. *Mark knows that his idea for fund-raising was not original or particularly good, but he meant it more or less as an Aunt Sally.*

beginner's luck unusual, unexpected success in one's first attempts at doing something. *Diane had never been bowling before, but she scored every time! Beginner's luck, I suppose.*

a bit of all right (slang) something/someone that finds someone's approval. *'Richard's got a new girlfriend.' 'I know, I've seen her. She's a bit of all right.'*

a bit on the side 1 (slang) a sexual relationship outside marriage. *Have you heard the rumour about Steve? They say he's got a bit on the side, but I don't believe it.* 2 (informal) **make** ~ earn money other than from one's regular job. *We need someone to help at the race-course. Ask Jim if he'd like to make a bit on the side.*

a blessing in disguise a mishap or unlucky event that turns out to be advantageous or fortunate after all. *Failing to get the job in Edinburgh was a blessing in disguise. If I had gone to work there, I would never have had the travel opportunities that my present job offers me.*

a blot on the landscape something or someone that spoils a situation; a factor one would like to remove. *Ted's job is running very smoothly. He says the only blot on the landscape is the prospect of having Dawson for a boss next year.*

a breath of fresh air a thing or person that brings a refreshing and welcome change to the present dull or routine situation. *We're thoroughly enjoying having Betsy staying with us. She's so lively and interesting – a real breath of fresh air for my parents, who never go out or see a new face.*

the calm before the storm a period of calm or inactivity before an expected period of trouble, frenzied activity etc. *'No one would believe that there's going to be a general election in this country in six weeks' time. It's so quiet.' 'It's just the calm before the storm. Once the campaigning starts, there'll be talk of nothing else.'*

castles in the air, usually **build ~** make impossible plans, have ideas which cannot be realized. *Mandy is talking about taking a sailing holiday in the Caribbean next year. All castles in the air, of course; she'll never have enough money.*

'**child's play** a very easy task. *Persuading Jack to join us should be child's play compared with the tremendous difficulties we had in getting Sam to support us.*

a cloud on the horizon a matter for concern, something unpleasant which is threatening. *Sarah and Jim have only been married a couple of weeks and already there's a cloud on the horizon. Jim thinks he may lose his job.*

a (small) cog in the machine/wheel an unimportant person in, or a small part of, a large organization. *Brian asked me to try to get his son a job with the company. I explained to him that I'm only a small cog in the machine and haven't got any authority.*

the corridors of power high level places in government where important decisions are made, power struggles are fought etc. *You should read this book. It gives you tremendous insight into the corridors of power on Capitol Hill.*

a/the devil's advocate someone who deliberately takes the opposite side or criticizes what he secretly favours, in order to test opposing arguments and reactions before committing/declaring himself. *Everyone was outraged when Jefferson announced that he thought a merger of the two companies would be a good thing. No one realized at the time that he was simply playing the devil's advocate.*

a dose/taste of one's own medicine treatment of the same kind as one has received from or has given someone else; retaliation using the same methods. *Anthony has been plotting to ruin Michael's good reputation in the company. It's time someone gave him a dose of his own medicine!*

a drop in the ocean a very small amount (in comparison to another very large amount). *'Mr O'Neill donated two hundred pounds to our hospital charity. A very generous donation, but unfortunately only a drop in the ocean – we need half a million.'*

a feather in one's cap an accomplishment of which one can be proud. *'Trevor has won a scholarship to Cambridge.' 'Oh, that's wonderful – certainly a feather in his cap!'*

a flash in the pan something which lasts only a short time; an effort or partial success which soon turns to failure; a short-lived outburst of enthusiasm for something. *Janet is thinking about a career in nursing. Her intentions seem to be serious, so we hope it's not going to be just another flash in the pan.*

food for thought a situation, something someone says etc. that stimulates thought and careful consideration. *Thank you so much for your constructive criticism and suggestions. They have certainly given me food for thought.*

force of circumstances a sequence of events or a situation that leaves one with no choice in one's course of action. *Unfortunately, we had to sell the house owing to force of circumstances. We desperately needed capital.*

the gift of the gab   the natural ability of being a fluent, persuasive speaker. *'Alan is hoping for a career in politics.' 'Well, he certainly has the gift of the gab.'*

grist to/for someone's mill   information etc. that someone can use to his advantage, that will strengthen his arguments, case etc. *Mr Thomas decided that he would write a letter of complaint to the travel company, so he interviewed several of the other tourists in the hotel. Many of them were dissatisfied, which all added grist to his mill.*

a home from home   a place at which one feels very welcome, happy and comfortable, as in one's own home. *We enjoy visiting Aunt Maud and Uncle Leonard. They're just like my parents, so their house is a home from home.*

the icing on the cake   something additional that is pleasant/helpful etc. but not the essential, most important thing. *The police didn't manage to trick the suspect into an admission of guilt, but that was only going to be the icing on the cake, anyway. They had enough evidence to charge him without a confession.*

a jack of 'all trades   a person who is capable of doing many different kinds of jobs, who is skilled in many ways. Note the saying **jack of all trades (but master of none)** a person who does many different kinds of jobs but who is not expert at any of them. *Why don't you let Joe do the electrical wiring in your new house? He says he would put in the heating as well, and tile the bathroom.' 'That's just the point – Joe's a jack of all trades.'*

the 'jet set   active, fashionable people with expensive tastes who travel widely for business and pleasure and enjoy a life of luxury. Note: a 'jet-setter. *Don't go to Cannes in the summer months for a family holiday – unless you want to get in with the jet set, of course!*

jobs for the boys   (informal) favouritism in the employment world; the system of getting well paid jobs for favoured people through influential friends, connections etc. *There won't be a chance for young university graduates like me. It's usually jobs for the boys in government administration, isn't it?*

a kick in the pants   strong criticism that shocks one into positive action. *Christopher's tutor told him that all the teaching staff were expecting him to fail his exams. That was a real kick in the pants for him. From then on he started to take his studies seriously.*

'kids' stuff   a very easy task that requires no effort. *Change the spark plugs? Of course I can do it myself! It's kids' stuff!*

the law of the jungle   the principle that the strongest and most unscrupulous will survive and do well in a competitive situation. *It's all very well having a degree in business administration, but you don't learn the law of the jungle at university.*

a law unto one'self   someone who acts without consideration for others of his group or community and who does what he wants regardless of written or unwritten rules. *You're wasting your time explaining business ethics to Roger – he's a law unto himself and acts in any way he pleases.*

a leap/shot in the dark a risky attempt/action, a random guess/idea which one hopes will be correct. *His answer was only a shot in the dark but luckily it was correct.*

the lesser of two evils the slightly better of two bad alternatives/ choices/solutions. *Patricia decided that telling Tom a lie would be the lesser of two evils. She didn't want to hurt him by telling him that her career was more important to her than he was.*

the life and soul (of the party) the person who is the centre of attraction because he is the most lively or amusing and provides fun for others. *We had a good time at Penny's get-together. Of course, Mick was the life and soul of the party, as usual.*

the luck of the draw good or bad luck as decided by chance, which one cannot influence. *The Millers had a very efficient au-pair girl last year, but they aren't happy with this year's at all. It's the luck of the draw.*

the man of the hour a person who is in demand/very popular because of a success or something he is admired for. *Congratulations on your success! How does it feel to be the man of the hour?*

the man in the street the average person. *In this country, the man in the street is extremely well informed on political issues.*

money for jam/old rope money earned without any effort. *All you have to do is to stand here and count the people coming into the store. Then write down the numbers per hour. It's money for jam.*

a 'mug's game something that only a foolish person would do, as it is not beneficial and often harmful. *Bernie? Take drugs? Never! He knows it's a mug's game.*

a nail in someone's coffin something bad that contributes towards someone's failure, downfall, ill health etc. *I'm trying to persuade my office colleague to stop smoking. Every time he lights a cigarette, I tell him it's another nail in his coffin.*

the name of the game the main factor, the essential ingredient that counts. *Well, now let's talk about the pay you are offering. Money – that's the name of the game these days, isn't it?*

the nuts and bolts (of something) the essential, practical details. *Just give me the nuts and bolts of the conversion plans for the house and tell me what it will cost.*

one's own man a free and independent person who makes his own decisions and manages his own life. *Why do you let Ralph push you around? I always thought you were your own man.*

a pack of lies something that is completely untrue. *Don't believe a word of it! The story's a pack of lies!*

par for the course (informal) what is expected, usual or normal in the given situation. *'John has been banned from driving for six months, with a fifty-pound fine.' 'Well, when you're found guilty of dangerous driving, that's about par for the course, isn't it?'*

pie in the sky a promise of better things that is unlikely to be fulfilled. *When the Prime Minister talks about reducing unemployment by fifty per cent within three months, everyone knows it's only pie in the sky.*

a piece of cake   a very easy task to do successfully. *After the gang had successfully broken into three banks, it was a piece of cake to break into a few private houses.*

a pillar/the pillars of society   a person/the people considered to be upholding society's moral and traditional values most reliably (because of social standing and profession, e.g. teachers, doctors, judges). *Dr Isaacs is surely above all suspicion of bribery. He's been regarded as a pillar of society in this town for over forty years.*

the pros and cons   the arguments for and against a matter. *Before we can come to a decision, we shall need to hear all the pros and cons of the matter.*

the rank and file   the ordinary people in an organization who have no special position; the masses. *The rank and file are definitely influenced by a party's pre-election promises.*

a rule of thumb   a practical rule which has proved through experience to be a useful method of assessment but which ignores finer points of detail. *Are there any rules of thumb for English prepositions?*

the run of the mill   the average thing in kind or quality; the everyday, routine thing. *'What kind of goods does the new shop sell? Anything special?' 'No. Just the run of the mill, as far as I could see.'*

the salt of the earth   ordinary people with high ideals and an upright character; valuable members of society. *People who devote their free time to community or social work may rightfully be called the salt of the earth.*

a share/slice of the cake   a share/portion of the profits, benefits etc. *When Richard realized that the partnership was more successful than had been expected, he demanded a larger slice of the cake.*

a skeleton in the cupboard   a past event/fact (usually something embarrassing or shameful) which is kept secret. *A presidential candidate must have an immaculate past record, but most influential families have a skeleton in the cupboard somewhere.*

a spoke in someone's wheel   a hindrance to someone's plans, something that causes a setback, delay etc. *Jones didn't expect any members of the board to challenge his authority. The votes against him were certainly a spoke in his wheel.* Often **put** ~.

a step in the right direction   an improvement; something done that brings one nearer to one's final goal/aim. *Jill wants to become a fashion designer eventually. She's just been offered a place at the local art college, so I suppose that's a step in the right direction.*

a 'stick-in-the-mud   a person with fixed views and ideas, without desire for progress or change. *Why won't you let your sons computerize the business, Mr Thomas? Don't let it be said that you are a stick-in-the-mud.*

a stone's throw   a short distance. *We could visit the Railway Museum as well. According to this guidebook, it's only a stone's throw from here.*

a storm in a teacup   a lot of excitement and discussion about a trivial matter. *The papers are full of some incident that took place at the Russian Embassy – probably just another storm in a teacup.*

a straw in the wind an incident, happening, statement etc. that indicates how a future situation might develop, how a person/group/country etc. might act. *This reaction can surely be regarded as a straw in the wind. There are definitely some major policy changes ahead.*

a thorn in the flesh/someone's side something/someone that is a source of annoyance/distaste/trouble for someone. *The new associate has been a thorn in Patterson's flesh ever since he joined the company. Patterson thought that three partners were enough.*

the tip of the iceberg only the beginning or a small part of a problem/ difficult situation etc. which is known to be much bigger. *This incident is just the tip of the iceberg. If you ask me, there's much more to come.*

a tower of strength a person who can be relied upon for help/comfort/ encouragement in a time of trouble or grief. *Aunt Jessica was a real tower of strength when Father died.*

the tricks of the trade the best, most effective methods of doing a particular job, learnt by experience. Often **teach someone/learn** ~. *Bob hasn't been in business very long and he often has trouble with suppliers. He needs someone to teach him the tricks of the trade.*

a turn-up for the book(s) something that is unexpected, a surprise development. *'There's Bill Davis on the phone for you.' 'Well, that is a turn-up for the books. He swore I should never hear from him again!'*

the writing on the wall an event or indication which points to impending dangers, misfortune or difficulty; a warning of bad things to come. Often **see/recognize** ~. *The steep drop in sales orders was recognized as the writing on the wall. The firm immediately began to diversify.*

Adjective + noun

the 'acid test the ultimate, most severe test that proves the ability, truth, worth etc. of someone/something beyond all doubt. *Jim thinks he is a shrewd businessman with a first-class product, but the acid test will come when he has to face up to Japanese high-tech competitors.*

ancient/past history a subject/story/person in someone's past that is no longer important or relevant and which he often prefers to forget, e.g. a past mistake, a former love affair. *Bob doesn't like to talk about his first wife. He says that for him she's past history.*

an armchair critic/expert etc. a person who offers criticism or advice on a subject or area of knowledge in which he was never actively involved. *Uncle Tom loves to tell the boys how to play cricket. He's a real armchair expert.* Note also: **armchair travel etc.** reading about travel. *If you enjoy armchair travelling, turn to page 14 and find yourself in Kingston, Jamaica.*

an awkward/tough customer an unpleasant, difficult or dangerous person to deal with. *If a Mr Jack Evans phones, give me the call. He's an awkward customer and I like to deal with him personally.*

a back seat   a position in which one has little or nothing to say in the managing or running of affairs, without importance, influence or responsibility. Often **take** ~. *Dick has been running the business for three months, but as soon as his father gets out of hospital, he'll be forced to take a back seat again.*

a back-seat driver   1 a passenger who gives unnecessary and unwanted advice or criticism to the driver.   2 an interfering person of no authority who tries to influence the actions/methods/decisions etc. of others. *No back-seat drivers, thank you, Uncle Richard. We're perfectly capable of bringing up our children without your help.*

(the) 'backroom boys   a group of people who do important work for prominent public figures, but who are not in the public eye themselves, e.g. scientists, research workers, political aides. *It's the backroom boys who really run a country, not its leader. Without their invaluable work, no important political decisions could be taken.*

a 'bargaining counter   a special position or advantage in politics, business or a private dispute with which one can bargain and thus weaken the position of one's opponent. *The students' protest against the new matriculation regulations was ineffective, because they had no real bargaining counter.*

a/one's besetting sin   a dominant fault of character or bad habit. *Mark is quite a likeable type of person, but his besetting sin is his ambition to be best at everything.*

a bitter pill (for someone) (to swallow)   something that is unpleasant or difficult to accept, e.g. a disappointment, defeat, rejection, setback, refusal etc. *It was a very bitter pill for Gwen to swallow when Michael fell in love with her younger sister.*

a blind alley   1 a short, narrow street closed at one end.   2 something that has no future, e.g. a job without prospects. *Tom thinks the job of motor mechanic is a blind alley, as in ten years' time, all cars may be electronic and computer-driven!*

a blind date   (usually **go on/have/meet on** ~) an arranged social meeting of two people of opposite sexes who do not know each other. *Karen and Doug have been happily married for over ten years. Did you know that they met on a blind date?*

a/one's 'blind spot   lack of will or ability to understand/accept something or to judge something/someone objectively or rationally, often because of a prejudice, lack of knowledge, emotional involvement etc. *I'm afraid poetry is a blind spot with me. I like people to say what they mean in plain words.* □ *Brian has a blind spot as far as Sheila is concerned. She treats him abominably, but he accepts it all without question.*

the bright lights   the entertainment, opportunities and excitement associated with city life. *Valerie is starting a job in London next week. After village life in Scotland, she's looking forward to the bright lights.*

a 'bright spark a lively, intelligent person with a quick wit; a bright, clever child. *'Anne gave an excellent talk, full of ideas and wit.' 'Yes, she was a particularly bright spark at school, too.'*

the burning question a question/issue much discussed; an important matter/problem that needs to be solved urgently. *The bank will definitely give us a loan, but the burning question is, will they let us have as much as we need?*

a carbon copy (of someone/something) 1 someone who is very like someone else in character, personal qualities etc. *You say your uncle's teaching you how to succeed in business, but haven't you noticed that he's turning you into a cold, calculating carbon copy of himself?* 2 something that is very like something else in detail, appearance, method etc., e.g. a crime. *The two supermarket break-ins on Portsmouth Road were a carbon copy of the ones on Holborn Road. Obviously the same gang was involved.*

a caretaker government/chairman etc. a temporary government etc. that is in office only until a new one has been elected. *We all hope that Robin will remain caretaker chairman until his successor has been appointed.*

the casting vote the deciding vote which is given by the last person (the chairperson at official business meetings etc.) when votes for and against something are equal. *That's four votes for, and four against. Kathy, you have the casting vote.*

a clean bill of health a positive confirmation given by someone in authority after an examination/investigation that someone/something is in good health/condition/order. It can refer to a person's health but also to his conduct, methods, honesty etc. *The Justice Department examined the case thoroughly, but after finding nothing incriminating, gave the company a clean bill of health.*

a clean slate/sheet 1 a past record of conduct/work/achievement without discredit. *Jacobs has been one of our most trusted workers. He's had a clean slate for over twenty years.* 2 an opportunity for a fresh start, forgetting past mistakes. *Patrick was in trouble for stealing at school, but soon afterwards his family moved away, so he was able to start again with a clean sheet at another school.*

a 'clever dick/a smart alec(k) a person who enjoys showing his superiority in front of others, and who readily corrects/criticizes others. *'What's your opinion of the new man?' 'Well, if you ask me, he's a clever dick!'*

a close call/shave/thing a narrow escape from anything unpleasant, e.g. from danger, accident, death, defeat, loss, failure, embarrassment. *That was a close call! That van came speeding round the corner and didn't see me crossing the road!* □ *'Did Oliver pass his exam?' 'Yes, but it was a close shave and he knows it!'*

a close-run thing a race, competition, election etc. in which the results are very close. *As the election drew near, it became increasingly clear that it would be very close-run thing.*

a closed book 1 a subject that one person or people in general know(s) little or nothing about. *I'm afraid nuclear physics is more or less a closed book to me.* 2 a subject of the past that should no longer be discussed because it is ended and thus no longer interesting or relevant. *Patricia regards her first marriage as a closed book. She never mentions Rob and doesn't expect other people to mention him either.*

cold comfort   poor consolation, very little help or sympathy after some misfortune. *When John lost his job, it was cold comfort telling him that he was only one of five hundred.*

(the) cold war   war carried out not by fighting, but by propaganda, economic sanctions, break-off of diplomatic relations etc. *Cold war between the two superpowers has long been a thing of the past.*

the common touch   the ability to adapt to people of all types and classes, being accepted and liked by them. *Adams was asked to speak to the workers on the management's behalf, as he was regarded as having the common touch.*

a confirmed bachelor   a man who has decided never to marry on principle, or who is unlikely to marry because of his set habits and life-style. *Robert's a confirmed bachelor – unlike his brother who was married three times.*

a cool customer   1 a self-assured person who in a calm manner often presumes on others. 2 a person who remains cool and calm under pressure, stress or emotional strain. *The police knew that Barker was a cool customer and that he would lie convincingly in court.*

creature comforts   enjoyable things which satisfy our physical needs, e.g. good food, clothing, comfort in the home. *Rita refuses to go on a camping holiday. She insists that she needs her creature comforts and little luxuries, especially on holiday.*

a damp squib   something that is meant to cause excitement or to be sensational (e.g. news, an event, a story/publication) but which does not provide the expected effect. *The story about the latest spy case turned out to be a damp squib. It couldn't be proved and was soon forgotten.*

a different/a whole new 'ball game   a separate issue or matter very different from the matter under discussion etc.; a new situation very different from the present one. *Now that Mark has voting shares in the company and a seat on the board, it will be a whole new ball game in the boardroom. He will be able to influence all the board's decisions.*

a different kettle of fish   something entirely different, usually more difficult, complicated, demanding. *Mary enjoys playing the piano for her own pleasure, but she says playing in the school concert will be a very different kettle of fish.*

a distressed area   part of a country which has continued unemployment problems with resulting economic hardship. *There are several distressed areas in Scotland and in the North of England due to mass unemployment.*

a double bind   (usually **be in/find oneself in/put someone in** ~) a dilemma with two possible choices/courses of action which are equally undesirable. *The company's reorganization programme put Jim in a double bind. He could either choose an immediate transfer to Glasgow – which he didn't want – or he could risk being transferred to a place of the company's choice at a later date, which he might like even less.*

double Dutch unintelligible written or spoken language, difficult to understand and seemingly meaningless. *I'm sorry but I can't understand this legal jargon, It's all double Dutch to me!* □ *Mary's little boy is learning to talk now. He chats all day – mostly double Dutch, of course!*

(a) double think two contradictory opinions about someone/something at the same time, which lead to contradictory actions. *As far as Jenny is concerned, there's a bit of double think on Mr Baxter's part. On the one hand he asks her to represent the company at the annual trade congress, but on the other he won't give her any authority inside the department.*

a doubting Thomas a sceptic; a person who only believes what he has seen himself or what can be proved to be true. *Hugh has always been something of a doubting Thomas. He won't believe what you say until you show him the letter to prove it.*

a down payment partial payment paid when a purchase deal is made or when an order is given, before one is in possession of the goods. *We've made the down payment on a new house. We're moving in next month!*

a dry/dummy run a trial or practice performance to see how successfully a project, machine etc. works. *There were a few setbacks with the new factory equipment, but on the dummy run everything went smoothly.*

Dutch courage courage which one gets from drinking alcohol. *When Bob failed his exam for the second time, he resorted to Dutch courage before he went home to break the news to his family.*

a Dutch treat entertainment (a meal, a film etc.) where each person pays his own share. *It's very kind of Martin to invite us all to a celebration meal, but it will cost him too much, so let's make it a Dutch treat instead!* Note: **go Dutch**.

easy/fair game someone who is easy to attack or take unfair advantage of because of his weak/exposed position. *After his shattering political defeat, he was fair game in Fleet Street.*

an easy rider (mainly US informal) an opportunist, a person who takes what advantages society or the situation has to offer but who gives nothing in return. *Every social system will be abused by its easy riders who claim benefits that they are not entitled to.*

the eternal triangle a situation of emotional conflict involving two men and one woman or two women and one man. *Marilyn was too proud to accept the eternal triangle situation, so she started divorce proceedings in spite of her husband's promises that he would never leave her.*

a fair crack of the whip a fair chance to do something. *You've been given a fair crack of the whip, my boy, but you haven't proved to me that you are fully competent to run the business. So now it's your brother's turn.*

a fair weather friend a person who stops being a friend when one is in trouble or difficulties. *When Barry lost his job and was no longer able to lead an expensive social life, he discovered he had many fair weather friends.*

a far cry (from something) very different from, often much better than, the object/situation that is being compared. *Today's modern cookery books with their tempting illustrations are a far cry from the old-style cookery books of our grandmothers' days.*

a fast/quick buck (informal, buck = dollar) usually **make/earn** ~. Earn money quickly and easily, usually at the expense of others. *Ben has never been opposed to making a fast buck, so I'm sure we can include him in the deal.*

fast living a life-style devoted to pleasure and luxury. *Simon looks tired and pale. All this fast living of the past months is beginning to show.*

a fast worker a person who is quick at attracting and making contact with members of the opposite sex. *We had only been in the disco about ten minutes and Paul was already surrounded by a group of girls. He's certainly a fast worker!*

a final/last fling the last opportunity for pleasure or amusement before a time of restraint. *Jason is getting married tomorrow, and since his wife-to-be doesn't approve of him going to pubs with friends, he's meeting us in the Red Lion tonight for a final fling.*

a flash Harry a non-complimentary term for a self-assured man whose dress shows expensive but vulgar taste, often characterized by loud colours and extravagance. *We were having a quiet drink at the bar when some flash Harry came in and started ordering champagne for everybody!*

a flying visit a very short visit often made on the way to somewhere else or between doing other things. *Hello, Rita. I can't stay long. I have a hairdresser's appointment, so this is just a flying visit.*

a foregone conclusion an obvious or inevitable result that can be predicted. *With two of our best men injured, it was a foregone conclusion that the other team would win the match.*

foul play 1 unscrupulous dealings. 2 murder or violent crime. *At first the girl's death looked like suicide, but later the police began to suspect foul play.*

a Freudian slip an unintentional mistake in speaking, which is thought to reveal the speaker's true thoughts, wishes etc. *We're going to Brighton for a month in July. Sorry. I mean for a week, of course. That must have been a Freudian slip.*

'funny business (often **be up to some** ~) dealings/actions that seem to be improper, not quite in order or straightforward in a legal or moral sense. *Make sure you get a solicitor to check the contract before you sign it. I have the feeling that Ted Parsons is up to some funny business.*

a gentleman's agreement (usually **come to** ~) an unwritten agreement based on mutual trust and good faith. *When I bought the car from Trevor, we simply came to a gentleman's agreement. I didn't sign anything, and neither did he.*

a 'ginger group a group within a political party or associated with it which is particularly active. *He's always been a political activist with a reputation for forming or joining ginger groups.*

a going concern a successful and active business, shop etc. *I hear that Kate is doing very well with her new boutique. Apparently, it's quite a going concern.*

the going rate the usual price to pay for some service or goods at any particular time. *Ask Judith if she'll do the translation for us, but tell her I want no favours – I'll pay the going rate.*

a golden handshake a gift of money given to an employee by his employer, company etc. for good service when he retires. *He received a golden handshake for forty years' faithful service to his company.*

(the) grass roots society at the local level. Mostly used in a political context, e.g. *grass roots opinion, at grass roots level, a grass roots movement.*

'growing pains difficulties, problems, mistakes etc. that occur at the beginning of a new business concern, enterprise, movement etc. before it is properly established. *Since the state was granted its independence four years ago, it has been going through a continual phase of growing pains.* See also **'teething troubles.**

the 'gutter press those newspapers which specialize in scandal and sensation, crime, sex etc. *If you want correct information read a serious newspaper, not the gutter press.*

a/the happy medium a/the middle course, which avoids two inconvenient/unfavourable extremes. *When Frances has an exam to take, she either studies day and night or does nothing at all. She can never find the happy medium.*

a/the 'hat trick (often **do the** ~) three wins/successes in succession, often in sport, a game etc. *Another hat trick, Peter. You're so lucky at card games!* □ *Margaret Thatcher does the hat trick! A third term of office for Britain's Premier!*

a 'hatchet man/job a person whose job it is to get rid of unnecessary and unwanted factors, e.g. to reduce staff and costs in a company, to discredit opponents (often political); a job with these aims. *In an effort to reduce government spending, a hatchet man was employed to cut costs in several local government departments.*

Hobson's choice a situation where one has no choice at all, as one is forced to take what is offered or nothing. *The reorganization of the company left several workers with Hobson's choice – a job at the new factory in Birmingham or no job at all.*

a hole and corner business/affair etc. secretive, dishonest dealings; some activity which is not carried out openly, as others would disapprove. *I refuse to be involved in some hole and corner affair. Either we declare the new company under our own names or I want nothing to do with it.*

home truths honest criticism which often hurts, but which is meant to help the person criticized. *You will have to learn to face up to a few home truths, my boy, before it's too late.*

a hung jury/parliament a jury which is not in agreement on a verdict; a parliament without a majority for any one party. *The verdict in the murder trial will take longer than expected. There's a hung jury.*

ill-gotten gains money and other advantages obtained by dishonest methods. *The politician was indirectly accused of having accumulated wealth through ill-gotten gains. There was a rumour that he had accepted bribes.*

an Indian summer a period of hot, dry weather in the late autumn. *After three months of continual bad weather, we had an Indian summer in September and October.*

inside information reliable and correct information from someone who has access to it, e.g. because he receives this information at his place of work; information that is not available to everybody. *You are on the short list for the job at the bank. I know the manager's secretary very well and she gave me some inside information.*

an inside job a theft/crime arranged or committed by someone who is employed inside the building or who is connected with it, not by a stranger. *The police are interrogating all the bank staff. They are sure that the robbery was an inside job.*

an/one's ivory tower a way of life, a state, that is out of touch with reality, often associated with individuals who pursue academic or artistic studies. *If Des would only come down from his ivory tower now and again, he might save himself a lot of trouble. He hasn't filled in any tax forms for years.*

a jaundiced eye the prejudice of someone who is determined to find fault and reason for criticism because of jealously or spite. *Peter is always critical of Ben because he doesn't like him. He judges everything Ben does with a jaundiced eye.*

a Job's comforter someone who means to comfort an unhappy person but who manages to depress this person even more. *Don't let the neighbour in after the funeral. Mother has no need of a Job's comforter at the moment.*

kid gloves (usually **treat/handle someone with** ~) treat someone with care, gently, so as not to hurt his feelings or give offence. *Now remember, Janice is very sensitive and needs treating with kid gloves on occasion. So just be very careful what you say to her.*

a knotty problem a difficult, intricate problem to solve. *The advertisement must be only five lines long. Getting all this information into so little space will be a knotty problem.*

the last ditch one's last defence/resource/advantage/effort in a difficult situation, contest, argument etc. before defeat. *The young minister was prepared to fight to the last ditch to defend his good name.* Note also: **a last-ditch attempt/effort.** *In a last-ditch attempt to escape from the police dogs, the thief tried to climb a ten-foot high wall.*

the last straw an additional problem or difficulty that makes present problems intolerable; the ultimate provocation. *The children had been very badly behaved all afternoon, but when they deliberately wiped their sticky fingers on the freshly washed curtains, that was the last straw!*

a leading light someone in a prominent position of respect in a community, branch of study etc. *Mrs Dobson has been a leading light in our local archaeological society for years.*

a leading question a question which suggests the answer one wishes or hopes for. *'I know you will be making a generous donation to our hospital fund again, won't you Mr Pollard?' was her leading question. So I had to get out my cheque-book!*

a left-handed compliment one of doubtful sincerity or which is ambiguous. *Phil said he had never seen anything quite like my paintings – a bit of a left-handed compliment, I thought.*

level pegging the state whereby competitors in a race, participants in an argument etc. are equal, i.e. as good as each other. *'Which presidential candidate will win the TV debate in your opinion?' 'I really don't know. It's level pegging at the moment, I would say.'*

a **'live wire** a very active, forceful and lively person. *Susan's always full of energy and enthusiasm in everything she does. A real live wire.*

a **loaded question** a question which is intended to trap someone into saying or admitting something which will betray him. *'Where were you at the time of the break-in?' 'At 11.35 I was in bed,' replied the suspect. But the police didn't know the time of the break-in, only the thief did. It was a loaded question.*

loose talk careless revelation of information; gossip. *Remember that the information you are dealing with is classified, so there must be no loose talk outside the office, not even to your wife. Have I made myself clear?*

a **lost cause** an ideal, project, cause to which only few people have given their support and which therefore cannot be successful. *Sheila is trying to get everybody in the neighbourhood to sign her petition for an old people's home to be built, but I think she's supporting a lost cause again. She's only got twenty signatures so far.*

a **low profile** quiet behaviour which does not arouse attention or attract notice. (Usually **keep ~**.) *It would be advisable to keep a low profile for a time, until this unpleasant scandal has died down.*

the **lunatic fringe** a small group in a community with radical or fanatical views and conduct. *As always it was the lunatic fringe that turned a peaceful demonstration into chaos.*

a **man/girl Friday** a person who does all the different kinds of jobs that are necessary in an office etc. *They need a man Friday at Jeff's garage, to do everything from cleaning the tools and machines to making tea.*

a **marked man** one who is observed with suspicion or enmity because of some past misdeed or scandal. *When the news leaked out that Jones had been in prison, he became a marked man in the neighbourhood.*

a **'meal ticket** a reliable provider of money and comfort, often taken advantage of and receiving nothing in return. *I don't think Miriam really cares much about John. She just regards him as a convenient meal ticket.*

the **missing link** a person or thing needed to solve a mystery or problem, to explain a situation etc. *The police have made some progress in the murder case, but the motive for the crime is still the missing link.*

a/the **mixed bag/bunch/lot** a group of people of very different types, character, ability, interests etc.; a collection of objects of differing sizes, values, usefulness etc. *'What kind of people had Iris invited to her party?' 'Oh, the usual mixed bag. Everything from the City man to the bohemian artist.'*

a **mixed blessing** someone or something which brings pleasure and which one is pleased to have, but which also brings trouble, disadvantages etc. *Working in the city centre is really a mixed blessing. It's an advantage to be close to the shops in a modern office block, but the traffic and the noise are a real problem.*

a narrow escape an escape, either from danger or from someone/ something unpleasant, which almost failed. *That was a narrow escape! I've been trying to avoid my neighbour all day, and I almost bumped into him in the lift!* See also **a close call/a near miss.**

a nasty piece of work a dangerous, dishonest or cruel person. *Take a word of warning from me. Don't deal with Bill Watson. He may seem friendly and fair at first, but underneath he's a nasty piece of work.*

a near miss/thing a fortunate escape from danger, accident, mishap. *Aeroplanes seldom crash, but, because of bad working conditions of air traffic controllers in certain countries, apparently there are several near misses every month.* See also **a close call/a narrow escape.**

a necessary evil something which is undesirable or unpleasant, but which one cannot do without. *Colin is naturally lazy. He has always regarded work as a necessary evil.*

a new broom (sweeps clean) (saying) a person of responsibility or authority who begins a new job by changing or reforming the existing system. These changes are often not welcomed. *The new boss also turned out to be a new broom. Within three months she had totally reorganized three departments with the result that no one quite knew what he was supposed to be doing!*

the nitty gritty the basic, practical facts; the essential points. *Cut all the background details. Let's get down to the nitty gritty of Webster's proposal.*

a Nosy Parker an interfering person who wants to know all about other people's affairs and things that do not concern him. *I have the feeling that the new neighbour will turn out to be a real Nosy Parker, so it's best not to get too friendly.*

odd jobs different small jobs or tasks, usually manual. *My husband's very good at doing odd jobs around the house and garden.*

an/the odd man 'out a person/thing that is different from or does not fit in with the others of a group; one too many. *Charles seems to be something of an odd man out. He never joins in any of the social activities arranged by the club.*

an 'olive branch (usually **carry/hold out** ~) a token/sign of the desire for peace or reconciliation, end of hostilities etc. *Political experts expect at least one of the nations at war to enter negotiations carrying an olive branch.*

an open and shut case a legal case or other matter whose end is predictable because there can be no doubt about the verdict, outcome etc. *It's an open and shut case, unfortunately. All the evidence is against Roberts. His defending counsel will have a very hard time.*

an open book someone or something straightforward and honest, without mystery or secrecy. *Jerry's life is an open book. He's one of the most uncomplicated fellows that I know.*

an open secret one that has become generally known but which is still supposed to be a secret. *It's an open secret that Philip and Jessica are going to get engaged, but I shall pretend to be surprised when they tell me!*

a parting shot a last hurtful comment, criticism or attack made just before one leaves. *Mildred couldn't resist a parting shot as she opened the* door to leave: *'Oh, and by the way, the job you wanted in the personnel department was offered to me!'*

a passing fancy a temporary liking for something or someone. *We don't like Roger's new girlfriend at all. Both Mark and I are hoping that she's just another of his passing fancies.*

a/the 'pecking order a hierarchical system which determines who dominates. *Who do I go to to get this signed? I'm new here, so I'm not familiar with the pecking order in the firm yet.*

plain sailing a plan or course of action without obstacles or difficulties which is easy and straightforward. *Now that she's mastered the major obstacle in her career, it should all be plain sailing from now on.*

a plum job etc. an easy, well-paid job etc. *Teaching used to be regarded as a plum job, but nowadays it's very hard work.*

a private eye a private detective/enquiry agent. *Walker believed that his son was involved with criminals, so he engaged a private eye to find out.*

a put-up job a pre-arranged matter usually with the intention to swindle or incriminate someone, or to get someone falsely accused. *Don't you see? It was all a put-up job to discredit me. I know nothing about the stolen money!*

a queer customer/fish a person who is difficult to deal with because of his unusual character, nature, attitudes etc. *Gregson is a bit of a queer customer, I suppose. He has no sense of humour at all.*

a quixotic project/plan/scheme etc. one which is considered foolish or extravagant and totally unrealistic. *Paul has some quixotic plan to raise money for charity. He wants us to sponsor him for a parachute jump, but he's never been in an aeroplane in his life!*

a random shot a wild guess that is not expected to be correct. (Often take ~.) *I don't know the year so I'll have to take a random shot at it. 1848?*

a raw deal unfair, harsh treatment usually of a moral or financial nature. *We all think that Polly has been given a raw deal, and that it is the duty of the firm to find her another job in one of its branches.*

ready money cash which is immediately available. *William will probably give you a cheque. He hardly ever has any ready money.*

a ready wit a quick mind, prompt to answer, able to make fitting comments and jokes. *I've always envied people with a ready wit who always know just what to say and when.*

a ringside seat a position from which one can observe or experience clearly what is happening. *June is being transferred to headquarters for six months for management training, so she'll have a ringside seat.*

a rolling stone a person who moves from place to place, job to job, without staying anywhere very long. *For years, Mike was a rolling stone – until he met Anne.* Note the saying **a rolling stone gathers no moss**, i.e. such a person does not acquire anything permanent, such as good friends.

rose-coloured spectacles (usually **look at life/see things through ~**) a way of looking at life or seeing a person with a positive, optimistic and often unrealistic attitude. *Samantha looks at life through rose-coloured spectacles. She simply refuses to see problems or difficulties.*

a rough diamond an uncultured, often rough-looking person with a kind heart and good personal qualities. *Jack may be a rough diamond, but he's honest and reliable and always willing to help.*

a rough guess an approximate estimate or calculation. *Well, it's only a rough guess, but I'd say a caravan of that size would cost around fifteen thousand pounds.*

a rough/smooth passage a difficult/easy time. *We had better be prepared for a rough passage when we start up the business. We'll have large overheads and a huge overdraft to carry – and not many sales in the first few months.*

a rough patch a time of personal or financial difficulty or trouble. (Usually **go through** ~.) *Their marriage is going through a rough patch, true, but they are sensible enough to sort matters out.*

a rough ride a painful or unpleasant experience; strong criticism etc. (Usually **give someone** ~.) *The managing director sent for Maxwell and apparently gave him a very rough ride for losing the Japanese contract.*

a rude awakening an unpleasant shock; the sudden realization or awareness that things are worse than one believed. *I don't think Yvonne realizes just how precarious the situation is. It will be a rude awakening for her when the bank manager tells her that we are forced to sell the house.*

a/one's ruling passion a passion or motive which dominates a person's life or character, e.g. a love of money, desire for power etc. *Peter's ruling passion is his ambition. He wants to be the best in everything he does.*

a safe bet something that is sure to be successful, correct, what one expects it to be. *Put your money on Flying Lady in the 3.30 race. She's a pretty safe bet.* □ *Kate is a safe bet for the protest march on Saturday. She's always taken part in marches in the past.*

a saving grace a good quality or characteristic which redeems or excuses a person who has otherwise only rather bad qualities. *There's not much good to be said about Jason, but his saving grace is his deep affection for his little son.*

second fiddle a person or position that is not the most important; someone of little authority and influence. (Usually **play** ~ **to someone.**) *I've been playing second fiddle to my brother for long enough. Now it's my turn to control the business.*

second nature some skill or practised ability that comes very easily. *When you've used the computer a few more times, it will become second nature to you.*

second thoughts further thoughts on a matter which lead to a changed decision or opinion. *I hope you're not having second thoughts about the dance on Saturday. Please say you'll still be coming.*

sharp practice(s) dishonest methods/dealings in business. *There are some sharp practices going on in the building trade. Inferior building materials are sometimes used.*

a/the/one's sixth sense the power of intuition that warns one against danger and makes one sensitive to people and situations. *I saw an* *unattended parcel in a corner of the room, and a sixth sense told me that I should leave the building immediately. Could it have been a bomb?*

a skeleton staff the smallest number of employees needed to keep the office, service etc. going, e.g. at holiday times. *The firm doesn't close in August. We keep it open, if only with a skeleton staff.*

small beer/potatoes (informal) something of little importance or value. *I know it's small beer compared with your valuable collection, but I do own an original Picasso sketch. □ What you've seen today in the atelier is really only small potatoes. When Gina is working on a new collection, her dress designs are superb.*

'small fry people or groups not considered to be very important or influential; small businesses. *Most public companies regard family businesses as small fry, no matter what their volume of business is.*

the small print those parts of a legal document which often contain important exceptions and exclusions etc. and which are difficult to read and easily overlooked because of the small type. *You should never sign an insurance policy until you have read all the small print carefully.*

'small talk trivial, unimportant conversation. *The meeting started off with the usual small talk which seemed to go on for ages.*

a smooth operator a calculating person who can easily persuade and manipulate others into doing things to his advantage. *Don't agree to let Joe look after your finances. He's a smooth operator and you may not realize what his real intentions are until it's too late.*

a snap decision/judgement a decision etc. made immediately because there is not much time to think about it; a decision, judgement etc. made too quickly without enough thought. *Consider the matter very carefully. I don't want a snap decision that you will regret later.*

a 'soap opera a popular TV or radio series often of many years' duration about the life and fortunes of a family or community, e.g. 'Dallas', 'Dynasty', 'Coronation Street'.

a soft option an alternative course of action which is easier or more agreeable. *Rebecca realized that if she stayed in her present job it would mean competing with an envious rival. Leaving the firm would probably be a soft option. □ Pupils tend to regard music and art as soft options for school certificate examination purposes, but this is a mistaken belief.*

soft soap (informal) flattery designed to get what one wants from someone. *Remember, no soft soap with Uncle Eric. If he wants you to work for him, he'll offer you a job in any case.* Note the verb **to soft-'soap someone.**

a soft spot a special liking or weakness for someone/something. *You know that Uncle Bill has always had a soft spot for you, so if you need advice or help, ask him. □ Liz has always had a soft spot for animals. She does voluntary work for the Battersea Dogs' Home at the weekends.*

a soft touch a person who readily lends or gives money, who does not notice that he is being used, taken advantage of, overcharged etc. *I feel sorry for Harry. His so-called friends realize that he's a soft touch, so they always invite him to the pub, knowing that he will pay for the drinks.*

sour grapes   Describes someone's attitude towards someone else's good fortune or towards something which he can't have and therefore despises. *'Robert said that he doesn't like Don's new Volvo.' 'Well, that sounds like sour grapes to me. Robert would love a Volvo himself but he can't afford one.'*

the spitting image (of something/someone)   the exact likeness. *You can't mistake the fact that Jackie is Rosemary's daughter. She's the spitting image of her mother.*

a spot check   (usually **do/carry out** ~) a random test, examination or investigation carried out without warning. *If you follow the green signs at Heathrow Airport, you won't have any trouble going through customs. They only do an occasional spot check.*

a square deal   fair treatment morally, a fair bargain financially. *Do you think the estate agent gave us a square deal when he sold our property?*

a square meal   a substantial meal of good basic food. *The poor man looked thin and pale. I thought he looked very much in need of a square meal, so I invited him to have lunch with us.*

a square peg (in a round hole)   someone who is not suited to his position, job, surroundings etc.; someone who does not fit in. *Bernard used to be a research scientist before his institute had to close down. He got a part-time job teaching, but he's a square peg. He can't handle the children and obviously can't adapt to school life.*

a standing joke   a joke which always causes amusement to certain people who know its origin. *I didn't understand why everyone started to laugh when I said 'cricket'. I later learned that it was a standing joke in the family.*

a 'stepping stone   a job/position/success which helps towards something better/higher in someone's profession, social status or educational level. *The pop group's tremendous success in America was an important stepping stone in their international career.*

a stiff drink   a strong alcoholic drink usually taken to calm oneself after some bad news. *Well, after that shocking news I feel in need of a stiff drink.*

a stiff upper lip   (usually **have/keep/maintain** ~) a state of great self-control in the face of danger or difficulties, bad news, unpleasant situations, defeat etc. *When the doctor told Bill that his heart was in a critical state, he kept a stiff upper lip and replied with a smile: 'Then I suppose I'll have to take life a little more slowly, won't I?'*

a straight answer/talk   a frank, open and unambiguous answer etc. (Usually **give someone/ask for/want** ~.) *You said you wanted a straight answer, so I'll give you one. Yes, it was me who told the police where you were hiding. □ It's time we had a straight talk about your future, my boy.*

a straw poll/vote   an unofficial opinion poll which tries to establish public attitudes on matters of current interest. *On election day a straw poll was taken outside six constituencies in London, and from those figures they were predicting strong Conservative gains.*

a stuffed shirt   a pompous, conceited person. *Pete, now you're behaving like a stuffed shirt. Mr Littleton may not be rich or influential, but that's no reason not to accept his invitation.*

a sugar daddy a rich, elderly man who favours a young woman financially in return for special attentions. *No sugar daddies for Marilyn! She told old Parkinson to get lost!*

a sure-fire method/way/solution a sure, reliable method etc. *If you need a sure-fire method to improve the working morale of the staff, just promise them more money for better results.*

a sweeping statement a very general statement which leaves out details, restrictions, exceptions etc. *Aren't you making a rather sweeping statement when you claim that private doctors use the same methods as calculating businessmen?*

a tall order a task which is difficult to accomplish or a request which is difficult to grant. *That's rather a tall order, Mrs Lewis. I can have your car repaired by tomorrow, but I really can't do it by this afternoon.*

a tall story a statement or narrative that is difficult to believe because it seems impossible or unrealistic. *Don't believe a word of what Nick told you about his adventure in Bangkok. It sounds very much to me like another of his tall stories.*

'teething troubles the difficulties and setbacks which arise at the beginning of a new enterprise/project and which are expected to become fewer with experience. *We can improve the new engine design; we don't need to change it completely. The failure of the engine test was only due to teething troubles.*

the third degree (usually **give someone/put someone through** ~) harsh and intensive interrogation. *I've given you time to recover from the shock of the accident before putting you through the third degree, but now I need some answers to some very important questions.*

a third party another person besides the two already in question. *Now you say that your car was damaged by his car. Was there a third party involved in the accident?*

the Third World the developing countries. *Several countries of the Third World are making definite progress on their way to economic independence.*

a tight spot/corner a difficult or awkward situation. *I wish you hadn't told Chris about my plans to move house. It put me in a very tight spot when he asked me why I hadn't told him.*

a tight squeeze (e.g. in a vehicle) crowded, allowing very little room. *'Can all five of us get in your car?' 'Well, it will be a tight squeeze, but it's only for a short distance.'*

a (little) tin god a person who is mistakenly held in great respect or credited with great knowledge, influence etc. *Don't regard your professor as a little tin god. If you think he's mistaken, just tell him why you think so.*

(the) top brass (informal) people of the highest position, rank or authority. *It's obviously going to be an important occasion. All the top brass will be attending.*

an unknown quantity an unknown factor which cannot be calculated or predicted and is therefore a risk. *I can say with certainty how five of the members will vote, but Stevens is an unknown quantity this time.*

(the) upper crust the aristocracy, the highest social classes. *In certain working situations, belonging to the upper crust can create more problems than belonging to the underprivileged classes.*

a vested interest an interest in or connection with some enterprise that involves personal gain. *Don't expect an unbiased opinion from Morgan. He has a vested interest in the project.*

a vicious circle a situation which cannot be altered or improved because the cause and the effect of the problem lead to each other. *If you earn more, you have to pay more for things; if you have to pay more you want to earn more; so it's a vicious circle, unless wages and prices are frozen.*

a wet blanket a person who spoils a jolly atmosphere or who does not join in the fun of others, thereby reducing it. *Matthew, don't be such a wet blanket! Grab a glass and let me pour you some wine. Come and join in the fun!*

wishful thinking imagining something to be true because one wishes it to be true. *'That must be John', she thought as the telephone rang, knowing full well that it was only wishful thinking on her part.*

a working breakfast/lunch/dinner a meal at which the participants discuss work or business. *There are still a lot of details to discuss, so we're meeting for a working lunch at 12.30.*

4 Idiomatic pairs

Pairs of adjectives

alive and kicking (informal) well and active. *I had a letter from Rod. He's still very much alive and kicking, working on an Australian sheep farm.*

born and bred born and brought up; having spent one's early years. *Born and bred in Yorkshire, she wrote novels containing much autobiographical detail and description of the Yorkshire countryside.*

bright and breezy in a cheerful, bright mood, doing things quickly and in a lively manner. *Larry is a very bright and breezy sort of person. Everybody likes him.*

bright and early very early in the morning. *Let's get up bright and early and set off at seven!*

bright-eyed and bushy-tailed looking very cheerful, bright and lively. *Sue must have had some good news. She's looking very bright-eyed and bushy-tailed this morning.*

cut and dried settled, decided, final (arrangements, plans, opinions etc.). *Our holiday arrangements are all cut and dried. We're going to Crete for the last two weeks in August.*

fair and square (informal) 1 in a fair way. *Let's settle the bill for the damage fair and square. We were both at fault, so we'll both pay half.* 2 exactly, directly. *He raised his fist and hit him fair and square on the chin.*

free and easy casual, relaxed; unconcerned about social convention. *I hope it won't be formal dress for dinner in the hotel – I like to be free and easy when I'm on holiday.*

hale and hearty physically strong and fit. *Grandfather was hale and hearty right up to his death at ninety-three.*

home and dry sure of success, no longer in danger of failure, losing etc. *If the team makes the next round, we'll be home and dry for the semi-finals.*

meek and mild quiet, not self-assertive or bold. *Pru should have defended herself and told Lucy what she thinks of her, but she's too meek and mild.*

rough and ready only approximate; not exact. *I can't tell you how to use prepositions correctly, but I can give you a few rough and ready rules.*

safe and sound unharmed. *After his three months' trip on foot through Africa, our son is glad to be back home safe and sound.*

short and sweet brisk, without unnecessary detail (speech, letter, explanation etc.). *Remember, no one wants to hear a long speech, so just keep it short and sweet.*

sick and tired (informal) thoroughly bored or annoyed with someone/ something. *I hope Sid doesn't start telling us about his adventure in Algiers again – I'm sick and tired of hearing about it.*

slow but sure slow but good. *He doesn't rush things. He's a slow but sure worker and the end product is always worth waiting for.*

spick and span clean and tidy, in very good order. *How do you manage to keep your house so spick and span with three children?*

Pairs of nouns

aches and pains (small) health complaints. *I met Hilary yesterday. She talked about her aches and pains all the time.*

bag and baggage (with) all one's luggage; (with) all one's possessions. *Valerie soon got tired of Malcolm's bohemian way of life and moved out of the flat, bag and baggage.*

beer and skittles fun and pleasure. (Often in the phrase **life is not all beer and skittles**.) *It's a good summer course, but it isn't all beer and skittles. You'll have to do some work.*

one's best bib and tucker (informal) one's best or formal clothing. *I've got an extra ticket for the ball. Why don't you put on your best bib and tucker and join us?*

bits and pieces 1 various small things, e.g. someone's belongings. *This looks like Mike's cigarette lighter. He's always leaving his bits and pieces lying around.* 2 small jobs. *I shall be home late. I still have some bits and pieces to attend to at the office.* 3 small parts, extracts of a conversation etc. *I didn't hear all they said, only bits and pieces, but it sounded as if they were dissatisfied with the organization as well.*

board and lodging (expenditure on) food and accommodation at a private house or small guesthouse. *I paid about £200 for the week, including petrol, board and lodging.*

body and soul physical and mental energy. *Bob puts body and soul into his community work. He loves every minute of it.*

one's bread and butter one's means of earning money/making a living. *He paints only for pleasure. He earns his bread and butter as a photographer.*

bricks and mortar buildings and property, especially for investment purposes. *Forget stocks and shares. Put your money into bricks and mortar.*

chapter and verse usually **give ~ (for something)**. Give an exact source for something stated, quote an authority. *If there's anything you want to know about tax exemption, ask Jim. He knows all the details and he'll give you chapter and verse.*

the cut and thrust 1 the energetic exchange of words and ideas in an argument etc. *I've always enjoyed the cut and thrust of a clever debate.* 2 the characteristic methods of attack and counter-moves between rivals, e.g. in business or politics. *George was advised to retire early for health reasons, but he knew he would miss the cut and thrust of business competition too much.*

by/in dribs and drabs in small amounts, at irregular intervals. *At three o'clock people started arriving in dribs and drabs, and by four o'clock the exhibition was crowded.*

fun and games 1 pleasurable activity, lively amusement. *You'll enjoy summer school, but it won't all be fun and games.* 2 (ironic) trouble or difficulties, an argument etc. *You've just missed all the fun and games. Ken's been trying to repair the kitchen tap and he's soaked us all through!*

give and take compromise; willingness to do what the other wants. *With a bit of give and take from both partners in a marriage, a wife and mother can also make a success of a job.*

hammer and tongs (usually **be/go 'at it** ~) argue/quarrel loudly and energetically. *There was a dreadful argument in the room above. They were at it hammer and tongs for over an hour.*

the haves and the have-nots people with money, privilege and influence and people without these. *In several countries there appear to be two kinds of justice – one for the haves and another for the have-nots.*

heaven and earth usually **move** ~ **(to do something)**. Use all one's influence; try everything possible to attain one's goal. *The parents and teachers are prepared to move heaven and earth to stop the kindergarten from being closed.*

hook, line and sinker completely; in every way or detail etc. (Usually **swallow/fall for something** ~.) Believe an untrue story in all details. *I didn't think he would believe my excuse, but he swallowed it hook, line and sinker.*

by hook or by crook in spite of any difficulty, by any method whether fair or unfair. *I'll get the money somehow, by hook or by crook.*

a hue and cry loud and outspoken protest. *There was a great hue and cry when it was announced that the factory would be reducing staff.*

hustle and bustle hurried activity. *I hate big airports. It's all hustle and bustle.*

ifs and buts excuses. *No ifs and buts, just do the work and tell me when it's finished.*

the ins and outs intricate details often difficult to explain and understand. *The ins and outs of the British parliamentary system are often difficult for foreigners to understand.*

life and limb one's life, survival, as in **risk/escape with** ~. *The rescue team risked life and limb trying to get the three young climbers down the mountain.*

lock, stock and barrel everything; every item. *Jock has decided to go and live with his daughter in Portsmouth, so he's selling up here, lock, stock and barrel.*

man to man openly and sincerely, as in **talk** ~. *We talked man to man for over an hour and managed to clear up a lot of misunderstandings that there had been between us.*

every nook and cranny every possible small place, as in **search** ~. *I've looked everywhere possible, searched every nook and cranny, but I can't find the ring.*

odds and ends 1 small things, articles, e.g. one's belongings. *I've almost finished packing, but there are still a few odds and ends in the bathroom that I* *have to put in.* 2 small jobs. *There are still some odds and ends to tie up at the office before I go to Japan.* See also **bits and pieces**.

part and parcel part of something. *The recent radio and TV information programmes on smoking are all part and parcel of a government campaign against it.*

peace and quiet a period of quiet and calm. *Turn that music down! Some people in this house are trying to get some Sunday morning peace and quiet.*

rack and ruin state of bad repair or ruin due to neglect, as in **go to ~**. *What a pity that this lovely old house is just going to rack and ruin.*

without rhyme or reason (someone's actions, a situation etc.) not making sense, illogical. *Why should Wilson close down the store when it's making such profits? It's without rhyme or reason!*

the rough and tumble rough (emotional) conditions, e.g. of competition, politics, business etc. *Spencer is a young idealist. I don't think he'll be able to stand up to the rough and tumble of the political arena for long.*

stuff and nonsense foolish talk, ideas, beliefs etc. (an expression of disagreement). *'They say that Bob's going to retire on his sixtieth birthday.' 'Stuff and nonsense – he won't leave the company unless they carry him out!'*

the thrills and spills successes and failures, excitement and disappointment. *I hear this is your first day on the newspaper. Welcome to the thrills and spills of journalism!*

touch and go critical, close to both success and failure, life and death etc. *Greg is in a critical state after the accident. They say it's touch and go.*

ups and downs good and bad moments, happiness and sadness etc. *There's no need to be so unhappy. Every relationship has its ups and downs.*

wear and tear deterioration through daily use (e.g. of clothes, furniture, one's health). *The material is very strong. It should stand lots of wear and tear.*

wheeling and dealing complicated (often dishonest or immoral) negotiating in politics, business etc. for personal gain. *I don't understand the council's decision to make a nature reserve into a property development area. Obviously a lot of wheeling and dealing has gone on.*

the whys and wherefores the reasons for something, the purpose behind something. *For the present we must simply accept the new regulations, but we shall expect to be told the whys and wherefores very soon.*

Pairs of adverbs

as and when whenever. *New catalogues will be sent to you from time to time, as and when they appear.*

back to front the wrong way round. *Jimmy's got his pullover on back to front.*

by and large taken as a whole, generally speaking. *By and large, it's been a pretty good year for the local team.*

far and wide everywhere. *I've hunted far and wide for those documents and they're nowhere. I must have left them on the train.*

few and far between seldom. *We enjoy having Uncle Alex here, but unfortunately his visits are few and far between these days.*

first and foremost most important, coming before all other things. *First and foremost, the new sales orders will mean employing extra staff to deal with the extra work.*

here, there and everywhere in many different places. *'Could this bag belong to Roger?' 'Oh, yes, quite possibly. He leaves his stuff here, there and everywhere.'*

in and out coming in and going out several times. *Colin wants to speak to you. He's been in and out all morning looking to see if you were in your office.*

left, right and centre everywhere; to extremes. *There was this eccentric outside the town hall. He was handing out five-pound notes, left, right and centre! □ He spends money left, right and centre.*

loud and clear very clearly. *'It's a bad telephone line. Can you hear me?' 'Yes, loud and clear!'*

more or less approximately, roughly; practically. *'Is this the sort of design you were thinking of?' 'Yes, more or less.' □ He more or less told me to start looking for another job.*

neither here nor there not important, not relevant. *The fact that she's Lord Dunvale's daughter is neither here nor there. She'll lose her driving licence, as would anyone else caught driving a car in that condition.*

now and again/then not often; occasionally. *'Do you still go to the theatre every week?' 'Only now and again, not as regularly as we used to.'*

on and off/off and on at irregular intervals; not all the time. *He's been working at the garage in his spare time on and off for over five years now.*

over and out the message which signals the end of a radio communication. *Position understood. End of message. Over and out.*

to and fro one way and then the other, up and down. *That poor man's very nervous, he's been walking to and fro in the corridor for an hour. His wife's expecting twins!*

up and about recovered and in good health. *Barry's much better now, thanks. He's up and about again.*

Pairs of verbs

bow and scrape behave in a humble, servile manner, often because one wants something from someone. *I've asked him politely for his help. Surely he doesn't expect me to bow and scrape to him!*

chop and change change one's mind, opinions, plans, wishes etc. often. *I do wish the boss wouldn't chop and change so much. I booked three flights for him today, but then he changed his mind and I had to cancel them all.*

do or die make the greatest possible effort, or fail. Used when referring to a final attempt or to a one-and-only opportunity. *Colin's taking a university entrance exam tomorrow. He knows it's do or die, so he has been working very hard.*

fetch and carry fetch things, do small jobs for someone at his will, especially when the person concerned could do these things himself. *Mrs Hollings is always complaining that her teenage son is very lazy, but he won't change as long as she's willing to fetch and carry for him.*

forgive and forget be prepared to be reconciled; forget enmity. *This is the second time you've cheated Jim. I don't think he'll be prepared to forgive and forget again this time.*

give and take yield; make compromises. *If Barbara were prepared to give and take a little more, our relationship would be much smoother.*

grin and bear it (informal) suffer something unpleasant with optimism, because one cannot change it. *Our hotel room was over the disco. We couldn't get another room or another hotel, so we had to grin and bear it.*

hit and miss inexact, random, sometimes good and sometimes bad. *'How's Carol doing with the new computer?' 'Well, at the moment it's very much a question of hit and miss, I'm afraid. She doesn't know all the commands yet.'*

hum and haw not say directly what one thinks, be hesitant because one is undecided or because something is unpleasant. *When I asked him what he thought of my new designs, he just hummed and hawed.*

you live and learn become wiser, gain more experience with age. *I trusted John and he cheated me. But you live and learn. I won't be so trusting with strangers next time.*

live and let live be tolerant towards others of different opinions, life-styles etc. *There are some strange people in the flat above us, very bohemian in dress and behaviour. But I've told Sam it's a question of live and let live. They're probably very nice.*

pick and choose take time and trouble to choose very selectively. *I'm afraid you won't be able to pick and choose. There's a trade fair in Frankfurt, so it's a case of taking any hotel that has a vacant room.*

rant and rave protest or complain in a loud, excited way. *There was an old chap in the butcher's ranting and raving about the price of meat.*

scrimp and save/scrape try hard to save money, spend only the minimum because one has very little. *If we buy a house, we'll have to scrimp and scrape for the next twenty years.*

sink or swim survive/be successful or fail. *It's sink or swim at the audition, Paul. You won't get another chance to act in a film with a big star.*

toss and turn not sleep peacefully, because of worry etc. *Eric's very worried about his business. Joan says he tosses and turns for hours before he can get to sleep.*

wait and see wait patiently. *It's too early to say whether or not the plan will work. We'll just have to wait and see.*

wine and dine have a meal with wine at a restaurant, often on a special occasion. *After the show we shall wine and dine at Annabel's. I've booked a table.*

Identical pairs

again and again repeatedly. *I've told Henry again and again that he shouldn't smoke so much. He has a dreadful cough.*

all in all considering everything. *We didn't agree on all points, but all in all, I'd say we had a successful meeting.*

bit by bit in small stages/steps; gradually. *Don't try to write the essay at one go. Do it bit by bit and think about it as you go along.*

blow by blow (when giving an account of something) including all the details, events etc. in order. *Sarah gave me a detailed account of the argument with her landlady – blow by blow.*

by and by as time goes by; in the course of time. *By and by, I came to realize that my decision to leave home and go to work abroad had been the right one after all.*

from door to door going to all the houses in a street/in the area. *There are some children going from door to door, collecting for the Boy Scouts.*

little by little gradually; at a slow rate. *'How's your father after his heart attack?' 'Well, I suppose he's making progress, little by little.'*

on and on (usually **go** ~) go further, continue without stopping. *If you are tired of hearing Grandfather's stories, tell him so! Otherwise he'll just go on and on.*

over and over (again) repeatedly, continually. *We told him over and over again not to drive so fast on his motorbike.*

round and round (often **go** ~) moving in circles; spinning. *I suddenly felt dizzy. Everything was going round and round in my head.*

step by step one step at a time; slowly. *Don't try to learn everything at once. Take it step by step.*

through and through completely, thoroughly. *Emlyn is a Welshman, through and through.*

on the up-and-up improving (e.g. one's health, general situation). *'How's business these days?' 'On the up-and-up at last, thanks.'*

5 Idioms with prepositions

above

above board legal, without secrecy; (a person) correct, honest. *The rumour that money was transferred illegally to Switzerland was not true. The bank transfer was completely above board.* □ *In business Ross is always above board, but they say that he can be unscrupulous in private life.*

above par better than usual (one's health, achievements, performance etc.). *'How's Jack after his illness?' 'Oh, he's fine now. Above par, I'd say. Better than ever!'*

above suspicion too honest to be suspected of doing something wrong. *Surely you don't suspect Mr Rogers of stealing the money? He's been a teacher here for years and is completely above suspicion.*

across

across the board affecting everyone, all groups; without exception. Used of an offer, wage/price/tax increase/cut etc. *The 2% tax cut goes across the board, so everyone will benefit.*

after

after a fashion in an unsatisfactory manner, not devoting much time or care. *'Has Richard finished his French essay?' 'Well, yes, he's done it – after a fashion.'*

after hours after the normally permitted business hours. *Ted is careful not to serve drinks after hours. He would lose his pub licence.*

against

against the clock against time. *Paul's working against the clock. The report has to be out by Tuesday lunchtime.*

against the grain usually **be/go ~ (with someone)**. Be contrary to one's wishes or one's normal standards of behaviour; be displeasing. *When Pam finds out that we have to work overtime next week, it will definitely go against the grain with her.*

against all/the odds in spite of great opposition or disadvantages etc. *Mason knew that in trying to save his company from ruin he was fighting a losing battle, but he carried on against all odds.*

at

at the Bar working as a barrister. *Many of Simon's Oxford contemporaries have already established themselves in the City or at the Bar.*

at bay (usually **keep/hold someone/something ~**) keep/hold someone/something at a distance in order to protect oneself. *Keep those* *dogs at bay until I've jumped over the wall!* □ *Williams can't pay his debtors. He won't be able to keep the bailiffs at bay for long.*

at someone's beck and call continually at someone's disposal to carry out his wishes. *I don't mind your mother staying with us, but I won't be at her beck and call all day!*

at bottom fundamentally, in reality. *Howard says he isn't envious of his brother's intelligence and good looks, but at bottom I think he is.*

at close quarters very near. *The insurance man climbed up the ladder onto the roof to inspect the damage at close quarters.*

at cross purposes (especially **be/talk/argue** ~) each speaking about different things; misunderstanding each other. *Just a moment, I think we're talking at cross purposes. I was referring to John, not to his father.*

at a/the crossroads at a crisis; a turning-point where a decision has to be made. *At forty, she found herself at a crossroads – should she risk giving up a dull but secure office job to go into full-time freelance journalism?*

at daggers drawn (two people or groups) enemies. *Thomas and his brother have been at daggers drawn for years. They have different ideas about the running of the family business.*

at the double quickly; without delay. *Father wants to speak to you, so off you go, at the double!*

at the drop of a hat willingly and immediately; without prompting. *If you asked Celia to go with you to Athens, I know she would do so a the drop of a hat.*

at (one's) ease relaxed; comfortable in one's surroundings. *Max is a good conversationalist. One always feels at ease in his company.*

at every turn always and everywhere; whatever one does. *Valerie finally managed to open her own language school, although she had met with opposition at every turn.*

at one's (own)/someone's expense paying oneself/with someone else paying. *I expect to make the journey at my own expense.* □ *Bill does all his travelling at the company's expense, even when his wife accompanies him.*

at face value as things appear to be on the surface. *You can't take what Robin says at face value – there's always a catch somewhere, with some advantage in it for him.*

at one fell swoop with only one single effort or action. *You can't expect to pay off all your debts at one fell swoop.*

at first sight when seen/considered for the first time. *At first sight it would seem to be a straightforward case of suicide, but the police suspect foul play.*

at the helm in charge/command, as leader. *With Dr Jacobs at the helm, we are expecting to make better progress with the appeal fund.*

at home (with someone, in/on/with something) familiar, relaxed; well acquainted with, knowledgeable about something. *They gave us such a warm welcome that we soon felt at home in their company.* □ *I'm not really at home with Kandinsky, so I won't offer an opinion on his paintings.*

at issue (the subject) being discussed. *The point at issue is not how much to invest, but whether to invest in the scheme at all.*

at large 1 taken as a unit, a whole group. *The Prime Minister appealed to the nation at large on the subject of capital punishment.* 2 (a prisoner) escaped and still free. *The escaped prisoner is still at large and thought to be armed and dangerous.*

at one's leisure at one's own speed, not under pressure. *I'd be obliged if you would read the article at your leisure and let me have your opinion.*

at length in detail, very fully. *Chapter 9 deals at length with Rembrandt's late self-portraits.*

at loggerheads (with someone) in a state of disagreement or dispute. *Robert always seems to be at loggerheads with one or other of the team.*

at a loss (to do something) puzzled; not able to decide what to do, how to do it etc. *Victoria is at a loss to know how best to deal with her teenage son. He doesn't respond to anything she says.*

at a loss for words not knowing what to say, often due to surprise, shock etc. *The offer took me so much by surprise that I was at a loss for words.*

at a low ebb lacking in interest, enthusiasm, activity. *After the failure of the disarmament talks, relations between the two countries were at a low ebb for months.*

at odds in disagreement. *Why do we have to be at odds on this matter? Surely everyone is for the abolition of nuclear weapons.*

at the outside at the most. *I don't think John and Sarah will like city life after living in the country. I'll give them six months at the outside – then they'll be back in their country cottage.*

at a pinch/push if absolutely necessary, if circumstances make it essential. *The car will hold six at a pinch.*

at a price with a sacrifice (of time, money, effort, happiness etc.) or with disadvantages. *Martin has reached the top in his career, but at a price. His health and his marriage are both ruined.*

at random haphazardly, without a deliberate choice or intention. *She chose six books at random, and fortunately all made excellent reading.*

at the ready ready for use. *She quickly entered the room with the rest of the journalists, pencil and notebook at the ready.*

(all) at sea confused or uncertain. *I thought I understood the principles of the theory, but now I realize that I'm all at sea after all.*

at sight on seeing something. *I can't translate this document at sight. I shall need a dictionary.*

at a standstill not moving at all, at a halt. *Negotiations on arms reduction had been at a standstill for months before the Geneva talks.*

at a stretch for a certain period of time without a break. *When working with a microscope, I find I can only concentrate fully for about two hours at a stretch. Then I need a break.*

at a tender age while still very young. *He had learnt about poverty and hardship at a tender age, and consequently was never wasteful, even when rich and famous.*

at will whenever one wants, as one wishes. *A good actor must be able to laugh and cry convincingly at will.*

at one's wits' end greatly troubled, not knowing what to do next. *Falsely arrested and charged, in a strange country and all alone, Walker was truly at his wits' end.*

behind

behind bars in prison. *He spent a couple of years behind bars as a youth but has since been a responsible member of society.*

behind closed doors in private; without the press or members of the public being present. *The preliminary hearing of the case was behind closed doors.*

behind the scenes not seen by the public, without public knowledge. *There was endless activity behind the scenes days before the visit of the royal couple.*

behind schedule later than the time planned or agreed. *Production for this quarter is already three weeks behind schedule.*

below

below the belt (usually **hit** ~) fight/attack/argue unfairly. *Unfortunately, politicians often hit below the belt to discredit their opponents.*

below par not as good/well as usual. *Grandfather had been feeling a bit below par for a few days before he was taken to hospital.*

by

by degrees gradually, slowly, little by little. *Max has been improving since he came out of hospital, if only by degrees.*

by/in fits and starts not continuously; at irregular intervals. *The work on her new novel is going by fits and starts at the moment because she's writing a TV script as well.*

by/in leaps and bounds with great or rapid progress. *My teacher says my English has improved by leaps and bounds since I started using idioms.*

by the look of it/things as the situation, matter etc. seems to be; judging by appearance. *By the look of it, John won't be coming. He said he'd be here by lunchtime and now it's two o'clock.*

by rights according to how circumstances should really be, but are not. *I know that by rights it's Jean who should have been given the credit for the success, as the idea was hers, not mine.*

by the same token for the same reason, based on the same argument. *You believe that Britain needs a nuclear deterrent because it is a small country. By the same token, more than half the countries of the world should have nuclear weapons!*

for

for the asking (usually in **be someone's/can have something** ~) if you only ask for it. *If you like this bracelet, it's yours for the asking.*

for the best with the best intentions. *When parents send their children to* *private boarding schools, they do it for the best, but young children often take a long time to adapt.*

for a change   as an alternative, different from before. *The Pearsons are going to Brighton again for their holiday. I'm surprised they don't go abroad for a change.*

for dear life   as if trying to save one's life. *When the pony started to gallop, Ben lost the reins, so he threw his arms round its neck for dear life.*

for fun   for amusement, not being serious. *Don't be hurt by Jeremy's remark. He only said it for fun.*

for keeps   for ever. *You don't have to give me the bracelet back. It's yours for keeps, if you'd like to have it.*

for kicks   (informal) for the excitement one gets. *'Is it really necessary to rewrite the whole of that report?' 'Well, you don't think I'm doing it for kicks, do you?'*

for laughs/a laugh   for the amusement one gets. *They put salt in his coffee just for a laugh, but he didn't think it was very funny.*

not for love nor money   under no circumstances. *I wouldn't walk through that part of town after dark – not for love nor money!*

for 'my money   (informal) in my opinion. *For my money, this is the best book of its kind on the market.*

for real   (informal) not in pretence. *When Jack said he was phoning from Australia, I didn't think it was for real – until his letter arrived postmarked Sydney.*

for the record   so that it can be recorded/noted. *Just for the record, it was Ken's idea to come to this terrible party, not mine.*

for 'two pins   (informal) without much provocation. *For two pins, I'd tell Rogers that he can stuff his stupid job!*

from

from A to Z   completely and thoroughly. *Mr Charlton's a good teacher. The pupils like him, and he knows his subject from A to Z.*

from cover to cover   (of a book etc.) in total; all the way through. *The novel is so exciting that I read it from cover to cover in just two days.*

from pillar to post   in several different directions/places. *Peggy has been moved from pillar to post by the company in the last four years. She's tired of never being in one place for more than a few months.*

from scratch   (informal) from the beginning. *If you had been on the project from scratch, you would realize just how much these successful results mean.*

from where one/someone is standing   from one's/someone's position or situation. *I know you don't agree with Jenny's decision to leave college and sign a recording contract, but try to look at it from where she's standing – it's her one chance to do what she really wants.*

in

(up) in the air   (plans etc.) still undecided, not definite. *Our plans to go to India are still very much up in the air. We probably won't have the cash.*

in the bag (informal) certain of success; already decided in one's favour; finalized. *We've done it! We've got a two million pound contract in the bag!*

in the balance undecided, at a critical point/situation. *His future as a politician was in the balance. If he lost this election, he would have little chance of ever becoming a member of parliament.*

in someone's book in someone's opinion/moral judgement; according to someone's beliefs. *I don't know how you judge the situation, but in my book, it's fraud!*

in the can (informal) practically achieved. *I've just been promoted with a 20% rise in salary. A new car's already in the can!*

in the cart (informal) in trouble/difficulties, facing punishment or failure. *Tomorrow we are running the critical engine test. If it doesn't perform this time, we'll all be in the cart.*

in the chair as chairperson at a debate, meeting etc. *Who's in the chair at the meeting on Friday?*

in the clear not in danger; not under suspicion. *Jones has an alibi for the time of the crime, so he's obviously in the clear.*

in clover (usually be/live ~) in great material comfort. *Fiona has lived in clover all her life. She doesn't know what work is!*

in the dark (especially be/leave someone ~) without information, not knowing what is happening. *The company sent Richard to the States at short notice and left his family in the dark as to whether the posting would be temporary or permanent.*

in deep water(s) in great difficulties, in a complicated or dangerous situation. *In my opinion, it's a political cover-up. If you try to expose it, you'll find yourself in very deep waters with no one to pull you out.*

(down) in the dumps depressed, in low spirits. *What's wrong with Pete? He's been down in the dumps all day.*

in one's element in a situation or with people that give one great pleasure. *Jack's in his element when he has someone's old car to tinker around with.*

in a fine/pretty pickle in a mess; in a difficult or unpleasant situation. *You would be in a fine pickle if John weren't here to help you to put the car engine back together again!*

in a fix/scrape (informal) in a difficult position. *I'm in a bit of a fix – six unexpected people to dinner and nothing to eat in the house!*

in a flash very suddenly or quickly. *We told the doctor on the phone that we suspected a heart attack, and the ambulance was here in a flash.*

in the flesh in real life (i.e. not in a photograph or picture). *I have a cousin in Australia. I've never seen her in the flesh, only in photographs.*

in a flutter in a state of nervous excitement, often because of some small unexpected difficulty. *Aunt Betsy was in a flutter when we arrived. The dog had just knocked over a bucket of water in the kitchen.*

in a fog confused; uncertain of the facts. *The lecture left us all in a fog. The book said one thing and Professor Taylor said another.*

in full swing in fully active operation. *When we arrived, the fashion show was already in full swing.*

in hot water (informal) in trouble; facing punishment. *You'll be in hot water when your father finds out that you've knocked the heads off his best roses.*

in a jiffy (informal) very quickly, very soon. *Just excuse me a moment. I have to go out, but I'll be back in a jiffy.*

in the know well informed; knowing facts that those not closely involved do not know. *I'll ask the secretary what went on at the meeting. It's her job to be in the know.*

in limbo put aside because temporarily not needed; forgotten at the present time; having an indeterminate fate. *The decision on the new project is in limbo until market research studies have been completed and evaluated.*

in the limelight the centre of attention or publicity. *I'd hate to be a popstar, in the limelight all the time with no privacy.*

in the money earning a lot of money. *June's really in the money now. Her computer software shop is very popular.*

in a nutshell concisely, reduced to the essential facts. *I don't need to know the contents of your speech in detail, so can't you put the main message in a nutshell for me?*

in the offing likely to materialize/happen. *Mark's going up to Glasgow tomorrow. He says there's a good job in the offing.*

(out) in the open revealed to everyone, generally known, not secret. *I've told the police everything and I feel relieved that my story is now in the open.*

in the pipeline receiving attention, in preparation. *Oh, good! It says in this magazine that six new episodes of my favourite TV series are in the pipeline.*

in raptures (about/over something) delighted, thrilled. *David is in raptures about his new car.*

in the raw (usually life, nature) as it really is, with all its unpleasant aspects revealed. *The film is certainly realistic – too much life in the raw, in fact.*

in a rut in a state of dull routine; in a fixed repetitive pattern of life. *Peggy feels she's in a rut and badly needs a change, so she's going to do voluntary work overseas for a year.*

in the same boat (as someone) in the same difficult position or circumstances. *If the firm has to close down, we'll all be in the same boat, whether manager or mechanic.*

in seventh heaven in a state of extreme happiness. *Barbara was in seventh heaven when Elton John gave her his autograph and talked to her for a few minutes.*

in step (with someone/something) in agreement/harmony/conformity. *Every statement he made was in step with Conservative policy.*

in a stew (informal) in a state of nervous confusion. *The boss is expecting an inspector from headquarters this afternoon. He's been in a stew about it since yesterday.*

(out) in the sticks in an isolated, remote part of the country. *Bert has bought himself a little cottage somewhere out in the sticks – much too lonely, if you ask me.*

in stitches in uncontrollable laughter. *Ask Peter to tell you his joke about the woman with the poodle. He'll have you in stitches!*

in store forthcoming; about to happen to someone. *There's a nice surprise in store for Jane when she gets home. Her brother is back from Nigeria.*

in the swim informed and up to date, actively engaged in social events. *If you want to know what's going on around town, ask Margaret. She's always in the swim.*

in a tight squeeze in a difficult situation, either financially or in a personal matter. *Phil, I'm afraid I'm in a tight squeeze. Can you lend me fifty pounds?*

in tow following behind. *There comes Joe laden with suitcases, wife and children in tow.*

in trim in good physical shape; fit and slim. *Staying in trim is much easier these days with low-calorie foods on the supermarket shelves.*

of

of one's own accord voluntarily. *He told her of his own accord that he had been married twice before.*

of a kind/sort, of sorts (follows a noun) of an inferior kind in the speaker's opinion. *Freddie is a pianist – well, a pianist of a kind. He can only play jazz.*

of note (formal) with a good reputation; well known. *His ambition was always to become a writer of note.*

off

off the air (TV, radio) not broadcasting or being broadcast. *Win or Lose has been off the air for years, ever since the presenter died unexpectedly.*

off one's own bat (informal) independently; using one's own initiative, without help or advice from others. *He set up the business entirely off his own bat. It was his idea, and his alone.*

off beam (informal) having the wrong answer, ideas, approach to something. *David usually has some good ideas, but he's certainly off beam with this one. It will never work!*

off the beaten track away from the usual routes and roads. *We found ourselves off the beaten track, miles from anywhere.*

off colour unwell; not looking or feeling as well as usual. *Jan's been feeling a little off colour recently. Too much work, I suppose.*

off the cuff without preparation or previous thought. *'Can you tell me the figures from the last test run?' 'Well, not off the cuff, but I can give you the test report.'*

off form not performing as well as usual, either physically or mentally. *David's hitting all the balls into the net. He's definitely off form today.*

off limits outside the allowed limits. *Look at that sign. This part of the building is off limits for unauthorized personnel. Let's go.*

off the map (a place) not shown on the map; remote or insignificant. *Sheila's living down in Cornwall, in a tiny little place way off the map. I can never remember its name.*

(way) off the mark 1 incorrect or mistaken. *I guessed at the answer, but unfortunately it was way off the mark.* 2 **be quick/slow** ~ be quick/slow to take action; react quickly or slowly. *'Peggy got her name on the list, but I didn't.' 'Well, she was quicker off the mark than you, wasn't she?'*

off the peg (usually clothing) ready-made; displayed in the shops, not made especially for the customer. *Since Max is extremely tall, he finds it difficult to buy his suits off the peg.*

off the rails (informal) confused; disorganized. Especially **go** ~ start behaving in an unreasonable, unconventional manner. *When his wife left him, Steve went completely off the rails. He stopped coming to work and joined a weird sect.*

off the record (information) told in confidence, unofficial. *'This is strictly off the record, but you are to be put in charge of manufacture in Scotland.'*

on

on the air (TV, radio) broadcasting or being broadcast. *The radio series Woman's Hour has been on the air for years, and it's still very popular.*

on balance when all points for and against have been considered. *On balance, the team has had a pretty successful season.*

on the ball (informal) intelligent, mentally alert and shrewd. *It's a great advantage these days to be on the ball in money matters.*

on the beat (a policeman) on regular patrol duty through the streets. *Luckily, there was a policeman on the beat just round the corner, so he came to our help.*

on the boil in an active state, at a high level of activity. *The company is obviously anxious to keep the investors' interest in the new shares on the boil until they are finally put on the market.*

on the bottle drinking a lot of alcohol. *Eric's obviously been on the bottle again. He's very unsteady on his feet.*

on call (doctor etc.) available for duty. *Dr Murphy is always on call, even at weekends.*

on the cards likely to happen/materialize. *Have you heard the latest? It's on the cards that a new art gallery is to be built in Birmingham.*

on the carpet (informal) be reprimanded, usually by one's employer, someone in authority etc. *Keith's in the manager's office. I expect he's on the carpet again for messing up another export order.*

on the cheap (informal) at a low price, even if the quality is bad. *We travelled through the States from New York to San Francisco on the cheap, either by bus or hitching a ride.*

on the dole (informal) receiving unemployment benefit from the state. *Millions of unemployed workers have been on the dole for years.*

on the dot punctual(ly)/precisely. *I'll meet you at 12 on the dot. Don't forget!*

on edge nervous, tense, irritable because of worry or fear. *Tom's terribly on edge. He's waiting for his new passport to come by post. He's flying to Madrid tomorrow.*

on an even keel in a state of financial solvency or emotional balance. *We've been through a tough period trying to keep the business alive, but I'm glad to say that we're back on an even keel now.*

on form performing well physically or mentally. *Bob's the best chess player I know. You should see him when he's really on form.*

on/over the grapevine through an unofficial information network, by the passing of news from person to person. *'How did you hear that Robson had resigned?' 'The usual source – on the sailing club grapevine.'* □ *I heard over the grapevine that White Enterprises had bought up a prime piece of property in Mayfair.*

on the hop (especially **catch someone ~**) unprepared and therefore at a disadvantage. *Sorry about the mess, but you've caught us on the hop. We weren't expecting you until tomorrow.*

on the house free for the customer; at the expense of the business establishment (hotel, bar etc.). *To celebrate Jim's birthday, drinks and refreshments are on the house tonight.*

on the job working. *Nothing to eat, thanks. Not while I'm on the job.* Note: **sleep/lie down ~** not work properly. *Now remember, we want results to be proud of – no sleeping on the job this time!*

on the level honest and sincere. *This suggestion sounds too good to be true. Are you quite sure that Andrew's on the level?*

on the loose escaped (prisoner, wild animal etc.). *There have been several radio warnings that there's a lion on the loose near the zoo.*

on the make (informal) trying to make money, profit, be more successful than others etc. as one's main aim. *George never does anything without a view to making money. He's continually on the make.*

on the mend improving (one's state of health), recovering after an illness. *Harry was still quite ill when he came out of hospital, but thankfully he's on the mend now.*

on one's mettle (usually **be/put someone ~**) eager, determined to perform well. *It's particularly important for new MPs to be continually on their mettle during the first parliamentary debates of the session.*

on the move active, moving from place to place. *Since Joe was made redundant, he's been on the move up and down the country trying to find work.*

on the nail (of payments, informal) immediately. Often **pay (cash) ~**. *Our landlady doesn't really trust students. She insists on cash on the nail on the first day of every month.*

on the never (-never) (informal) by a system of instalment payments. *If you can't afford to pay the full price for the freezer now, why not get it on the never-never? Other people do.*

on the 'off chance without a fixed arrangement, hoping that one will be lucky. *We called round to see Joan on the off chance, and luckily we found her in.*

on a par with equal in quality, on a level with. *Mary's paintings really are quite good, but I wouldn't say they're on a par with yours.*

on one's plate (usually **have (got) a lot/enough/too much ~**) have a lot of work, responsibility, problems, troubles which one must deal with and attend to. *I don't want to trouble Mike at the moment. I know he's got enough on his plate with the exhibition he's organizing.*

on the quiet secretly, unofficially. *Fred takes bets for a bookmaker. He's been making money on the quiet that way for years.*

on the rack (informal) in an unpleasant state of suspense, tension, anxiety. *Well, please don't leave me on the rack, doctor! What's wrong with me?*

on the rebound recovering from an unhappy love affair or relationship. *Jane was on the rebound when she met Tony. She didn't really love him and should never have married him.*

on the road travelling. *I'd hate Steve's job. He's on the road six days a week.*

on the rocks (informal) 1 in a critical state, in serious trouble, failing (e.g. a marriage, business, project). *Their relationship has been on the rocks before, but it always survives.* 2 (an alcoholic drink) served with ice. *'What's your drink?' 'Whisky on the rocks, please.'*

on the run escaping pursuit, especially from the police. *Two of the escaped prisoners have been caught, but the third is still on the run.*

on a shoestring at low cost, with little money. *Tom bought the business cheap and ran it on a shoestring for years before it started to show a profit.*

on the side (informal) as an additional source of income, often unofficially or secretly, i.e. not declared to the tax authorities. *She's a secretary, but she does some hairdressing in the evenings on the side.*

on the sly secretively so as to deceive. *I remember when I was a boy smoking in school was forbidden, but we used to do it on the sly in the lavatories.*

on the spot 1 present when and where something happens etc. *Within minutes of the shooting, the Standard had a reporter on the spot.*
2 immediately; without stopping to think. *We made him a good offer, but he refused it on the spot.* 3 **put someone ~** put someone in a difficult situation where he is unprepared. *I know I'm putting you on the spot, but I need a decision now.*

on the stocks in preparation; being developed. *The first volume of the dictionary has just been published, and there are two more volumes on the stocks.*

on tap available; ready for action/use. *I've got six people coming to help us tomorrow, and three more on tap if we should need them.*

on target having the right answer, idea, approach to a problem. *It must be the spark plugs that need renewing. Yes, that's it. We're right on target this time.*

on tenterhooks in a state of nervous anxiety or suspense. *Jim's been on tenterhooks all week, waiting to hear the results of his audition.*

on thin ice (especially **be/skate** ~) in a dangerous, precarious position or situation. *Remember that we're on thin ice with the maintenance contract. One wrong move and we lose it.*

on tick (informal) on credit. *You'd be surprised, You can get most things on tick these days.*

on the tiles (informal) (usually **a night** ~) enjoying oneself in an unrestrained manner, drinking, dancing etc. *The last time we had a real night on the tiles was when England won the European Cup.*

on one's tod (informal) alone. *Well, I don't really want to come with you, but then I don't want to be left on my tod, either.*

on the trot 1 active, busy, having many things to do. *I've been on the trot all day with the wedding preparations.* 2 in succession, following each other. *What's wrong with Nicola? She's been late for rehearsals three days on the trot.*

on the wagon (informal) deliberately abstaining from drinking alcohol for a long period. *I'll have orange juice, please. The doctor's put me on the wagon again!*

on the warpath preparing to vent one's anger, dissatisfaction etc. *Daddy's on the warpath, looking for a culprit. Someone's pinched his gardening gloves.*

out

out of bounds a place, area etc. to which one is not allowed to go. *The club rooms are normally out of bounds for non-members, unless they are brought in as guests.*

out of character not corresponding to a person's usual behaviour. *Telling rude jokes is very out of character for Simon – unless he has been drinking, possibly.*

out in the cold (usually **be left** ~) not be included or informed; be left out, ignored or neglected. *We ought to inform Bill of our plans. We can't leave him out in the cold.*

out of condition not in good physical form. *How about a run in the park tomorrow before breakfast? It's the best thing when you're out of condition.*

out for the count unconscious; sleeping heavily, e.g. when very tired or drunk. *He lay down on the bed and was out for the count within seconds.*

out of one's depth in a position/situation that is too difficult for one to handle, because of lack of knowledge/ability. *The discussion took a rather philosophical turn, so I was soon out of my depth.*

out of the frying-pan into the fire (saying) from one bad situation to another which is equally bad or even worse. *Sheila found that she'd jumped out of the frying pan into the fire when she changed lodgings. The new landlady was worse than her former one.*

out on a limb in a risky position alone. *No member of the club is likely to put himself out on a limb by voting against the merger.*

out of the ordinary something special, unusual, unconventional. *'What do you think of Fiona's paintings?' 'Well, they're something out of the ordinary, that's for sure.'*

out of place inappropriate (a remark etc.); not in suitable surroundings. *Peter's remark about archaeologists wasting the country's money was quite out of place, I thought. □ Don't you think that big cupboard looks rather out of place in such a small room?*

out of pocket made poorer by a financial transaction. *Archie buys paintings at auctions, cleans them up and sells them. He's hardly ever out of pocket.*

out of the question impossible, not worth consideration. *A new car is unfortunately out of the question this year.*

out of reach not obtainable; too far away to get. *The children will soon be back, so I'll put these tablets on top of the cupboard out of reach.*

out of the running no longer in the competition; having no further chance of winning, being successful, participating etc. *Of course, Black's injury means he is now out of the running for a place in the Olympic team.*

out of sorts a little unwell; not in one's normal good state of health or mood. *Brenda won't be coming along tonight. She's feeling a little out of sorts.*

out of touch no longer having close contact or knowledge of a person, subject etc. *Not having much time for reading, I'm afraid I'm rather out of touch with modern novelists.*

out of the wood(s) no longer in danger, difficulties or trouble. *Uncle Joe is still in hospital but the doctor says he's out of the woods.*

over

over the hill 1 over the worst/most difficult part of something. *We've already run six out of the seven scheduled tests. The results are good, so I think we're over the hill now.* 2 past one's youth, in mid-life. *I suppose, to teenagers, anyone over 35 is over the hill.*

over the moon delighted, very happy about something. *When I showed Rita the tickets for the Rod Stewart concert, she was over the moon.*

over the odds (informal) more money than expected; more than the usual price. *He does all his shopping at expensive boutiques. He believes that it's worth paying a bit over the odds for quality.*

over the top (informal) (especially **be/go** ~) 1 act wildly, in an unrestrained manner. *The children went completely over the top when they saw their new bicycles.* 2 do something daring, bold or exaggerated. *Fashion designers have really gone over the top this season.*

round

round the bend/twist (informal) mad, crazy. Especially **be/drive/send someone** ~. *That dreadful noise from the building site is enough to send anyone round the bend.*

to

to date up to the present time, so far. *How many tickets have we sold to date?*

to the core in every way, completely. *He's an English gentleman, to the core.*

to a fault excessively, too much. *The headmistress is conscientious to a fault, and she expects the same of all of us.*

to the full as thoroughly as possible. *My philosophy is to enjoy life to the full and to regret nothing.*

to the letter exact in every detail. *We carried out your instructions to the letter, but we couldn't find the error in the programme.*

to the manner born (especially **as/as if ~**) with natural skill, as if having done something all one's life. *Felicity can host a dinner party for over twenty guests as if to the manner born.*

to a T/tee exactly, in all details. *We saw a woman on TV who could imitate Mrs Thatcher to a T.*

to the tune of (informal) for the large sum of. *You could, of course, hire a top model to show your new designs – to the tune of roughly two thousand dollars a day.*

under

under one's belt achieved by practical experience. *Jack's got forty years as a building contractor under his belt. He could build you a house with his eyes closed.*

under one's breath in a low whisper to oneself, so that others can hardly hear. *He left in an angry mood, muttering and swearing under his breath.*

under a cloud under suspicion, out of favour. *Although the charge of espionage could not be proved, the affair put him under a cloud for several months.*

under the counter secretly and illegally. *There are laws against the copying of video tapes for commercial use, but a lot of it still goes on under the counter.*

under the doctor receiving treatment from a doctor. *Mrs Carson has serious heart trouble. She's been under the doctor for years.*

under the knife (informal) having a surgical operation. *Harry goes under the knife next week, but it's nothing serious, only an ulcer.*

under one's own steam by means of one's own efforts or initiative; without help. *There won't be room for us in Jeff's car, so we'll have to get there under our own steam.*

under the sun (used with a superlative for emphasis) anywhere in the world. *Don't believe a word Angus tells you! He's the biggest story-teller under the sun.*

under the weather unwell. *Jill has a nasty cold and is generally feeling a bit under the weather at the moment.*

under wraps (especially **keep something/stay ~**) hidden, secret, not made available to the public. *Information about the new model was kept under wraps for months before it eventually leaked out.*

up

up in arms strongly protesting. *The unions are up in arms again about the proposal to close down part of the production plant.*

up the creek (informal) all wrong. *Jeremy, these statistics are completely up the creek. You've used the wrong computer programme again.*

up for grabs (informal) (especially **be** ~) available for anyone to get. *The thought that the family estate would be up for grabs within the week filled her with nausea.*

up a 'gum tree (informal) in a difficult or awkward situation. *In Karachi I discovered that my luggage had been put on a wrong flight, so there I was up a gum tree with just a camera and my duty-free.*

up to the mark up to standard, good enough. *James is doing well at school. It's only in maths that he's not quite up to the mark.*

up the pole (informal) mad, out of one's senses. *Giles must be up the pole if he expects me to finalize deals in Tokyo, Rio and Chicago all in one week!*

up to scratch (especially **be/come/bring something** ~) up to the expected or required standard. *If your work isn't up to scratch by April, there's no point in entering your name for the exam.*

up the spout (informal) wasted, lost, ruined. *Over a thousand pounds up the spout. The wonder cure for rheumatism didn't work.*

up someone's street (informal) exactly the thing that someone enjoys/is good at etc. *Here's an interesting book on old aircraft. Should be right up Robert's street.*

within

within one's means not more than one can afford, corresponding to one's income. *Many people find it difficult to live within their means and are constantly borrowing money.*

within reason reasonable. *'Dick, can you do me a favour?' 'Yes, of course. Anything within reason.'*

6 Phrasal verbs

A particular difficulty experienced by learners is the correct handling of expressions consisting of verbs in combination with prepositions or adverbial particles, for example, **take off, sit in on, leave out**. Such verbs are a typical and frequent occurrence in all types of English, but most especially in everyday spoken English.

Sometimes, the combination of verb + preposition or particle results in a separate unit of meaning which is highly idiomatic. The total meaning of the combination may bear no relationship to the meaning of the individual words of the combination. For example, the verb **pack something 'in** presents no difficulty in the sentence
She opened her suitcase and packed all the clothes in.
However, in the sentence
He decided to pack his job in
the individual meanings of **pack** and **in** do not convey the true meaning 'leave, abandon'. Likewise the example **take someone 'off**. This may mean 'take away to another place' as in the sentence
As soon as Tom arrived, Bob insisted on taking him off.
However, it may have the meaning 'imitate humorously', which cannot be guessed from the individual meanings of **take** and **off**:
Liz can take the Queen off very well.

As shown above, verb combinations with prepositions and particles can have a non-idiomatic meaning as well as an idiomatic meaning. Of the idiomatic ones, some are more idiomatic than others. It is these 'more idiomatic' combinations which are presented in this chapter.

Any one combination may have several idiomatic meanings, depending on the words which accompany it, i.e. its 'collocations'. Here are some of the collocations and meanings of **take off**:
1 *The aircraft/flight/pilot/passenger took off*
   i.e. left the ground.
2 *The thief/boy/dog* (persons or animals) *took off*
   i.e. ran away in a hurry.
3 *The sales/product/economy took off*
   i.e. began to improve greatly, make a profit.

The collocations and meanings of **take something 'off** are also numerous and varied:
1 *take weight/pounds/inches/surplus fat off*
   i.e. lose, reduce.
2 *take a bus/train/flight off*
   i.e. withdraw from service, stop providing.
3 *take tax/duty/a sum of money off*
   i.e. remove.

An additional problem is knowing how the combination is used in a sentence, i.e. the problem of word order. The word order depends on whether the verb is followed by a preposition or by a particle. Consider the following:

A 1 *I read the letter through.*   B 1 *I saw the plan through.*
   2 *I read through the letter.*   2 *I saw through the plan.*

In A, **through** is a particle in both sentences (although it looks confusingly like a preposition in A2!). Because it is a particle in both, there is no difference in meaning. In B, **through** is a particle in 1 and a preposition in 2, so there is an important difference of meaning between the two sentences. B1 means: 'I persevered until the plan was completed', and B2 means: 'I recognized the deception of the plan.'

In order to solve difficulties of word order, the combinations treated in this chapter indicate exactly where the direct object and preposition or particle stand. The words **someone** and **something** stand for the object in its correct place, for example, **see something 'through, see 'through something**.

This chapter is based on the scheme of verb patterns presented by A.P. Cowie and R. Mackin in their *Oxford Dictionary of Current Idiomatic English*, Volume One. Six basic verb patterns are given, three for transitive verbs (i.e. with a direct object) and three for intransitive verbs (i.e. without a direct object). The three patterns for each set are:

Verb + Particle
Verb + Preposition
Verb + Particle + Preposition

This gives six patterns:

1 Intransitive + Particle
   e.g. **slow 'down, get 'on, take 'off**

2 Intransitive + Preposition
   e.g. **go 'off someone/ something
       'count on someone**

3 Intransitive + Particle + Preposition
   e.g. **put 'up with someone/ something
       come 'up against someone/ something**

4 Transitive + Particle
   e.g. **pack something 'in
       take someone 'off**

5 Transitive + Preposition
   e.g. **put someone 'off something
       get someone 'through something**

6 Transitive + Particle + Preposition
   e.g. **put someone 'up to something
       take someone 'up on something**

Pattern 4, **pack something 'in,** must receive extra attention. In this pattern it is possible to say:

He decided to pack his job in.
He decided to pack in his job.

The object can stand *before* or *after* the particle without a change of meaning. However, when the object is a pronoun (*me/you/him/her/it/us/them*) it can only stand *before* the particle, as in:

He decided to pack it in.

Here are more examples:

I rang up my brother/I rang my brother up.
BUT: *I rang him up.*
He cleaned out the room/He cleaned the room out.
BUT: *He cleaned it out.*

The use of **someone** and **something** in the entries does not only indicate the position of the object. It also indicates differences of meaning within the structures. The meaning may be different according to whether the object is a *person* or a *thing*. For example, **take someone 'in, take something 'in.** If there is no difference in meaning, the slant (/) is used, for example, **walk 'out on someone/something.**

The examples indicate typical collocations, e.g. **'answer for something** gives the example *answer for the consequences.* Secondly, the examples indicate how a verb is typically used, e.g. often in the passive:

There are few problems that cannot be ironed out.
We can't move into the house until the electricity has been laid on.
All cheques are to be made out to Global Enterprises.

Sometimes, nominalized forms are noted or are given in the examples. These are nouns formed from verbs, e.g. **an outbreak, a breakthrough, a sell-out, a write-off, a screw-up.** British English absorbs many such nominalized forms from American English, which is very flexible.

Stress marks (') have been included for all verbs in order to make correct learning easier. They indicate stress when the verb is in its *basic* infinitive form. Within the sentence, sentence stress prevails. This means that the stress patterns given may sometimes be changed minimally by sentence intonation patterns.

However, there are some pattern 4 phrasal verbs which have a fixed direct object position (*before* the particle), for example **get someone 'round,** and a small number which have their noun object *after* the particle. These phrasal verbs, such as **give 'up something, keep 'up something, put 'up something** and **take 'up something,** look like pattern 2 phrasal verbs but are in fact pattern 4 phrasal verbs because their pronoun object must come *before* their particle. For a fuller description of all six phrasal verb patterns, including these pattern 4 exceptions, see *English Idioms: Exercises on Phrasal Verbs* by Jennifer Seidl (Oxford University Press, 1990).

act 'up (informal) cause annoyance through awkward behaviour. *The children always start acting up when it's time to go to bed.* □ *The car's been acting up again this week; I've been late to work every day.*

add 'up make sense, be logical. *When the police found a motive for the murder, the facts of the case suddenly began to add up.*

add 'up to something amount to something, mean something. *This new information adds up to very little, I'm afraid.*

a'gree with someone suit someone's health/digestion. *The fish didn't agree with me. I feel ill.* □ *The Brighton air must agree with you. You look marvellous!*

al'low for something take something into consideration, plan for something. *We'll set off an hour earlier to allow for traffic jams and stops on the way.*

answer (someone) 'back return a criticism or a rebuke in a rude manner, especially to a teacher/parent/someone in authority. *Answering your teachers back is not the best way to make yourself popular with them.*

'answer for something take the blame or responsibility for something. *If you drive that car without a licence, you'll have to answer for the consequences.*

'answer to someone justify one's actions to someone, explain the reasons for one's behaviour and accept probable punishment. *If you stay out until after midnight again you'll have to answer to your father!*

'ask after someone inquire about someone's well-being. *I saw George yesterday. He asked after you and the children.*

ask someone 'in invite someone to come into one's house. *Don't leave Mrs Parker standing in the cold, John. Ask her in!*

ask someone 'out invite someone to go out for a meal, to the theatre, to a dance etc. *If you'd like to repay your neighbours for their help, why not ask them out?*

at'tend to someone/something look after, manage, deal with someone/something. *A good salesman is always polite when attending to customers.* □ *I can't attend to everything – please come and help!*

back 'down withdraw a statement, accusation etc. because it is not true, accurate etc. *Wilmott's statement could easily damage our reputation. We'll have to get him to back down.*

back 'out (of something) withdraw (from an agreement, one's obligations or promise). *You can't back out of a contract once you've signed it.* □ *If you promised to help Sylvia with the organization of the conference, you can't back out now.*

back someone/something 'up 1 support someone/something morally or physically. *Will you back me up when I tell the story to the police?* 2 supplement in order to improve. *We could back up the lecture with video materials.* Note: **a 'back-up** and **'back-up** (adjective). *We could use these materials as a back-up to the lecture.*

balls something 'up (slang, taboo) ruin, mess up the organization of something, mismanage. *Don't let Speakes handle your advertising campaign. He'll balls it all up for you!* Note: **a 'balls-up.**

'bank on someone/something rely on someone/something; expect. *Bill is banking on Jane to lend him the money he needs.* □ *The forecast said it was going to be sunny at the weekend – but I wouldn't bank on it.*

(not) 'bargain for something (not) expect something; (not) be prepared for something. *When Sheila offered to look after the neighbour's four children, she got more than she had bargained for.*

be 'after something aim at getting something, want something. *Jack's after a promotion to head of department.* □ *Jim visits his old uncle every week. He may be after the old man's money.*

be 'at someone (informal) try to persuade someone through continual complaining. *Jill wants her husband to stop smoking. He says she's continually at him.*

be 'at something (informal) touch, use, interfere with something that is another's property. *Where are all those chocolates that were in this box? Somebody's been at them.*

be 'down for something have one's name registered or listed for something. *The Smiths have been down for a council flat for over a year, but there's a long waiting list.*

be 'down on someone/something (informal) be critical of or unfavourable towards someone/something. *The critics are very down on Stevenson's new book, but I like it.*

be 'in for something (informal) be due for or likely to get something. *Barry's in for a nasty surprise – he's about to lose his job.*

be 'in on something be informed about something, involved with something, participate in something. *Who's in on the plan apart from you and me?*

be (well) 'in with someone (informal) be on favourable, familiar terms with someone. *Janet always makes sure she's in with the most influential people at the sailing club.*

be 'into something (informal) be very interested in something, occupy oneself with something (usually a subject or an area of knowledge). *How fascinating! I didn't know you were into astronomy.*

be 'on 1 be planned, be going to take place. *Janet had planned a meeting with Wilson for Friday morning, but I heard that he was ill, so I don't know whether the meeting will still be on.* 2 (a film, theatre, play etc.) being shown. *What's on at the Odeon this week?* 3 the phrase you're 'on! (informal) I'll accept your challenge, offer, bet, suggestion etc. *'I'll give you twenty pounds for your old bike.' 'All right! You're on!'* □ *'How about a game of tennis this afternoon?' 'Okay! You're on!'* 4 not be 'on (informal) not be acceptable, be too unreasonable. *I can't possibly be expected to do my own work and yours as well. It's just not on!*

be 'on something be taking medication. *After his accident, he was on painkillers for over a week, but he isn't on them now.*

be 'on about someone/something (informal) talk about someone/ something persistently. *Fred's always on about some crazy plan of his to get rich quick.*

be 'on to someone/something (informal) be on the track of someone/
something; discover, search for and be close to finding someone/
something. *The police are on to the gang who did the supermarket break-ins.*
□ *An experienced reporter knows when he's on to a good story.*

be 'out for something (informal) be determined to get something, aim
directly at getting something. *He's out for all he can get, whether it's money
or favours.*

be 'out of something have none left. *We're out of sugar.* □ *Don't ask me for
any more help. I'm out of ideas.*

be 'up be at an end, over. *Time's up!* □ *The Prime Minister's second term of
office will be up in June.*

be 'up against someone/something (informal) be confronted with
someone/something, have someone/something as competition. *Sarah
will be up against tough competitors in her new job.* □ *David's up against a
tricky problem with his latest computer programme.*

be 'up to something 1 be doing something, be involved with something
(often something undesirable). *It's very quiet. I bet little Jimmy's up to some
mischief again!* □ *Tony is very secretive about his whereabouts these days. I
think he's up to something.* 2 be of a good enough standard, be capable of
something. *Ted wants to go to university, but his teachers don't think he's up
to it.*

be 'with someone 1 follow someone's line of argument/explanation;
understand someone. *Would you repeat that, please? I'm not with you.*
2 support/encourage someone. *We're all with you one hundred per cent!*

bear something 'out support, confirm as true. *I hope you'll bear my story
out when I tell it in court.* □ *I'm afraid that my suspicions are borne out by the
facts.*

bear 'up manage to cope, remain strong in times of grief, pain, hardship
etc. *How is Mrs Jones bearing up after her husband's tragic death?*

'bear with someone be patient/tolerant with someone. *If you'll just bear
with me a little longer, madam. I've almost finished the demonstration.*

beef something 'up (informal) add more interest, spice, vitality to
something that is a little dull. *It's a good lecture, but I suggest you beef it up a
bit with a few jokes, humorous comments, personal experiences etc.*

blow 'over (informal) cease to arouse interest; be forgotten. *The
unpleasant affair has caused a lot of trouble, but it will all have blown over in a
few weeks.*

blow 'up 1 suddenly become angry. *I'm sorry, I didn't mean to blow up at
you in that way.* 2 arise and develop to a crisis. *Some trouble has blown up
at the factory. The workers are very dissatisfied.*

blow someone 'up (informal) reprimand someone angrily. *The boss blew
Deborah up for erasing his notes from the dictaphone.*

blow something 'up 1 exaggerate something in importance. *The incident
has been blown up in the press just for publicity's sake.* 2 enlarge
photographs etc. *These prints would look great blown up.* Note: a 'blow-
up. *I'd like a blow-up of this for my study wall.*

boil something 'down (informal) reduce in length, summarize. *The report's too long. Can you boil it down to, say, ten pages?*

boil 'down to something be reduced to something, be summarized as something. *The whole issue boils down to the same old problem – how to fight inflation without lowering the standard of living.*

bottle something 'up (informal) suppress emotion, anger etc., keep one's feelings to oneself. *Tell him exactly how unjust you think it all is. Let him know your feelings. Don't bottle them up.*

bounce 'back recover after any kind of difficulty or failure. *Don't worry about Matthew. He's been bankrupt twice before and he always bounces back.*

break 'down 1 stop functioning through mechanical defect. *Jan's car broke down again this morning, so she had to take a bus.* 2 come to nothing, fail, be discontinued. *Negotiations over the pay dispute have broken down again.* 3 lose emotional control because of grief/shock. *Mrs Roberts broke down completely when she heard the news of her husband's accident.* 4 collapse because of bad health. *Mr Hill had been overworked for some time when he finally broke down and had to be rushed to hospital.* Note: **a 'breakdown.**

break something 'down 1 overcome/conquer something. *Some people experience shyness as a barrier to communication, but this can be broken down gradually.* □ *It will prove difficult for the management to break down the union's resistance to the new scheme.* 2 analyse, reduce to details. *We can break down expenditure into three main factors – hardware, software, man-hours.* Note: **a 'breakdown.** *Can you submit a breakdown of your expenses by tomorrow?*

break 'in 1 interrupt to speak. *At meetings, Ray always breaks in with some trivial matter and holds up the proceedings.* 2 enter illegally by force. *Burglars broke in last night and stole over four hundred pounds.* Note: **a 'break-in.** *There's been a break-in at the college. A lot of video equipment is missing.*

break someone 'in help someone to adjust to something new, train someone. *I'll give you an easy task first, to break you in gently.*

break 'off 1 stop speaking. *Jackson had to break off in the middle of his speech because of shouts of protest from the audience.* 2 stop one's work for a break. *Shall we break off for lunch and continue this afternoon?*

break something 'off discontinue something, bring something to an abrupt end. *Frank and Liz have broken off their engagement.* □ *Negotiations have been broken off and are not expected to be resumed.*

break 'out 1 escape, free oneself. *After only one year in prison, he broke out and was on the run for several months.* Note: **a 'break-out.** *There has been another prison break-out.* 2 appear and spread rapidly. *Fighting has broken out again on the border.* Note: **an 'outbreak.** *There's been a second serious outbreak of food-poisoning.*

break 'through make a major discovery or advance. *Nuclear physicists claim to have broken through in several new aspects of the nature of the atom.* Note: **a 'breakthrough.** *The medical profession feels confident that there will be a major breakthrough in the fight against cancer within the next few years.*

break 'up 1 come to an end. *The partnership is expected to break up.* □ *People started to leave at 11 o'clock and the party finally broke up at midnight.* Note: **a 'break-up.** *I was sorry to hear of the break-up of Susan's marriage.* 2 finish for school holidays. *When does school break up for the summer vacation?*

break something 'up stop something (often by force). *A fight started in the High Street last night, so the police were called in to break it up.*

'break with someone/something end a relationship or association with someone/something. *He broke completely with his son when he found out that he was taking drugs.* □ *We intend to break with tradition and spend Christmas on Gran Canaria this year instead of at home.*

bring something a'bout cause something to happen, initiate something. *The new regime has already brought about a large number of improvements.* □ *This failure has been brought about by his own negligence.*

bring someone 'down 1 cause someone to be defeated. *This scandal may well bring the government down at the next election.* 2 persuade someone to reduce something in price. *After much argument, we managed to bring the car-dealer down to a price of £450.*

bring something 'down reduce something. *Government expenditure has been brought down radically by large defence cuts.*

bring someone 'in 1 arrest someone; detain someone for questioning at the police station. *Constable Crowther has just brought a man in for disorderly conduct. The man's been brought in before for the same thing.* 2 cause someone to be involved. *The legal situation is too complex. It's time we brought in an expert.*

bring something 'in introduce something. *A new bill has been brought in against terrorism.*

bring someone 'in on something tell someone about something, give someone a part in something. *I think we should bring Julia in on the scheme. She's always full of good ideas.*

bring something 'off (informal) complete something successfully. *I must admit that I didn't think you would bring the deal off.* □ *The dinner party won't be an easy thing to organize but you can rely on Felicity to bring it off with her usual flair.*

bring something 'on cause something, lead to something. *I often get bad headaches. I think it's concentrated reading over long periods that brings them on.*

bring someone 'out 1 help someone to become less shy. *Carol was very shy before she met Peter. He's brought her out a lot.* 2 cause to strike (i.e. stop work). *The union leader is threatening to bring his miners out again.*

bring something 'out 1 publish something, put something on the market. *The same publisher is bringing out a new edition of Ian Fleming's novels next year.* 2 reveal, show clearly. *It's difficult to bring out the exact meaning of certain English idioms in translation.* 3 develop. *A good teacher tries to bring out his pupils' individual talents.*

bring someone 'round 1 restore someone to consciousness. *Tom fainted, but the fresh air soon brought him round.* 2 persuade. *Michael didn't like our suggestion at first, but we soon brought him round to our way of thinking.*

bring someone 'up educate someone, rear someone. *Alan's wife is French, so they are bringing up their children to be bilingual.* □ *I was brought up in Sussex.*

bring something 'up introduce something for discussion, mention something. *Who brought this matter up in the first place?* □ *The question of higher membership fees was brought up at the last meeting.*

brush something a'side disregard something, reject something as unimportant. *I didn't expect him to brush aside my idea in such a rude way.*

brush 'up (on) something revise past knowledge/skills; improve something. *You'll have to brush up on your typing if you intend to get a part-time secretarial job.*

build 'up develop; increase in intensity. *Tension really builds up towards the end of the novel.*

build someone 'up 1 develop someone's physical strength, especially after illness. *The doctor says David is much better, but he now needs building up with vitamins and fresh air.* 2 increase someone's fame by praise. *He's only an average performer, but the critics have built him up to be a star of television.* Note: a '**buildup.** *The new television series was given a terrific buildup by the popular press.*

build something 'up develop something; increase or extend something gradually. *Mr Green built up his business from nothing.* □ *Her fortune has been built up over the years by careful investment.*

bump someone 'off (informal) kill someone. *Do you really believe that people who go around bumping others off deserve better themselves?*

bump something 'up (informal) increase a price, amount, number etc. *Get them to give you a fixed price before you give your name. Otherwise they might bump it up by a few hundred.* □ *It was an editorial decision to bump up the print run to 60,000.*

burst 'in enter suddenly in an excited manner. *Jeremy burst in with the news that he had won a holiday for two in Paris.*

buy someone 'off pay money in order to protect one's interests. *The blackmailer will have to be bought off, or he will ruin our good name.* □ *If you think you can buy me off, then you're wrong.*

buy someone 'out buy someone's business, all someone's shares in a company etc., often in order to gain a controlling interest oneself. *We offered to buy him out at 2% above the market value.* Note: a '**buy-out.** *We don't simply want a controlling share. It must be a full buy-out, 100% or nothing.*

buy something 'up buy as much of something as is available. *Speculators have bought up the entire building land in this area.* □ *All supplies of this material have been bought up by the chemical industry. There's none available to private householders.*

buzz 'off (informal) go away, leave. *I wish he'd buzz off and leave us alone. I hate anyone looking over my shoulder when I'm trying to concentrate.*

call 'by make a short visit. *Don't go out. Jeff's calling by this evening.*

'call for someone/something 1 collect someone/something. *I'll call for you on my way to the hairdresser's.* 2 demand or require someone/ something. *This position calls for a person of absolute integrity.* □ *Congratulations! This good news calls for a celebration.*

call 'in stop somewhere on the way to somewhere else. *I'll call in at the video shop on the way to the post office.*

call something 'off cancel something. *If it rains the tennis match will have to be called off.* □ *Jenny and Debbie have decided that their planned trip to Malaysia will cost too much money, so they're calling it off.*

'call on someone 1 visit someone. *The agency said that a representative would call on us next week.* 2 invite/request someone to speak. *The chairman called on the guest speaker to address the gathering.*

call someone 'up 1 (mainly US) telephone someone. *I'll call you up again later.* 2 summon someone for military service. *Jack wasn't called up until the war was nearly over.* Note: a **'call-up.**

carry someone a'way fill with emotion or enthusiasm. *She's a wonderful actress. She just carries you away.* □ *Lyn was completely carried away by the thought of a honeymoon in Hawaii.*

carry something 'off make a success of something, handle something well. *The situation requires tact and diplomacy. If anyone can carry it off, Grace can.*

carry 'on 1 continue. *Please carry on with your story – sorry I interrupted.* 2 (informal) argue, make a fuss. *Mrs Green was carrying on to her butcher about the poor quality of his steak.* Note: a **carry-'on.** *There was such a carry-on when Edward was invited to stand for chairman and not Simon.* 3 (informal) have an affair with. *There were rumours that a junior minister was carrying on with his secretary – all untrue, of course.*

carry something 'out 1 perform/conduct something. *Many experiments have been carried out in the field of adult second language acquisition.* 2 fulfil. *The boss is in the States, but she left us with a long list of instructions to carry out.*

cash 'in (on something) (informal) exploit a situation (often financially), turn something/a situation to one's own advantage. *There are always plenty of competitors ready to cash in on a company's misfortune.*

catch 'on (informal) become popular, be generally adopted. *In the States, the idea of a lunch-break work-out at a fitness club soon caught on.*

catch 'on (to something) understand; grasp the situation. *Paula is very bright. She catches on to things more quickly than most kids of her age.*

catch someone 'out outwit/outsmart someone. *It's difficult to catch Moira out on a point of fact. She knows all the answers.*

catch 'up (on/with something) bring oneself up to date. *After two months away from home, there's a lot of local news to catch up on.* □ *It's a 14-hour flight, so it will give me a chance to catch up with my reading.*

catch 'up with someone overtake and affect someone in a negative way (old age, illness, the past, one's mistakes etc.) *Charles looks continually worn out. I think his hectic life-style is beginning to catch up with him.*

change 'down/'up change a vehicle into a lower/higher gear. *There's a funny noise every time I change up into third gear.*

charge something 'up (to someone) put something on someone's account for payment later. *Don't bring me a bill – just charge it up.* □ *I'd like to have these goods charged up to my wife, please.*

chat someone 'up (informal) talk to someone (of the opposite sex) in a friendly way in order to win his/her confidence or favours. *I run a mile from any salesman who starts to chat me up.* □ *When I arrived at the disco, Nicola was being chatted up by a man of at least forty!*

check 'in/'out register one's arrival/departure. *You should check in at the flight-desk about an hour before take-off.* □ *I'm sorry, sir. Mr Carmichael checked out of the hotel about an hour ago.* Note: **a 'check-in.** *Look! There's Mike over there at the Alitalia check-in.*

check something 'off mark something as correct on a list. *Will you check these names off as I read them out, please?*

check someone/something 'out investigate someone's background/past. *I had him checked out. He's telling the truth.* □ *She says she was with the CIA for five years. Check it out, will you?*

check 'up on someone/something investigate someone/something, test the truth of something. *We'd better check up on him before we use him as a witness.* □ *Check up on the figures again before the article goes to press.* Note: **a 'check-up** usually refers to a medical examination. *The doctor gave me a thorough check-up and couldn't find anything wrong with me.*

chew something 'over (informal) think carefully about something, take time to consider something. *I'll need some time to chew the matter over before I can give you an answer.*

chip 'in (with something) (informal) 1 interrupt when someone is speaking. *I did my best to explain the situation to them, but Robert kept chipping in with silly questions and comments.* 2 contribute a small amount of money. *If we all chip in with a pound or two, surely we'll have enough to buy a coffee-maker for the seminar room.*

chuck something 'in/up (informal) leave (job etc.), stop doing something. *Mike's going to chuck his job in and go into business with his brother.* □ *Sally started an Open University course in English Literature, but she soon decided to chuck it up because of the pressure of her job.*

clamp 'down (on something) use one's authority to stop/suppress something. *It's time the government clamped down on false claims for unemployment benefits.* Note: **a 'clamp-down.** *There are a lot of health-conscious people who would welcome a clamp-down on cigarette advertising.*

clean someone 'out (informal) take all someone's money. *If I have to buy a new car, it will clean me out completely.*

clean something 'up remove dirt etc. in order to make something clean. *What are they doing about cleaning up the oil spill?* Note: **a 'clean-up.** *After losing over a million gallons of crude, the tanker company is now facing a massive clean-up in the North Sea.*

clear 'off (informal) go away. *I told the children to take their football and clear off.*

clear 'out (informal) leave and not return; leave quickly. *Monica's cleared out with the kids. She was fed up with Clive's violence.* □ *We'd better clear out of here as fast as we can. It's off limits.*

clear something 'out make something tidy, empty a room/drawer etc. of unwanted things. *Would you like to help me clear out the writing desk?*

clear something 'up 1 make tidy something that is untidy. *I hope you're going to clear up that mess yourself!* 2 explain by finding out the true facts. *Can we clear up the matter ourselves, or shall we call in the police?*

cock something 'up (slang, taboo) spoil something, make a mess of something, do something badly. *Don't ask Jim to organize anything! He's had no experience and he'll cock it all up for you.* Note: **a 'cock-up.** *You made a real cock-up of the travel arrangements, didn't you?*

come a'cross be understood clearly. *Her speech was carefully prepared, but it didn't come across very well.*

'come across someone/something meet someone or find something by chance. *You'll never guess who I came across the other day. Our old maths teacher!* □ *Where did you come across these old documents?*

come a'long 1 hurry. *Come along, we haven't much time.* 2 arrive, exist. *If the chance of being posted abroad ever comes along, take it.* 3 accompany someone. *We're going to a show. Why don't you come along?* 4 develop, make progress. *How's your new project coming along?*

'come by something obtain. *A job with such good prospects is not easy to come by in these times of high unemployment.* □ *How did you come by this beautiful Indian carving?*

come 'down on someone criticize someone, punish someone. *The new traffic laws come down heavily on dangerous drivers.*

come 'in 1 become fashionable. *Pleated skirts are coming in again this season.* 2 take a place in a competition. *Julia came in third in the 400 metres.* 3 play a part. *The plan sounds just fine, but where do I come in?* Note: **come in 'useful/handy** prove to be useful. *Don't throw that big box away. It might come in handy for the move.*

come 'off 1 take place, happen. *There was a lot of talk about a takeover, but it never came off.* 2 succeed. *It was a good plan, but it didn't come off.* 3 fall off. *Fred was riding his bike when he came off and hurt his leg.*

come 'on 1 begin. *I've got a headache coming on.* 2 make progress, develop. *My cabbages and onions are coming on nicely.* 3 be broadcast on TV/radio. *My favourite programme comes on at 8 o'clock on Tuesdays.* 4 follow later. *Julie's arriving today and David's coming on tomorrow with the luggage.*

come 'out 1 strike (i.e. stop work). *There's no chance of the police force coming out.* 2 be published, be available on the market. *Elizabeth's book came out last month.* 3 result, be produced. *The photographs of the experiments came out very well.* 4 take a place in an examination. *Jonathan came out bottom in social studies and top in maths.* 5 become public, be made known. *When is the news of their engagement coming out?*

come 'out with something (informal) say or reveal something that may surprise. *You never know what children are going to come out with next.*

□ *When I asked him where he'd been, he came out with a very confused story which was obviously not true.*

come 'round 1 regain consciousness. *Hilary fainted, but she soon came round in the fresh air.* 2 pay an informal visit. *Would you like to come round tomorrow evening?* 3 change one's attitude, be persuaded. *Bob refused the job at first, but he soon came round when he heard how much money we were offering him.*

come 'to regain consciousness. *When she came to, she found herself in a hospital bed.*

'come to something 1 amount to something. *How much did the bill for the car repairs come to?* □ *What it all comes to, is that he won't offer us his support in the election campaign.* 2 be a question of. *Mandy's very good at painting and playing the violin, but when it comes to cooking a meal she's hopeless.*

come 'up 1 present itself. *Mary's been hoping to find work through the Job Centre, but nothing suitable has come up yet.* 2 be mentioned or discussed. *Dumping toxic waste is a matter that's always coming up these days.* 3 win, be successful. *If my number comes up in the lottery, it's champagne for everybody.*

come 'up with something produce an idea/suggestion/solution etc. *Marjorie usually comes up with some good ideas.*

cook something 'up invent, fabricate something (an excuse, a story etc.). *What good excuse have you cooked up for not attending the committee meeting?*

cool 'off (informal) become less angry, aggressive, excited etc. *Jeff's furious. Just give him a few minutes to cool off.*

count someone/something 'in include someone/something. *Shall we count you in on the plan?*

'count on someone/something rely on someone/something. *You can always count on Mary to give sound advice.* □ *We're counting on completing the research by Christmas.*

count someone/something 'out exclude someone/something, not consider someone/something. *If the trip's going to cost over five hundred pounds, you'd better count me out – I can't afford it.*

crop 'up happen, occur unexpectedly. *I was scheduled to fly to L.A. tomorrow, but something unexpected has cropped up so David's going instead.*

cry 'off (informal) withdraw. *Max promised to come, but now he's cried off at the last moment.*

cut 'back (on) something reduce. *On account of the huge surplus oil reserves, it was necessary to cut back production.* □ *If we don't cut back on expenditure, the company will be faced with serious difficulties.* Note: **a 'cut-back.**

cut 'down (on) something reduce (consumption). *Jim has cut down his daily calorie intake by half.* □ *It's difficult to cut down on little luxuries.*

cut 'in 1 interrupt. *I'm sorry, I didn't mean to cut in like that.* 2 drive sharply in front of another car when overtaking. *I wish big lorries wouldn't cut in like that. It unnerves me.*

cut 'off turn. *The police saw the suspect cut off down a dark lane and disappear into an empty building.*

cut someone 'off 1 break a telephone connection. *I got through to the right number, but then we were cut off.* 2 isolate someone. *The snow drifts and avalanches have cut several hundred holiday-makers off from the larger ski resorts.*

cut something 'off 1 interrupt the supply of a service (electricity, gas, telephone). *If you don't pay the bill, they'll cut your electricity off.* 2 isolate something. *The low-lying villages were cut off by flood water for several days.*

cut 'out stop functioning. *I'm having terrible trouble with the engine. It keeps cutting out.*

cut someone 'out (informal) eliminate/defeat someone. *He's managed to cut out all competition so far, so it looks as though he may win the chess championship.*

cut something 'out 1 stop something, do without something. *Cut out bread and potatoes and you'll soon start to lose weight.* 2 (informal) stop doing something because it is not desired (often with **it** as object). *We've had enough of that ridiculous talk, now just cut it out!* 3 exclude something. *If you cut out paragraphs five and seven, the essay will be fine.* □ *Let's cut out the preliminaries and get started on the important business.*

cut someone 'up 1 (informal) upset someone. *The bad news naturally cut him up a lot.* □ *He was terribly cut up by his wife's death.* 2 (informal) injure someone. *The car crash cut him up a bit but he's fully recovered now.*

dash something 'off produce something hurriedly. *I'll just dash off a few letters before lunch.*

'dawn on someone (an idea, fact) become clear to someone after a certain length of time. *Richard couldn't find his bicycle, and after he had looked everywhere for it, it dawned on him that it had been stolen.*

'deal in something sell/do business with something (goods). *They deal in hi-fi and video equipment.*

'deal with someone 1 trade with, buy from someone. *We've been dealing with Leach Brothers for over six years now.* 2 (informal) punish someone, take action against someone. *Richards has caused us enough trouble. Just leave him to me – I'll deal with him.*

'deal with something treat a topic/subject; be concerned with a question/matter etc. *The book deals with the topic on pages 35 to 48.* □ *It's time we dealt with the question of what new laboratory equipment we need.* 2 handle, tackle, solve something. *My job is mainly to deal with customer complaints and enquiries.* □ *Inflation is one of the most difficult issues for any government to deal with.*

die 'down decrease, lose in intensity. *Maureen was furious about the matter at the time, but her anger soon died down after she had had more time to think about it.*

'die for something (informal) want something very much, long for something. *After a busy day in town, I'm usually dying for a rest with my feet up.*

'do for someone (informal) 1 keep house for someone. *My grandparents have done for themselves for years.* 2 ruin someone. Note: be 'done for be ruined, finished. *If the bank forecloses on the property, we'll be done for.*

'do for something (informal) serve as something. *Don't throw that old shirt away. I'll cut it up and it will do for cleaning rags.*

do someone 'out of something (informal) cheat someone, prevent someone from getting something. *I still think it was Williams who did me out of the promotion.*

do someone 'over (slang) beat someone severely with fists. *Pete has stopped going to football matches since he got done over by a gang of youths.*

do something 'up 1 renovate something. *Mrs McDonald is having the old cottage done up.* 2 fasten (shoe laces, a zip fastener, buttons etc.) *Do up your shoes or you'll fall over the laces.*

'do with something 1 (informal) (used with could) want, need, benefit from something. *I'm hot and tired. I could do with a nice, cool drink.* □ *Sue's car could do with a good wash and polish.* 2 (used with have to) be concerned with something, be relating to something. *Patricia's work has to do with computer application for chemical problems, I think.*

do 'without someone/something 1 manage without someone/ something. *Fiona has bought a personal computer. Now she says she can't imagine how she ever did without one.* 2 (used with could) dispense with something; not require/tolerate someone/something. *I could do without Pamela coming tomorrow. I haven't really got time to see her.*

draw 'in 1 (daylight hours) get shorter. *The evenings are drawing in. It will soon be winter.* 2 (a train) arrive at a station. *The Bristol train drew in ten minutes late.* 3 (a vehicle) stop at the side of the road. *The lorry drew in and the driver got out.*

draw someone 'in attract someone. *Shoppers were drawn in by the special offers on wine and spirits.*

draw 'out 1 (hours of daylight) get longer. *As soon as January is over, the days begin to draw out noticeably.* 2 (a train) leave. *We arrived at the platform just as the train was drawing out.* 3 (a vehicle) move into the stream of traffic/onto the road. *The van drew out unexpectedly and almost caused an accident.*

draw someone 'out encourage someone to be less shy. *Peter was rather shy when he left school, but when he started work his colleagues soon drew him out.*

draw something 'out 1 take money from one's bank account. *I'm going to draw out all my savings to pay for the holiday.* 2 (informal) make something longer, prolong something. *Your speech is too short. Can't you draw it out a bit?* 3 extract information from someone who is unwilling to give it. *Johnny wouldn't tell us what really happened at school. We had to draw it out of him slowly.*

draw 'up (a vehicle) come to a stop. *The van drew up in front of the house.*

draw something 'up 1 place or pull near (a chair etc.). *Draw the armchair up to the fire.* 2 formulate something. *Has the agreement been drawn up by a lawyer?* □ *It's a carefully drawn up report, accurate and clear.*

dream something 'up use one's imagination to create a story, scheme, plot, plan etc. *Whatever wild scheme will Simon dream up next?*

dress 'up 1 put on one's best or formal clothes. *Is the reception going to be informal, or do we need to dress up for it?* 2 wear a disguise or fancy-dress costume. *What are you dressing up as for the Charity Ball?*

dress something 'up improve something; make something appear or sound better. *Your proposal is fine. Dress it up a bit and then submit it to the committee.*

drink something 'in (informal) listen to something or look at something eagerly. *Mrs Green drinks in all the gossip and spreads it as fast as she can.* □ *We stood on top of the hill, drinking in the breath-taking view.*

'drive at something try to express something, mean something. *David doesn't explain things very well, but I think I know what he's driving at.*

drop 'by/in/over/round pay someone a casual visit. *Do drop by when you're in the area.* □ *My neighbour often drops in for a coffee and a chat.*

drop something 'by/in/off/over/round bring or take something somewhere. *'Where did these video tapes come from?' 'Jill dropped them by for you this afternoon.'*

drop 'off 1 fall asleep. *I had just dropped off when the telephone rang.* 2 decrease. *Sandra doesn't talk much about wanting to become a nurse any more. Her interest must have dropped off.* Note: a **'drop-off.** *There was a sudden drop-off in attendance at the cookery class when the new teacher took over.*

drop someone 'off allow someone to get off a vehicle. *Ask the bus driver to drop you off at the racecourse.*

drop 'out stop attending or participating. *Frank started a cookery course but he dropped out after the first few sessions.*

drum something 'up encourage and obtain something, e.g. support, sales orders. *Frances is going to the States next week to drum up business for the new product.*

dry 'up 1 dry the dishes. *Be a darling and dry up for me, will you?* 2 (informal) be unable to speak further. *Poor old Arthur kept drying up in the middle of his speech, so he had to get out his notes.* 3 (informal) stop talking. *Sharon talks about nothing but her disco friends all the time. I do wish she'd dry up!*

'dwell on something spend too much time, discussion or thought on a topic. *His speech was too long. He dwelt too much on the school's achievements.*

ease 'off decrease tension, pressure or speed. *I've advised Jim to ease off a bit. He's been working too hard.* □ *Political tension eased off slowly when the heads of the two nations began talks.*

ease 'up become less urgent, slacken. *I'll be glad when the pressure of work has eased up a little. I'm working twelve hours a day and more.*

'eat into something consume, use up a large part of something (money etc.). *The holiday in Canada will eat into our savings.*

eat something 'up 1 (food) finish. *Make sure the children eat their vegetables up!* 2 consume/use a lot of something. *Bob's new sports car just eats up petrol.*

egg someone 'on (informal) encourage/urge someone to do something which one should not. *Stop egging him on to drink more! You can see he's had enough!*

end 'up (informal) do in the end, finish (by doing something). *If you don't slow down, you'll end up in hospital.* □ *I ended up by telling Penny the whole story, although that wasn't my intention.*

face 'up to something/someone (problems, difficulties) accept or confront something/someone. *Grandad just can't face up to the fact that he's too old to work any more.* □ *It's time Peter learnt to face up to his parents' demands.*

fall 'back on someone/something go back to someone/something for help; use someone/something as a reserve. *We can always fall back on Bill to drive us to the airport if we can't get anyone else.* □ *Thank goodness we've got our savings to fall back on.*

fall be'hind (with something) be behind with a schedule, things that must be done etc. *He's falling behind with the work on his book. It's more difficult than he thought.* □ *If you fall behind with the payments, they charge high interest rates.*

'fall for someone be romantically infatuated with someone. *Paula's fallen for her new professor.*

'fall for something 1 like something very much. *Sally always falls for the most expensive dresses in the shop.* 2 be tricked into believing something. *I wish my husband wouldn't fall for all this sales talk. He's just bought his third lawn-mower.*

fall 'in with someone get to know by chance and begin to associate with someone. *We fell in with some French tourists from the same hotel.* □ *When Ted worked in Soho, he fell in with some people of dubious character.*

fall 'in with something accept/agree to/comply with something. *George will fall in with any suggestion that involves having a good time.*

fall 'off 1 decrease. *Sales tend to fall off just after Christmas.* □ *Attendance at lectures fell off gradually towards the end of the course.* Note: **a 'fall-off.** *There was a gradual fall-off in attendance.* 2 become worse, deteriorate. *The service in this restaurant has been falling off for a long time.*

fall 'out (with someone) (informal) quarrel; not be on friendly terms with someone. *Ruth and Tony have fallen out again, but it never lasts long.* □ *Tommy is becoming quite a difficult child. He's always falling out with his friends.*

fall 'through (informal) fail, not develop or take place. *The holiday plans fell through at the last minute owing to illness.* □ *We're going on a picnic tomorrow, unless it falls through because of the weather.*

feel 'up to something feel capable of something physically or mentally. *Do you feel up to continuing with the work today?* □ *After three weeks in hospital, I don't feel up to decorating the house.*

fight someone/something 'off defeat/repel someone/something. *The police had a difficult job to fight off the reporters as the filmstar was getting into the car. The fans had to be fought off, too.* □ *I'm trying to fight off a cold by taking Vitamin C every day.*

fill 'in do a job temporarily to replace someone else. *The maths teacher is ill, so I'm filling in for a few weeks until she comes back.*

fill someone 'in give someone details/information about something. *Can you fill me in on Harrison's qualifications for the job?* □ *I've just been filled in by Peter on the latest changes in government policy.*

fill something 'in/out/up complete with written information (form, papers etc.). *Please fill in all your particulars on this form.* □ *Is this visa application form filled up correctly?* (US)

finish something 'off complete something; use something up. *'You haven't finished this letter.' 'Oh, I'll finish it off after lunch.'* □ *Has the last of the Spanish brandy been finished off yet?*

finish 'off/up with something end with something. *Let's finish up with a chorus of 'Auld Lang Syne'!*

'finish with someone (informal) end a connection or friendship with someone. *The butcher's overcharged me three times, so now I've finished with him.*

'finish with something finish using something, not need something any more. *When you've finished with the book, will you pass it on to me?*

fit 'in go into the space provided. *The shelf is too small. The big books won't fit in.*

fit 'in with someone/something match, suit, harmonize with someone/ something. *That modern picture doesn't fit in with the antique furniture.* □ *David doesn't really fit in with the rest of the group; he's too much of an individualist.*

fit someone/something 'in find time or space for. *I hope the hairdresser can fit me in today.* □ *The doctor can't fit in any more visits this week.*

fit someone 'up with something equip/supply someone with something. *Do you think Fred's garage could fit me up with some new car tyres?*

fit something 'up with something fix/equip something with something. *The laboratories have just been fitted up with new equipment.*

'fix on something (informal) decide on something. *Have you fixed on a date for the dinner party yet?*

fix something 'on fasten/attach something. *If you don't fix the top on properly, the juice will spill out.*

fix someone 'up with something (informal) supply someone with something. *Can you fix me up with a part-time job in the supermarket?* □ *He rang up the hotel for a room and was fixed up immediately.*

fix something 'up 1 (informal) arrange something. *I've fixed up an appointment at the dentist's for Tuesday morning.* □ *Have you got your holiday fixed up?* 2 install something. *Joe has fixed up a work-bench in his garden shed.*

follow something 'through continue something to the end. *Robert is determined to follow his plan through.* □ *If you follow the argument through to its logical conclusion, it means that what Jeff says is true.*

follow something 'up 1 investigate something; pursue something further. *The editor thinks the story is worth following up.* □ *We ought to follow up his suggestion; it sounds reasonable.* 2 follow something; reinforce something with something. *The series is to be followed up by another programme on a similar theme.* Note: **a 'follow-up.** *His first novel was a great success, so now he's writing a follow-up.*

fool a'round (with someone/something) (informal) 1 waste time, play foolishly. *If Kevin doesn't stop fooling around he'll never pass his exams.* □ *He was fooling around with this old gun, when suddenly it went off!* 2 interfere with someone/something. *When Jake realized that Dan was fooling around with his girlfriend, there was a big fight.*

get a'bout 1 travel. *Mary gets about all over Europe, even though she hasn't got a car.* 2 walk. *Old people can't get about very well in winter.* 3 spread. *News got about that the local radio station was closing down.*

get a'cross communicate clearly. *The new commercial gets across very well.*

get something a'cross to someone communicate something to someone, make one's ideas clear to someone. *A good speaker can get his ideas across to his audience without much effort.*

get a'long 1 (informal) leave, depart. *We must be getting along now, or we'll be late for the cinema.* 2 make progress, manage, succeed. *How are the builders getting along with your new house?* □ *How's Alec getting along in Canada?* 3 manage to do something under difficulties. *How are you getting along while your wife's in Scotland?* □ *The Robinsons only have a small pension, but they seem to get along all right.* 4 have a good relationship. *Robin and the new assistant aren't getting along at all well, I'm afraid.*

'get at someone (informal) 1 criticize someone. *She's always getting at her husband for not helping with the housework.* □ *No names were mentioned, but we all knew who was being got at.* 2 bribe someone, influence someone to do what one wants. *Someone has been trying to get at certain members of the jury.*

'get at something 1 reach something. *Put the documents somewhere where the children can't get at them.* 2 find out about something; get to know something. *The truth of the case will be very difficult to get at.* 3 mean, try to say, hint at something. *I'm afraid I don't know what you're getting at.* □ *What was Rosaline getting at with that strange remark about the money not being ours?* 4 start work on something. *If the rain stopped, I could get at the garden. There's so much to do.*

get a'way with something escape reprimand or punishment for something. *You shouldn't let her get away with telling lies.* □ *He stole once before and got away with it, which means that he may do it again.*

get 'back at someone get revenge on someone. *She'll get back at him for telling everybody her secret – that's for sure.*

get 'back to someone contact someone again later (with information, an answer etc.). *I don't have the information you need just now, so I'll get back to you later.*

get 'by manage. *If you want to speak a language well, you can't get by without mastering its idioms.*

get someone 'down depress someone. *This miserable weather really gets me down.*

get something 'down 1 manage to write something down. *Did you get the last sentence down or was I dictating too quickly?* 2 (informal) swallow something. *This medicine is so bitter that it's an effort to get it down!*

get 'down to something start serious work on something; tackle something. *It's time you got down to your studies or the other students will leave you behind.* □ *Calculus isn't difficult at all, once you get down to it.*

get 'in 1 enter. *The rain can get in through this window.* 2 arrive. *What time does your train get in?* 3 be elected. *Do you think the Conservatives will get in again?* 4 be admitted. *The school has a long waiting-list, so I don't think our son will get in this year.*

get someone 'in summon/call someone. *I can't fix this loose wiring myself, so I'll get an electrician in.*

get something 'in bring something inside. *It's starting to rain. We ought to get the washing in.*

get 'in with someone (informal) get on good terms with someone in order to gain an advantage. *James always tries to get in with influential people. That's why he's joined the riding club.*

get 'off 1 depart; start a journey. *What time did you eventually manage to get off?* 2 escape punishment, reprimand, injury etc. *Dick was lucky, he got off with a warning and a small fine of fifty pounds.* □ *Alex crashed his car, but luckily he got off with only a few scratches.*

get 'off something 1 dismount from a horse; alight from a vehicle. *She got off her horse and came over to talk to us.* □ *The conductor will tell you where to get off the bus.* 2 stop talking about something. *Can't we get off the subject of work for a change?*

get someone 'off save someone from punishment. *The lawyer got Smith off, but he wouldn't have got him off so easily if it hadn't been a first offence.*

get something 'off 1 take something off, remove something. *I can't get my boots off. They're too tight.* □ *'There's a coffee stain on my shirt.' 'I know. I couldn't get it off.'* 2 send off, dispatch. *Please get these letters off by the afternoon post.* 3 (informal) learn perfectly. *Jeremy's playing the king in the school play, but he hasn't got his lines off properly yet.*

get 'off with someone (informal) become friendly with someone of the opposite sex at a first meeting. *Michael got off with a very pretty Italian girl at Mick's party.*

get someone 'off with someone (informal) arrange for someone to become friendly with someone of the opposite sex. *Mark's always on his own. Can't his sister get him off with one of her girlfriends?*

get 'on 1 make progress. *How's the broken leg getting on?* 2 manage, succeed. *How's Tom getting on with his Spanish course?* □ *How would you get on without me?* 3 become late, grow older. *Time's getting on, we'd better go home.* □ *Mr Williams is getting on, he must be nearly seventy.* 4 have a good relationship, like each other's company. *They get on well at work but not socially.*

get 'on to someone 1 trace/detect someone. *The police have finally got on to the man who was blackmailing the politician.* 2 make contact with someone, consult someone. *I complained to the shop about the faulty washing-machine and they said they would get on to the manufacturers.*

get 'on with something continue to do something, make progress with something. *Turn the television off and get on with your homework.*

get 'out 1 (informal) go out and enjoy oneself. *You work too hard. You should get out a bit more.* 2 leave, escape. *When the fighting started, George thought it would be better to get out, so he came back to England.* 3 become known, leak out. *The news has got out about the takeover, although it wasn't to become public until next month.* □ *Don't let it get out that I knew about it!*

get something 'out 1 remove something. *The cork's stuck in the wine bottle. I can't get it out.* 2 make an utterance in spite of physical or emotional difficulties. *Mr Clarke managed to get out an apology, but only because he was under pressure to do so.* 3 publish something, put something on the market. *The publishers hope to get a third edition out before Christmas.* 4 borrow from a library. *How many books can I get out at a time?*

get 'out of something avoid having to do something. *Fred always gets out of doing the washing-up by saying he's busy in the garden.*

get 'over someone stop being emotionally involved with someone. *Andrew's married again now, but he never really got over his first wife.*

get 'over something 1 overcome something (usually difficult or unpleasant). *Has Walter got over his financial difficulties yet?* 2 recover from an illness, shock, surprise etc. *I thought Jessica would never get over the shock of losing all her money, but she's starting up in business again.* □ *I can't get over Jack leaving for Australia without telling us.*

get something 'over 1 communicate one's ideas. *Professor Wright knows his subject, but he's not very good at getting over his ideas to his students.* 2 complete something. *As soon as Brian gets his exams over, he's going on holiday.* □ *As soon as the formalities had been got over, the consulate was quick to issue the work permit.*

get 'round someone coax/persuade someone. *Jenny's trying to get round her father to buy her a horse!*

get 'round something avoid/evade something. *It's no use trying to get round paying your income tax!* □ *I'm sure the regulations could be got round if we studied them closely enough.*

get someone 'round call/summon someone. *Get Tom round, if you need someone to fix the broken lawn-mower.*

get something 'round take something to a place, send someone to a place with something. *I'll get the video tape round to you by this evening.*

get 'round to someone/something find time for someone/something. *I can't get round to all the applicants now. Ask the last four to come back later.* □ *I haven't got round to reading your essay yet, but I'll look at it this evening.*

get 'through 1 manage to pass through. *There's a hole in the fence where the dog gets through.* 2 succeed, pass a test. *The exam was difficult. Not all candidates got through.* 3 get a telephone connection. *All the lines to Glasgow were engaged. I just couldn't get through.*

get 'through something 1 finish something; complete something successfully. *I got through the book in one evening.* 2 use something up. *His salary's quite high, but he's usually got through it by the middle of the month.* 3 eat or drink a large quantity of something. *Jimmy got through a big plate of spaghetti and then asked for a second helping!*

get 'through to someone succeed in establishing an understanding with someone, in communicating with someone. *Jan and I had a quarrel, and since then I just haven't been able to get through to her.*

get someone 'through 1 help someone to pass an examination. *The teacher got all his pupils through without difficulty.* 2 connect someone by telephone. *By the time the girl at reception had got me through to Blake's extension number, he'd gone home.*

get something 'through 1 cause something to be approved or accepted. *It was the personnel manager who helped to get my transfer through.* 2 succeed in bringing through. *Alan always manages to get a double allowance of spirits through without the customs officials noticing.*

'get to someone (informal) 1 bribe someone, influence someone. *He should have been given a harsher sentence. Someone must have got to the judge.* 2 affect someone emotionally, influence one's state of mind. *It's that woman. She's getting to you, isn't she?* □ *Don't let the strain get to you!*

get 'up 1 get out of bed. *I'm not used to getting up early.* 2 (wind, storm) increase. *There's a strong wind getting up.*

get someone 'up 1 call someone from bed. *Can you get me up at six tomorrow?* 2 dress someone formally, dress someone in fancy-dress costume. *The children were got up in their best clothes for Granny's seventy-fifth birthday celebrations.* □ *We got Barry up as Long John Silver for the New Year's Eve Ball.*

get something 'up 1 arrange/organize something. *We're getting up an evening of folk singing.* □ *The students have got up a petition against the building of nuclear power stations.* 2 study, memorize. *Bill is getting up his maths formulas for the test tomorrow.*

get 'up to something 1 reach the standard or level of something. *I hope to get up to a hundred words per minute for the shorthand exam.* 2 be involved in/busy with something (usually something undesirable). *'Tim brought a dead mouse home yesterday.' 'Good grief! Whatever will he get up to next?'* □ *And just what have you two been getting up to in my absence?*

give someone a'way 1 betray someone. *Nobody knows I've done this, so please don't give me away!* 2 lead the bride to the bridegroom at the marriage ceremony. *The bride was given away by her uncle.*

give something a'way 1 distribute something free of charge. *Amanda didn't want her college books any more, so she gave them all away.* 2 betray something. *Please don't give my secret away!* Note: **a 'give-away.** *The guilty look on his face was a real give-away.*

give 'in surrender, yield. *You can't win the game now, so you may as well give in.* □ *The rioters were at last forced to give in to the police.*

give something 'in submit something. *Don't forget to give in your names, if you wish to be considered for membership.*

give 'out 1 come to an end, be used up. *We had just reached home when the petrol gave out.* □ *His strength had almost given out when the rescuers found him.* 2 stop functioning. *We were ten miles from the next town when the engine gave out!*

give something 'out 1 distribute something. *The President's wife gave out flowers to the soldiers.* 2 announce something. *The list of winners was given out over the microphone.*

give 'up lose interest and admit defeat. *Oh, I give up! I'm tired of trying to guess the right answer.*

give someone 'up 1 surrender/betray someone. *They knew he was a spy and a sense of duty forced them to give him up to the authorities.* 2 no longer expect someone to come. *We had already given Don up, when suddenly he walked in!* 3 no longer expect someone to recover after illness. *The doctors had given the patient up, but he made a remarkable recovery.*

give something 'up surrender/stop something. *I don't want to give my job up unless it's really necessary.* 2 renounce (beliefs, principles). *Will Ben have to give his religion up in order to marry Kathy?* 3 devote time to something. *All our weekends are given up to gardening.*

give 'up something 1 stop doing or having something. *If you gave up smoking, your health would improve a lot. Please give it up.* 2 abandon something, no longer try to do something. *They've given up the search for further survivors of the wreck.*

go a'bout 1 circulate. *There's another rumour going about that the President is going to resign.* 2 move or walk about. *Teenage boys tend to go about in groups.* 3 (with **in**) wear regularly. *Does Uncle Henry still go about in those old army boots?*

go a'bout something manage something; approach/tackle something. *Can you help me with this maths problem? I don't quite know how to go about it.* □ *She went about her work of discovering the truth very efficiently. She had her husband followed by a private detective.*

go 'after someone/something try to get someone/something. *Paul's gone after another job, in Manchester.* □ *They both went after the same girl.*

go a'long with someone/something 1 agree with someone. *I'll go along with you there. You're right!* 2 comply with something; do as someone suggests. *Suggest putting the child in a private school. Maybe the parents would see sense and go along with it.* 3 approve of something. *Do you go along with the idea of inherited titles?*

'go by someone/something trust as correct; form a judgement from what someone says. *People around here must be very friendly – if you're anything to go by.* □ *Don't go by that clock. It's fast.*

go 'down 1 be received. *How does the prospect of working again after the holidays go down?* □ *His speech went down very well with the audience.* 2 lose in value, fall. *The share index has gone down again by ten points.* □ *The tone of the neighbourhood has gone down a lot since those new houses were built.*

go 'down with something fall ill with something. *Most of my colleagues have gone down with flu.*

'**go for someone** 1 attack someone. *He went for the fat man with a knife.* □ *The newspapers really went for him over the bad handling of the crisis, but he wasn't the only culprit.* 2 admire someone, be attracted by someone. *It isn't true that dark girls usually go for fair men.* 3 apply to someone, include someone. *Listen carefully, because this goes for you all.* □ *Does that go for the senior pupils, too?*

'**go for something** 1 like something. *I don't really go for modern art, the old masters appeal to me more.* 2 try hard to get something, make something one's aim. *Joanna is going for the tennis championship this year.* □ *Catherine wants to make dancing her career, but she's unsure of herself. So I told her to go for it.* 3 be sold for a sum of money. *'How much did the house go for?' 'Actually, it went for far less than I had expected.'*

go 'in for something 1 compete in something. *Robin's going in for the 400 metres.* □ *She went in for a piano competition and won second prize.* 2 have as an interest or hobby. *Ronald goes in for collecting antique weapons.* □ *Public speaking? Goodness, no! I don't go in for that sort of thing.* 3 choose as one's career. *Sylvia's going in for nursing.*

go 'into something 1 investigate/examine something. *The solicitor said that he would go into the matter very thoroughly.* 2 state something in detail. *We haven't enough time to go into the history of the case, so perhaps you could summarize the main points.*

go 'off 1 explode. *The bomb went off without warning, but luckily nobody was seriously hurt.* 2 (foodstuffs) go bad. *Don't drink the milk, I think it's gone off.* 3 get worse. *The standard of his work has gone off over the last few weeks.* 4 (informal) fall asleep. *Dad's gone off in the chair. Don't wake him!* 5 result, succeed. *'How did the meeting with Sutherland go off?' 'It went off rather well, actually.'*

go 'off someone/something lose one's liking or taste for someone/ something. *Jane had a nice boyfriend, but he must have gone off her because she hasn't seen him for a long time.* □ *We've gone right off camping holidays. We're going to a hotel this year.*

go 'on 1 continue talking. *I was tired of listening, but he just went on and on.* 2 continue, resume. *We'll stop there for today and go on with the reading tomorrow.* 3 happen, take place. *Will someone please explain to me just what's going on here?* Note: **goings-'on**. *There are some very strange goings-on in that house.* 4 (informal) behave. *Patty was going on like a silly schoolgirl.* □ *The way she went on, you would think she owned the company.*

go 'on at someone (informal) grumble at someone, reprimand someone. *My last English teacher was very hard to please. Every day he went on at me about something or other.*

go 'out 1 cease to be in fashion. *I hope plastic coats will soon go out. They're not very comfortable.* 2 be sent, be announced. *Have all the wedding invitations gone out yet?* 3 emigrate. *She went out to New Zealand about five years ago.*

go 'over something 1 repeat something. *Could you go over the explanation once more, please?* 2 examine/check something. *Let's go over the figures again.* □ *We went over the facts again and again, but we couldn't find a* *solution.* 3 search something. *The police went over his room three times, but found nothing.*

go 'through be concluded, accepted. *I hear that the deal went through. Congratulations!* □ *The Conservatives are trying to prevent the bill from going through.*

'go through something 1 use something up, consume something. *How many pints of milk do you go through a week?* □ *I've gone through too much money this week.* 2 search/examine something. *The customs went through all our luggage at the airport.* 3 suffer pain, hardship, loss. *Most families went through quite a lot during the war.* 4 discuss something; review something. *Shall we go through the details of the plan again?* □ *The pros and cons of the matter have been gone through again and again.*

go 'through with something complete something, continue something to the end. *The plan was very daring, and at the last minute I felt I couldn't go through with it.*

go 'up 1 increase in price. *Wines and spirits are going up again next week.* 2 be constructed. *There's a new hypermarket going up in the town centre.*

'grow on someone appeal more and more to someone. *I didn't like the song at first, but it grows on you the more you hear it.*

grow 'up (people) mature, become adult. *Your children are growing up very quickly now.* Note: **a 'grown-up.** *Chris is at the age when he likes to spend his time with grown-ups.*

hammer something 'out discuss something at length until a solution is reached. *The discussion went on until the early hours of the morning, but they managed to hammer out a solution that would be acceptable to both parties.*

hand something 'down 1 pass something to someone else by tradition. *These paintings have been handed down to us through five generations.* 2 give something that is no longer needed to others. *These clothes have been handed down from Peter to his two younger brothers and they are still in good condition.*

hand something 'out 1 circulate something. *Will you help me to hand out the leaflets at the meeting?* Note: **a 'hand-out** is a written or printed leaflet/sheet etc. 2 give/offer something to others. *Uncle Bill is good at handing out advice that nobody wants to listen to.*

hang a'bout/a'round (informal) stand waiting idly. *That man has been hanging about here for half an hour. What does he want?* □ *Colin's not here at the moment, but if you hang around for a while you should catch him.*

hang 'back hesitate to come forward. *If you know the answer, say it. Don't hang back!*

hang be'hind linger at a place when others have already left. *Janice and Tony hung behind after the lecture to talk to the guest speaker.* □ *Walk faster! If you hang behind, we'll lose you.*

hang 'on (informal) wait. *Hang on and I'll get help!* □ *Just hang on a second and I'll tell Bob you're on the phone for him.*

hang 'on to something keep something; not sell or give something away. *You should hang on to those shares, they'll be going up again soon.* □ *Wilson should have retired years ago, but he's hanging on to his job.*

hang 'out (informal) live or spend one's free time. *Where's Dennis hanging out these days?*

hang 'up end a telephone conversation (often abruptly). *I don't know what happened. She just hung up in the middle of the conversation!*

hang someone/something 'up (informal) delay someone/something (often passive). *I'm sorry I'm late. I got hung up on the way here.* □ *The heavy rain hung up the work on the building site for three weeks.*

'happen on/upon something discover something by chance. *How do you like this jade ornament? I happened on it in a little side street in Bangkok.*

have someone 'in employ someone in one's home/office; invite to one's home. *I'm having the electrician in to fix these faulty switches.* □ *We had the Robinsons in for supper last night.*

have someone 'on tease someone with an untrue or exaggerated story etc. *Uncle Bruce said I would get a thousand pounds for my old car, but I know he was having me on.*

have (got) something 'on 1 wear something. *Gloria had her fur coat on and it was much too warm.* 2 have something arranged, have an engagement. *Would you like to join us for supper this evening, or have you got something on already?* □ *I'll come and see you as soon as I can, but I have a lot on at the moment.*

have (got) something 'on someone (informal) have proof or evidence against someone. *The police can't arrest him because they haven't got anything on him.*

have something 'out cause something to be extracted or removed. *Brenda's in hospital having her tonsils out.* □ *The dentist says I'll have to have this tooth out.*

have something 'out (with someone) (informal) argue or discuss something to the end. *It's time you had the whole matter out with Ruth. Just tell each other the truth.*

have someone 'up for something (informal) charge someone with something. *If you say things like that, they can have you up for slander.* □ *Mike's been had up for speeding again. He was doing 65 miles an hour through the middle of Southampton.*

head someone 'off divert/elude someone. *The thief realized that the police were following him, but he succeeded in heading them off at the junction.*

head someone 'off something prevent someone from talking about something. *We tried our best to head Henry off the topic, because we knew he would accidentally reveal confidential information.*

head something 'off avoid/divert something. *I knew he would try to head off awkward questions about his past.* □ *I've been trying to head a cold off by taking hot lemon drinks.*

help someone 'out help someone to overcome a difficulty, e.g. with advice or money or by lending someone something. *Chris and Debbie haven't got much money, but they've been helped out on occasions by Chris's father.*

'hit on something (informal) have a sudden good idea, plan or answer to a problem. *Brilliant, David! I think you've hit on the right answer!*

hold 'back hesitate; restrain oneself. *I held back because I wasn't sure of the way he would react.* □ *She was held back from telling him her real opinion by the thought of losing her job.*

hold something 'back not tell or reveal something; withhold something. *Angela told me most of the facts of the affair, but I think she's still holding something back.* □ *The research findings have been held back long enough. They should be published.*

hold 'off (usually weather) be delayed. *If the rain holds off, we can play tennis this afternoon.*

hold someone/something 'off keep someone/something back; restrain physically. *The police had to hold off the fans when the rock group came out of their hotel.* □ *The soldiers managed to hold off the enemy attack for three days.*

hold 'on wait. *Hold on until I fetch help!* □ *If you just hold on, I'll get the car and drive you home.*

hold 'out 1 last, continue to be sufficient. *The tank's half full, but I don't think the oil will hold out until Spring.* 2 continue to function (something old or broken). *I hope the engine will hold out until we get to a garage.*

hold 'out for something refuse an offer in the hope of getting more. *The union has been offered ten per cent, but the leaders are holding out for twelve.*

hold 'out on someone (informal) refuse to tell someone something; keep a secret from someone. *If I thought you were holding out on me, I'd be very annoyed.*

hold something 'over postpone something. *Can't we hold the matter over until the next meeting?*

hold someone/something 'up 1 delay/stop someone/something. *Sorry I'm late. I was held up by the traffic.* Note: a **'hold-up**. *'What's the hold-up?' 'There's probably been an accident.'* 2 threaten someone with a weapon and try to rob him. *The robber held up four bank employees at gunpoint and forced them to open the safe.*

'hold with something approve of something. *I don't hold with any kind of blood sport.*

hop 'off (informal) go away. *If you see that young rascal around here again, tell him to hop off before I get my hands on him!*

hot 'up (informal) become more intense/exciting. *The novel is pretty boring at first, but it begins to hot up half way through and has a terrific climax.*

hunt something 'up find something by investigation or research. *I managed to hunt up that quotation I needed in the library.* □ *These are very interesting statistics. Where did you hunt them up?*

hush something 'up not reveal something; prevent something from becoming public. *They did their best to hush the whole affair up.* □ *You can't hush it up for much longer. The money will be missed.*

iron something 'out solve/resolve something. *Have you managed to iron out your differences of opinion with Louise?* □ *There are few problems that cannot be ironed out, if people are prepared to talk about them.*

jack something 'in (informal) stop doing something, e.g. one's job. *Felicity got bored with modelling so she jacked it in and is trying to get a place at a training college.*

jack something 'up (informal) increase a price, raise a salary etc. *The company made good profits this year, so the employees are expecting to have their wages jacked up by a few per cent.*

jazz something 'up (informal) make something brighter /livelier. *The colour scheme in this room is dull. It needs jazzing up a bit with some pictures and brighter curtains.*

join 'in (something) participate in something. *We're having fun! Why don't you join in?* □ *Ask Celia if she wants to join in the game.*

join 'up enter the armed forces voluntarily. *I never thought Matthew would join up, but he says he's always wanted to be a soldier.*

'jump at something (informal) accept an offer etc. with enthusiasm. *Alice would jump at the chance of going to Egypt.* □ *It was the offer of a life-time, and Mark couldn't help but jump at it.*

'jump on someone (informal) criticize someone severely; suddenly become angry with someone. *Nobody likes being jumped on for trivial matters.* □ *Why did the boss suddenly jump on Veronica like that?*

keel 'over lose one's balance and fall. *Patrick managed to climb out of the wrecked car. Then he keeled over and landed flat on his back.*

keep 'at someone keep someone under constant pressure of persuasion. *You'll have to keep at him if you want your money back.*

keep 'at something persevere with something. *If you want to learn to play the piano well, you have to keep at it.*

keep 'in stay indoors. *It's best to keep in when it's so cold.*

keep someone 'in punish a pupil by detaining him after school. *If we don't get the work finished properly, the whole class will be kept in.*

keep something 'in store something in one's home; have something available for use. *We don't keep much beer in as we don't drink it.*

keep 'in with someone continue friendly relations with someone. *It's best to keep in with Mr Parkinson. He's my bank manager!*

keep 'on continue. *Keep on until you reach the traffic lights and then turn left.*

keep something 'on continue to maintain something. *Will the Jacksons keep on the big house now that their last son has married and moved out?*

keep 'on at someone (for/about something) (informal) worry/criticize someone continuously. *I do wish you wouldn't keep on at me about the money I lost. It wasn't intentional!*

keep 'out of something not get involved in something. *Brian, you keep out of this – it isn't your quarrel!*

keep 'up 1 remain unchanged (weather). *If this storm keeps up the crops will be destroyed.* 2 remain bright and cheerful. *Her spirits kept up in spite of all her troubles.*

keep someone 'up prevent someone from going to bed. *It's late and I'm keeping you up, so I'll go now.*

keep something 'up maintain something. *Their country house became too expensive to keep up.* Note: **the 'upkeep.**

keep 'up something continue something (e.g. friendship, an activity or study). *We've kept up our friendship for over twenty years now.* □ *I used to be quite good at French, but I didn't keep it up after school.*

keep 'up with someone remain at the same level or position as someone. *Are you keeping up with me or am I reading too fast?*

knock 'about (with someone) (informal) go/travel around; share the company of. *Does Lloyd still knock about in that little red two-seater car of his?* □ *I've seen Dobson's son knocking about with some very dubious types.*

knock someone 'back (informal) cost someone a sum of money; set someone back financially. *That meal the other evening knocked me back thirty pounds!*

knock 'off (informal) stop work. *The factory workers usually knock off at six.*

knock someone 'off (slang) kill someone. *In certain areas of the city at night, you're likely to get knocked off for no reason at all.*

knock something 'off 1 deduct something from the price. *I'll knock you something off if you buy two.* 2 (informal) write/compose something quickly. *He earns his money writing short stories for women's journals. He can knock one off in a couple of hours.*

knock someone 'up 1 (GB) wake someone by knocking. *Could you knock me up at seven, please?* 2 make someone ill by exhaustion. *You look knocked up. Come and sit down.* □ *Don't let Grandad do too much work in the garden. He'll knock himself up.*

knock something 'up (informal) produce something quickly (often food). *I'll knock up a few sandwiches. It won't take long.*

knock 'up against something (informal) be confronted with something. *I didn't expect that we would knock up against so many difficulties on the project.*

'land someone with something (informal, often passive) burden someone with something he does not want. *I've been landed with the conference organization!*

lap something 'up (informal) absorb something readily and eagerly (praise, flattery, information). *The new pupil is very bright. She laps up any facts and information you give her.*

lash 'out (on something) (informal) spend a lot of money on something. *At Christmas, Dad really lashes out on presents for the whole family.*

latch 'on to someone (informal) impose one's company on someone; attach oneself to someone. *Do you know why Sheila latched on to that weird crowd?*

latch 'on to something 1 pay attention to something; listen carefully to something. *I managed to latch on to their remarks, but they didn't know that I was listening.* 2 grasp, learn how to do something. *Betty didn't know how to use the computer at first, but she soon latched on just by watching.*

lay something a'side (money) save for the future. *They lay a little aside every week for their old age.*

lay 'into someone (informal) attack someone physically or verbally with great energy. *I saw young Atkins laying into a boy twice his size in the school playground.*

lay someone 'off dismiss someone temporarily because there is no work. *The car factory is having to lay people off again.*

lay 'off something (informal) stop doing something. *You know I don't like people smoking in here. Can't you lay off it for once?*

lay something 'on 1 provide (a service), supply something. *We can't move into the new house until the gas and the electricity have been laid on.* □ *The bus company intends to lay on two more buses for this route.* 2 arrange/organize something. *Who's laying on the refreshments for the conference?*

lay 'out something spend a large sum of money. *How much has already been laid out for books and teaching materials?* Note: **an 'outlay.** *The initial outlay for computer hardware wasn't as high as we had imagined.*

lead someone 'on try to persuade/encourage someone to believe something. *Salespeople do their best to lead people on to buy things that they don't need.*

lead 'up to something prepare the way for something, signify something. *I know what he's leading up to. He wants you to lend him some money.* □ *Whatever he says, it all leads up to the fact that he doesn't want the responsibility.*

let someone 'down disappoint/fail someone. *He won't let you down. He's very reliable.* Note: **a 'let-down.** *I've had so many let-downs that I've stopped asking people for help.*

let someone 'off forgive someone; allow someone to go unpunished. *I'll let you off this time, but don't do it again!*

let something 'off explode something. *We're letting fireworks off tonight.*

let 'on (informal) reveal something by telling. *You can tell me your secret. I promise that I won't let on to anyone.*

let someone 'out (informal) give someone an excuse not to do something unpleasant. *On the day of Phil's party I had a meeting in Bristol – so it let me out nicely!*

let 'up stop or become less; decrease (activity, pressure of work etc.). *I think the rain's beginning to let up at last.* □ *When Polly's doing a crossword, she never lets up until she's found all the solutions.* Note: **a 'let-up.**

lie 'in stay in bed longer than usual. *You ought to lie in tomorrow and catch up on your sleep.* Note: **a 'lie-in.** *There's nothing nicer than a Sunday morning lie-in!*

live something 'down cause something unpleasant in one's past to be accepted, forgotten or ignored. Usually negative. *We thought she would never live down the humiliation of being asked to hand in her resignation.* □ *Such a scandal won't be lived down for some time.*

live 'up to something reach and maintain an expected standard, either bad or good. *We bought the car four years ago and it's certainly lived up to our expectations so far.* □ *He was well known for squandering his money. In fact, he still lives up to his reputation.*

look 'after someone/something take care of someone/something; be responsible for the well-being of someone/something. *If you want to go out, I'll look after the children for you.* □ *Clive has always known how to look after his own interests.*

look 'down on someone/something regard someone/something as inferior. *Edward is a snob who looks down on people with a working-class background.* □ *But his views are certainly looked down on by his fellow students.*

look 'in (on someone) make a short visit; call to see someone. *I'll look in on Francesca when I'm in Rome.*

look 'into something investigate/research something. *The police are looking into the matter very thoroughly.*

look 'on watch inactively. *I couldn't just stand there looking on while the old lady struggled with her parcels, so I carried them for her.*

'look on someone regard, consider as. *I've always looked on Ian as someone with very special personal qualities.*

look 'out be careful. *Look out when you're crossing the main road!*

look 'out (for someone/something) keep a watch for, be alert so as to see/notice someone/something. *I'll look out for Mr Pearson and give him your message.* □ *I've just broken a glass, so look out for the pieces.*

look 'over someone/something examine someone/something. *The manager is looking over two new applicants at the moment.* □ Note: a **'looking-over.** *Those figures need a thorough looking-over. They're not accurate.*

'look to someone (for something) turn to/rely on someone (for help, reassurance, encouragement etc.). *If Terry needs advice he always looks to his mother.*

look 'up improve. *The weather's looking up at last.* □ *Share prices are starting to look up again.*

look someone 'up go to visit someone informally. *We could look Walter and Barbara up when we're in Liverpool.*

look something 'up search for something in a dictionary, timetable, map etc. *I've got a timetable here so I'll look up the time of the next train.* □ *If you don't know what the word means, look it up!*

look 'up to someone admire, have a very good opinion of someone. *Frank has always looked up to his uncle, who's a self-made man.* □ *It's a pleasure to be looked up to by one's colleagues.*

lose 'out (to someone) (informal) suffer as a result of being less popular/successful than someone. *Many small traders lost out to the big supermarkets and simply closed their doors.*

lose 'out on something (informal) suffer a (usually financial) loss. *The dollar is low just now so you'll lose out on the exchange rate if you change your dollars into Deutschmarks.*

'make for someone/something move straight towards someone/something. *When I entered the room, Claire made for me as if she had something urgent to tell me.* □ *When the dog started to growl, the little boy made straight for the door and disappeared.*

'make for something help to promote/advance something; be good for something. *A little more friendliness from one's colleagues would certainly make for a better working climate.*

make 'off hurry away, escape. *When the police arrived, the thief was making off down the road.*

make 'off with something steal something. *The thief made off with the jewellery and the contents of the safe.*

make 'out (with someone/something) manage; succeed with someone/something. *How did Judy make out at the interview? □ How's Scott making out with Sharon?*

make someone 'out understand someone. *Marion's friendly one minute and cold as ice the next. I just can't make her out.*

make something 'out 1 (bill, cheque etc.) write. *Would you make out the bill, please? □ All cheques are to be made out to Global Enterprises.* 2 manage to read/decipher/understand something. *I can't make out his handwriting. □ Why did Robert say he would come if he had no intention of coming? I just can't make it out.*

make something 'over to someone legally transfer something to someone. *For tax reasons, some people make their property over to their children long before they die.*

make 'up apply cosmetics to one's face. *Deborah doesn't make up as heavily as she used to.* Note: 'make-up.

make someone 'up apply cosmetics to someone's face for stage/TV purposes etc. *Sheila makes up the guests on the Wednesday night talk-show.*

make something 'up 1 invent something. *Don't believe him. He made that story up.* 2 compensate for something. *How can he make up his losses in such a short time?* 3 prepare/pack food. *If you won't be here for lunch, the hotel will make you up a packed lunch.* 4 complete something by supplying what is missing. *Won't you make up the total by contributing another five pounds?*

make 'up for something compensate for something. *I took yesterday afternoon off, so I'm working this evening to make up for it. □ David's charm doesn't make up for his lack of good manners.*

make 'up to someone attempt to win favour with someone by being particularly pleasant to them. *Fortunately, the managing director isn't the sort of man you can make up to. □ He seems to think that if he makes up to the women in the typing pool, they'll do his reports faster.*

make something 'up to someone compensate someone for something. *Mike has been away from home on business a lot recently. He wants to make it up to his wife by taking her to Cannes for a week.*

mess a'bout/a'round waste time, usually in a silly way. *Get on with your work and stop messing around!*

mess someone a'bout/a'round treat someone without consideration causing inconvenience; hurt someone's feelings etc. *Either tell Garry you will buy his car or that you won't, but don't mess him around like this.*

mess something 'up spoil something. *It rained rather heavily, messing up our picnic completely. □ Roger came in from the garage with his best trousers messed up with oil.* Note: a 'mess-up. *There was a terrible mess-up with the flights.*

miss someone/something 'out omit someone/something. *I can't find Kate on the list. You've missed her out.*

miss 'out on something (informal) not experience something; not profit from something. *Because Jeff has never taken part in a management training scheme, he feels that he has missed out on something.*

mix someone/something 'up confuse/muddle someone/something. *The teacher explained too much at one time and mixed us all up.* □ *He mixed the story up so much that I couldn't follow it.* Note: **a mix-up.**

mix someone 'up in something involve someone. *Don't mix me up in this. I want nothing to do with the matter.*

move 'in settle in, take possession (of a house, office etc.). *The new neighbours have just moved in next door.*

move 'in on someone move close to /surround someone; force someone into a difficult situation. *His creditors moved in on him like a pack of wolves.*

'move on something (informal) take quick action on something. *The property has just been put on the market. If you want it, you'd better move on this one, or you'll lose it.*

move 'out vacate a house, office etc. *The Watsons couldn't keep up the monthly payments on their new house, so they had to move out.*

move 'up make room for someone by changing one's sitting or standing position. *We'd better move up so that those people have more room.*

muck 'in (with someone) (informal) co-operate; work together on friendly terms. *If Dennis would muck in with the rest of us, he'd be much more popular around the office.*

muck something 'up (informal) spoil something. *The strike of the hotel staff certainly mucked our holiday up!*

mug 'up on something (informal) learn something thoroughly with effort, often hurriedly. *I have a chemistry exam tomorrow, so I'm mugging up on formulas tonight.*

mull something 'over deliberate and think about something for a long time. *By the time the management has finally mulled over my proposals, they'll no longer be up to date.*

muscle 'in on something (informal) use force or unfair practices in order to get a share of something. *I refuse to let that young upstart muscle in on my business.*

nail someone 'down try to make someone say something definite about his intentions etc. *I tried my best, but I couldn't nail Harold down on a completion date.*

narrow something 'down (to something) reduce a larger number/ amount to a smaller number. *There was a large number of applicants for the job, but we've narrowed the list down to four.*

nod 'off fall asleep, especially in a chair etc. *I was just nodding off when the telephone rang.*

nose a'bout/around (informal) search around, take interest in things that are not one's concern. *What's he nosing around here for? He has nothing to do with our department.*

open 'out lose one's reserve or shyness. *Jill soon began to open out when she started work at the factory.*

open 'up 1 start a business. *There's a new butcher opening up on Duke Street.* 2 talk frankly. *Jason talked around the matter for a few minutes, then he finally opened up and told me that Sarah had left him.* 3 emerge, develop. *New opportunities for the company have opened up and they must not be neglected.*

opt 'out (of something) choose not to do it. *Now the club hasn't got a treasurer. Why did Bess opt out at the last minute?*

own 'up (to something) confess or admit to something. *If you own up to what you've done, the teacher may be lenient with you.*

pack something 'in 1 (informal) stop indulging in something. *I've packed gambling in. I've been losing too much money.* 2 end a relationship, job etc. *Lucy has packed her new boyfriend in already.* □ *Stewart is seriously considering packing his job in and going abroad.*

pack 'up (informal) 1 stop work. *The workers on the building site packed up at two o'clock because of the rain.* 2 stop functioning. *We were going up a steep hill when the engine packed up.*

'pass for someone/something be thought to be someone/something; be wrongly recognized as someone/something. *Your accent is excellent. You'd pass for an Englishman anytime.* □ *Isabelle looks just like her younger sister, and she would pass for thirty easily.*

pass 'off gradually disappear or become less. *Take this tablet and the pain should pass off within an hour.*

pass someone/something 'off as someone/something falsely represent as someone/something. *He passed his secretary off as his wife.* □ *They pass the old portrait off as a family heirloom, just to impress. Actually, they got it at an auction!*

pass 'on (formal) die. *Mr Harvey passed on during the night.*

'pass on something 1 not know something; not be able to give an answer. *'Do you know Mercury's distance from the Sun?' 'Sorry, I'll have to pass on that one.'* 2 decide not to do something. *I thought of buying into the new hotel complex, but it's risky, so I think I'll pass on it after all.*

pass something 'on tell/give something to another person. *There's no choir practice next week. Will you pass the message on?* □ *This note was passed on to me. It's for you.*

pass 'out faint. *Flora passed out because of the heat and the stuffy atmosphere.*

pass 'over something ignore something; avoid a subject. *Gerald never talks about his first wife. It's a subject he prefers to pass over.*

pay 'off (informal) succeed, prove to be profitable. *The gamble on the stock exchange paid off after all! We're rich!* □ *Preparing a doctoral dissertation is an awful lot of work, but Don hopes it will pay off in the end.*

pay someone 'off 1 (informal) pay someone to keep quiet. *The blackmailer had to be paid off, but afterwards the police were informed.* 2 settle one's debts with someone. *Has Lawson paid off all his creditors yet?* 3 pay and dismiss someone. *We've had to pay off another ten employees because there's no work for them.*

pay something 'off finish paying for something. *We've just finished paying off the bank loan – what a relief!*

'pick on someone (informal) single someone out for criticism, teasing, etc. *They always pick on Tom when anything goes wrong.* □ *Particularly small or fat children often get picked on at school.*

pick someone/something 'out choose someone/something from among many. *Can you pick your brother out from that group of people?* □ *Have you picked out the photographs that you'd like to have?*

pick 'up 1 continue, start again. *We can pick up where we left off tomorrow.* 2 improve (health, business etc.). *Dad's been quite ill, but he's picking up again now.* □ *Share prices have picked up recently, I'm glad to say.*

pick someone 'up 1 collect/go to get someone. *I'll pick you up from the tennis club at six.* 2 make casual acquaintance with someone. *That's the girl Sam picked up at the disco.* 3 reprimand/correct someone. *I made a few mistakes in the calculations and the teacher picked me up for them.* 4 catch/arrest someone. *The police picked up the man they were looking for just outside the town.*

pick something 'up 1 learn something. *Where did you pick up your Russian?* □ *Fracture mechanics isn't a subject that can be picked up in a month.* 2 get/buy something. *I picked up this coat in the sales for only forty pounds!* 3 become infected with an illness/disease. *Influenza isn't as easy to pick up as most people tend to believe.* 4 collect/go to get something. *Did you pick up the clothes from the dry-cleaner's?*

pile something 'on (informal) intensify and make worse; exaggerate. *The news is bad enough – don't pile it on by telling me more!*

pin someone 'down make someone state something definite about his intentions/knowledge of something etc. *Jerry won't be pinned down. He only ever states very rough figures.*

pin something 'down state/describe something exactly. *I can't pin down what it is that I don't like about her.* □ *I have a strange feeling about Leslie, but I just can't pin it down.*

piss 'off (slang, taboo) go away. *Fred had been annoying me all day with his stupid remarks. In the end I told him to piss off.* □ *Now just piss off and leave me alone!*

piss someone 'off (slang, taboo) bore or annoy someone. *He says he's so pissed off with his job at the factory that he'd take the first job anyone else offered him.* □ *No one likes Miller, yet he gets put in charge of the whole department! It really pisses you off!*

play a'long (with someone/something) co-operate; agree to something etc. *I'm sure Jackie will play along once we have made all the arrangements.* □ *Play along with them to see what their intentions are.*

play someone a'long 1 (informal) keep someone waiting without knowledge of something. *They've played him along for long enough. It's time they told him whether or not he'll get the loan.* 2 pretend to agree or co-operate with someone for one's own advantage. *They'll play him along until they've got the information they need, then they'll take their business elsewhere.*

play something 'down/up make something appear less/more important. *If the press hadn't played it up so much, the affair would have been forgotten long ago.*

play 'up (informal) cause trouble. *I couldn't start the car. The engine was playing up again.* □ *I hope the children don't start playing up when the guests arrive.*

play 'up to someone (informal) flatter someone to gain an advantage. *Stop playing up to Miriam like that, Jim. It won't work.*

'play with something consider for a time, not very seriously (an idea, notion, plan, scheme etc.). *I played with the idea of going to work abroad, but I think I'd miss home too much.*

polish something 'off (informal) finish something quickly. *It didn't take the children long to polish off the rest of the cream cake.*

polish something 'up improve something. *The content of the essay is fine. Just polish up the style a bit.*

'press for something demand something repeatedly. *The workers are pressing for a 36-hour week.*

press 'on continue one's efforts. *Not finished yet? Never mind. Press on!*

price something 'out calculate the cost of something, enquire about costs. *Sales promotion on this scale would cost a lot of money. I'll price it out for you, if you like.*

psych someone 'out (informal) try to find out someone's mental or emotional state, the state of someone's nerves etc. (e.g. of a rival in a competition), in order to use this knowledge to one's advantage. *The day before the big race, the two sailing crews did their best to psych each other out.*

pull something 'off manage to complete something successfully. *He pulled the deal off splendidly, as I knew he would.* □ *I never thought she would pull it off, but she did!*

pull 'out 1 (a train) leave, move away. *The Tyne-Tees express pulled out at 8.27 on the dot.* 2 (a vehicle) move out of a line of traffic. *A lorry pulled out in front of me just as I was about to overtake.* 3 withdraw. *I don't like the latest developments in the plan, so I'm going to pull out before it's too late.*

pull 'round get better after an illness, shock etc. *The operation has weakened him, but he'll soon pull round now that he knows he's coming out of hospital soon.*

pull 'through recover from a serious accident or illness. *The patient has very serious injuries, but we have hopes that he will pull through.*

pull to'gether co-operate, help each other. *If we all pull together by not selling any stock, we should be able to block this takeover bid.*

pull 'up (a vehicle) halt. *The van pulled up in front of me, so I had to brake suddenly.*

pull someone 'up (informal) stop someone in order to reprimand/warn him. *The police pulled him up for overtaking on a bend.* □ *Jacqueline got pulled up for speeding again.*

'push for something demand/try to get something. *The union leaders are pushing for early retirement.*

push 'off (informal) leave. *Well, I'll have to push off now so I'll see you later at the club.* □ *Push off, will you?*

push 'on continue. *We're pushing on with our investigations as fast as we can.*

push something 'on to someone (informal) force or impose something on to someone when not wanted. *They're pushing all the unpleasant, tiresome jobs on to the new clerk. It isn't fair.*

put something a'bout circulate a story, rumour etc. *Don't believe what you hear about Jim Howard. It's just a rumour that someone has put about.*

put something a'cross express, communicate (ideas, thoughts etc.). *Her ideas are good, but they aren't always put across very carefully.* □ *Try to put your explanation across as simply as possible, so that no one will have trouble with technical terminology.*

put something a'way 1 save money. *He puts a little away every week for his grandchildren.* 2 (informal) eat or drink in large quantities. *I've never seen anyone eat so much. He put away a whole fried chicken and two platefuls of chips!*

put someone 'down (informal) criticize, speak badly of someone. *April never gives her boss credit for anything. She's always putting him down, although he's a very competent man.*

put something 'down to something explain something as; assign something to. *We put his rude manner down to ignorance of our British customs.* □ *Her behaviour has been put down to an unhappy childhood, but I don't think that's any excuse at the age of thirty.*

put 'in interrupt by speaking. *'But I object!' he put in, suddenly and unexpectedly.*

put something 'in 1 spend or devote time/energy/care etc. *I have to put in an hour's piano practice every day.* 2 install/fix something. *They can't plaster the walls until they've put the heating in.*

put 'in for something request/claim something. *Most of the staff have put in for a wage-rise after Christmas.*

put something 'off postpone/delay something. *The cricket match has been put off until next Saturday.* □ *Don't put off going to the dentist's if you have toothache.*

put someone 'off 1 allow a passenger to get out of a vehicle. *Could you put me off at the hospital, please?* 2 deter/discourage someone. *I wanted to see the new play at the Grand, but the newspaper review put me off.* 3 distract; disturb one's concentration. *I don't like music playing when I'm working. It puts me off.* 4 keep someone waiting for a decision. *He won't give me a definite answer. He keeps putting me off.*

put someone 'out 1 disturb/upset/inconvenience someone. *It isn't fair that I should be blamed for something I know nothing about. I feel very put out about the whole matter.* 2 knock someone unconscious. *The other boxer put Alfred out in the third round.*

put something 'out 1 circulate/publish something. *An official statement has been put out denying all rumours that the company is going to be taken over.* □ *The police have put out an official description of three terrorists.* 2 extinguish (fire, flames). *We just managed to put the flames out before any* *real damage was caused.* 3 dislocate a part of the body. *I put my shoulder out digging the garden.* 4 cause something to be inaccurate. *That one little mistake has put the whole calculation out.*

put someone 'through connect someone on the telephone. *Can you please put me through to the complaints department?*

put something 'through conclude/complete/process something. *I'd be glad if you could put the visa application through as soon a possible.*

put 'up stay overnight for a short time. *He always puts up at the Crown Hotel when he's in town.*

put someone 'up 1 give accommodation to someone. *We'd be glad to put you up for a few days if you'd like to stay.* 2 nominate as a candidate in an election. *The Conservatives are putting Ted up in the by-election.*

put someone 'up to something encourage someone to do something. *Who put Steven up to the idea of selling his bicycle?* □ *He was put up to it by his brother.*

put something 'up 1 build/erect something. *Another supermarket's been put up in Hill Street.* 2 increase something. *Everyone's expecting the government to put taxes up again.*

put 'up something 1 offer money/prizes etc. as a contribution; lend money. *Jenkins put up a lot of money for the art gallery.* □ *When the first loan had run out, he put up another thousand.* 2 advocate something; introduce something for consideration. *Mr Morgan is going to put up another proposal at the meeting.*

put 'up with someone/something (informal) tolerate/bear something. *I can't put up with anyone telling me how to run my own house!* □ *I've put up with her complaints long enough.*

'put upon someone (usually passive) take advantage of someone; exploit someone. *Don't let yourself be put upon by that lazy, selfish woman.*

rake something 'up (informal) reveal something unpleasant from someone's past. *Why did they have to rake up those old stories? It was obviously very embarrassing for everyone concerned.*

rattle something 'off say from memory or read something very quickly in an automatic manner. *When you're on stage, don't rattle your lines off as you did just now. Try putting some emotion into them.*

read something 'into something interpret something wrongly, understand more than was said or meant. *Pat's professor didn't say that anyone had failed the exam. She's reading more into his remarks than necessary.*

read something 'up acquire knowledge or information about a subject by reading. *I must read up what Roberts has written on the history of China.*

read 'up on something improve one's knowledge of a special subject by reading. *He's going to read up on plant classification again before the exam.*

'reckon on something expect something; include something in one's calculations. *Actually, we had reckoned on your help.* □ *I wasn't reckoning on having such problems to deal with.*

reel something 'off say quickly in succession from memory (poetry, lists etc.). *I was always good on history dates at school. I could reel dozens of them off!*

rest 'up have a complete rest. *After the operation I shall need to rest up for a few weeks.*

ring 'off end a telephone conversation. *I'll have to ring off now, but I'll ring you again tomorrow.*

rip someone 'off (informal) cheat someone out of money, charge very high prices. *Don't buy anything at that shop – I've been ripped off there a few times.* Note: **a 'rip-off.** *Did you hear how much the garage charged Ben for his car repairs? It was a rip-off!*

roll 'in 1 (people) arrive, come in casually. *Greg never says he's coming. He just rolls in when he feels like it.* 2 (money) come in quantity. *Since Fred opened up a business, money has been rolling in.*

roll 'on 1 (time) pass. *Times's rolling on. It will soon be Christmas!* 2 come soon (usually the statement of a wish). *Oh, yes! Roll on Christmas! I need a break.*

roll 'up (people) arrive, come to see. *Visitors have been rolling up in crowds all day to see the exhibition.*

rope someone 'in (informal) persuade someone to help with a task, activity etc. *Fiona has roped me in to serve the refreshments at the golf club annual meeting.*

round something 'off finish something in a satisfactory way. *Let's round off the evening with a snack and a drink over at my place.* □ *It's a good essay, but it needs a better final paragraph to round it off.*

round someone/something 'up gather people/something together. *Let's round up the whole group and ask them what they think about Bob's idea.*

rub 'off on someone influence someone; affect someone in attitude/mood/character etc. as a result of close contact with someone. *Arthur's in a very good mood today. Let's hope some of it rubs off on the other members of the group.* □ *Some of her father's business sense has obviously rubbed off on her.*

rule someone/something 'out exclude someone/something. *Anyone who has entered for the same competition before is ruled out by the regulations.* □ *These new facts rule out the possibility of accident and suggest either suicide or murder.*

'run across someone/something find someone/something or meet someone by chance. *Guess who I ran across this morning in town! Sally Bell!* □ *We ran across these carvings in Jaipur.*

run 'after someone 1 pay excessive attention to someone. *He's always running after the girls in the typing pool. What's he trying to prove?* 2 serve someone's needs. *Jerry's a man who likes people running after him all the time.*

run a'way with someone (imagination, temper, feelings etc.) take control of someone. *Now you're letting your imagination run away with you. The situation wasn't all that dangerous.*

run a'way with something use up/consume a lot of something (e.g. money, petrol, electricity). *I'm afraid the research programme is running away with the government loan.*

run someone 'down/over 1 (a vehicle) knock to the ground and injure someone. *My son was almost run down by a van this morning. Luckily, he only has a few bruises.* 2 speak badly of someone; criticize someone. *I wish Jack wouldn't run his brother-in-law down the way he does. I think he's jealous.*

run someone 'in arrest someone; take someone to the police-station. *The police have run old Sam in again for being drunk and disorderly.*

run something 'in (a new vehicle, engine, machine) drive carefully to prepare for full use. *If you take care to run the engine in properly, the car will give you a lot of pleasure.*

run something 'off 1 produce written material quickly. *She's a remarkable writer. She can run off a novel in a week!* 2 print, photocopy, duplicate. *The minutes for last week's meeting are finished, but I still have to run them off.*

run 'out 1 expire, terminate. *The contract runs out at the end of the year and will have to be renewed.* 2 come to an end, be used up. *We had just reached the motorway when the petrol ran out.* □ *Only two weeks before the deadline. Time's running out!*

run 'out of something use something up; have no more of something. *We've run out of milk. You'll have to drink your tea without.*

run 'over something practise/rehearse something. *I'll just run over my speech again. I'd hate to forget it in the middle.*

'run through something 1 rehearse. *He ran through his lecture in his mind.* Note: a **'run-through**. 2 read something quickly. *Just run through this article and tell me what you think of it, will you?* 3 use up. *We run through about ten gallons of petrol a week.*

'run to something 1 amount to something; reach. *The book runs to about three hundred pages.* 2 provide money for something; be sufficient for something. *My salary doesn't run to buying a new suit every week!*

run something 'up 1 make/sew something quickly. *I'm going to run some costumes up for the children's fancy-dress party.* 2 accumulate something. *She runs up bills everywhere in town.* □ *I've run up an overdraft, and now the bank's stopped my credit.*

run 'up against someone/something be confronted with someone/something; encounter someone/something. *Could you help me with this computer programme? I've run up against a few problems.*

rush 'into something decide to do something too quickly without considering the consequences. *I wish Carl would slow down his marriage plans. I think he's rushing into something that he may regret.*

rush someone 'into something cause someone to do something without considering the consequences. *The estate agent tried to rush us into buying the house but it isn't a thing one can be rushed into.*

rustle something 'up 1 prepare (usually food) quickly from whatever is available. *There isn't much in the fridge, but I'm sure we can rustle up a snack* *or a few sandwiches.* 2 gather together. *I hope we can rustle up a bit more good will and support for our campaign.*

screw something 'up (slang) spoil/mismanage something; do something wrong/badly. *That fool Joe! He's screwed up all the arrangements. Didn't he screw everything up last time, as well?* Note: **a 'screw-up.** *It's a fiasco! A total screw-up!*

'see about something deal with or attend to a matter. *Excuse me, I must see about the arrangements for lunch.* □ *We ought to see about a new car before the prices go up.*

see 'into something investigate. *I took my complaint to the manager. He's going to see into it.* □ *Yes, it's about time the matter was seen into.*

see someone 'off 1 accompany to the place of departure. *Will you be there to see me off at the station?* 2 persuade someone to leave against his will. *The dogs soon saw the intruder off.*

see someone 'out accompany someone outside/to the door. *I'll see you out, or you may get lost in the building.*

see something 'out 1 see to the end. *It was a rotten film, but we decided to see it out because the tickets were so expensive.* 2 last. *I don't think these old boots will see the winter out.*

see 'through someone/something recognize the true nature of something deceptive. *Alison thinks I believe her story, but I can see through her.* □ *I can see through his scheme. He won't cheat me so easily.*

see someone 'through help someone through a difficult time. *Don't worry about money. I'll see you through.* □ *Do you think two hundred pounds will see him through, or should I give him more?*

see something 'through persevere with something to the end. *Now that we've spent so much time planning the project, we'll have to see it through.*

'see to someone attend to someone. *Will you see to that customer, please?*

'see to something 1 attend to something. *I hope you'll see to the matter immediately.* 2 fix/repair something. *The electrician's come to see to the faulty switches.*

sell 'out (of something) have no more left to sell. *Sorry, but we've completely sold out of brown bread.* Note: **a 'sell-out.** *Moira's dress designs for the Lady Hamilton line have always been a total sell-out.*

sell 'out to someone (informal) betray secrets or information to the opposition. *Put under enough pressure, Gilbert could be persuaded to sell out to our competitors, so we'd better watch him carefully.*

send a'way for something request or buy something by post. *I've sent away for the spring catalogue.*

'send for someone call someone in. *The fever's getting worse. We ought to send for the doctor.*

set a'bout someone attack someone physically or with words. *When I revealed the true facts, he set about me in order to make my story look ridiculous.*

set a'bout something begin something. *As soon as she got home, she set about preparing lunch.* □ *Please help me with this exercise. I don't know how to set about it.*

set someone 'back 1 delay/hinder someone. *This hold-up will set us back about three hours.* Note: a **'set-back.** *The only major set-back to the trip was when the car caught fire!* 2 cost. *The new house must have set him back a few thousand!*

set 'in begin; establish itself. *The winter has set in very early this year – snow in November.*

set 'off begin a journey. *Let's set off nice and early tomorrow, shall we?*

set someone 'off cause someone to begin. *Don't mention the war or you'll set Grandfather off reminiscing for hours!*

set something 'off 1 cause something to explode. *The children are setting fireworks off in the garden.* 2 cause something to start. *I accidentally pressed the button and set off the alarm!* 3 show something to advantage; make something look attractive. *The red dress sets her blond hair off beautifully.*

'set on someone attack someone. *He was passing by the front door, when suddenly their dog set on him!*

set 'out 1 begin with the intention/aim of doing something. *He set out to cut the grass, but he chatted to the neighbour for an hour instead.* 2 begin a journey. *When did you set out on the last stage of your journey?*

set 'to start energetically; apply oneself vigorously. *She set to and finished cleaning the house within an hour.* □ *When Billy sets to, he can eat more than his father!*

set 'up establish oneself in a business or profession. *He now intends setting up as a hairdresser in Portsmouth.*

set someone 'up 1 provide someone with required facilities. *His father will set him up as a solicitor when he has all the necessary qualifications.* 2 improve someone's health. *Take a holiday in the mountains. The fresh air will set you up and make you feel much better.* 3 (informal) make someone appear guilty of something, cause to be falsely charged. *I know nothing about the stolen money. Don't you see? I've been set up!* □ *All right. I admit I set him up.*

set something 'up 1 erect; place something in position. *He sets up a vegetable stall in the market every Saturday morning.* 2 establish/institute something. *The government has set up a committee to examine the fishing industry.* 3 put forward/evolve a theory. *He set up the theory ten years ago and scholars have been discussing it ever since.* 4 (in sport) create a new record. *Freeman set up a new time in the 800 metres.*

settle 'down 1 marry and lead a routine life. *Harry is 40 already. I don't think he'll ever settle down.* 2 establish oneself permanently. *The Grants have lived in several parts of England, but they'd like to settle down in Norfolk.* 3 make oneself comfortable. *She settled down in the corner with her knitting and turned on the radio.*

settle 'down to something apply oneself to something; concentrate on something. *I've been trying to read this book all day, but somehow I can't settle down to it properly.*

'settle for something be prepared to accept something. *With my qualifications, I won't settle for a second-rate job.*

settle 'in establish oneself in new surroundings. *How's Richard settling in at his new school?* □ *The new neighbours seem to have settled in quite well.*

'settle on something decide on/choose something. *We couldn't decide where to go for a holiday, but we finally settled on Greece.*

settle 'up (with someone) pay the money owing to someone. *I owe you some money for the drinks, so we'll settle up at lunchtime.*

sew something 'up (informal) finalize arrangements, complete a deal, contract etc. *We got the whole deal sewn up and the papers signed within a week.*

shack 'up with someone (slang, expresses disapproval) live together with someone unconventionally without being married. *She told me that her husband had left her and shacked up with some rich woman who calls herself an artist.*

shake someone/something 'off escape from/avoid/get rid of someone/ something. *The bank robbers tried desperately to shake off the pursuing police car.* □ *I'm still trying to shake off a cold.*

shake someone 'up upset/disturb someone emotionally. *The news of her mother's death has shaken her up pretty badly.* □ *Father's rather shaken up about the prospect of losing his pension.*

shake someone/something 'up reorganize a body or group of people/ an organization. Note: **a 'shake-up.** *This department could do with a total shake-up if it's ever going to run smoothly.*

shop a'round (for something) compare prices in different shops before buying, compare offers of jobs etc. *We shopped around for weeks before we decided on the bedroom furniture.* □ *'Has Adrian accepted any of the job offers he got?' 'No, not so far. He's still shopping around.'*

shout someone 'down shout loud while someone is speaking so that he cannot be heard. *The Labour candidate was shouted down by the angry crowd.*

show 'off display one's capabilities to others. *Laura always shows off with her knowledge of literature if she thinks she can impress anyone.*
Note: **a 'show-off.** *Thomas is a terrible show-off on the golf course.*

show someone/something 'off proudly display someone/something to advantage. *Angela's showing off her new boyfriend to all her friends.* □ *There's Jimmy – showing off his new computer games again.*

show 'up appear. *Did Nicky show up at the party last night?* □ *You never know when Jan's coming. She just shows up when you least expect her!*

show someone 'up embarrass someone by bad behaviour in the presence of others. *Pam's children showed her up in a restaurant by spilling fruit juice and food over the table.* □ *Nobody likes to be shown up in public.*

shut something 'down close temporarily or permanently (factory, mine, business etc.). *There was a gas leak at the chemical factory, so the plant has been temporarily shut down.* Note: **a 'shut-down.**

shut 'up be quiet. *I wish Gloria would shut up – no one else has a chance to speak!* □ *Just shut up, will you?*

sign 'on register one's name for state unemployment benefit when one cannot find work. *If the glass factory has to close down, another three thousand workers will be signing on.*

sink 'in be grasped, be fully understood. *The teacher explained it to me twice, but it still hasn't sunk in.* □ *What you say is unbelievable. It will take a minute to sink in.*

sit 'back be inactive, remain in the background. *Tom's unfair. He just sits back and lets me do all the work.*

sit 'in demonstrate protest by occupying a building, by sitting on the floor and refusing to move. Usually in the form **a 'sit-in.** *The students are staging another sit-in in protest against the proposed new matriculation regulations.*

sit 'in for someone substitute for someone; take the place of someone at a meeting etc. *The chairman won't be here next week, so James will be sitting in for him.*

sit 'in on something attend as a listener or visitor. *When I was doing teaching practice, people often used to sit in on my lessons.*

'sit on someone (informal) rebuke someone; put someone in his place. *That new assistant is very self-opinionated. If someone doesn't sit on him soon, I will!*

'sit on something 1 (informal) neglect/obstruct a matter by doing nothing. *I wrote a letter of complaint to my bank, but there's been no reply. I expect someone's just sitting on it and hoping I'll calm down.* 2 keep hold of something; not part with something. *Brian knows I need that information urgently, but he's just sitting on it for some reason.*

sit 'out not take part. *Most people joined in the dancing. Only a few sat out.*

sit something 'out attend something until the end. *We didn't enjoy the play, but we sat it out.*

sit 'up 1 not go to bed until late. *I sat up until midnight writing letters.* 2 become attentive. *Martina was falling asleep in the lecture, but she sat up when the test results were read out.*

sleep something 'off recover from too much food or drink by sleeping. *Father ate too much at lunch, so now he's sleeping it off.*

'sleep on something postpone a decision overnight. *I can't give you a decision just now, but I'll sleep on it and let you know tomorrow.*

slip 'up make a mistake. *These figures aren't correct. I must have slipped up somewhere.* Note: **a 'slip-up.** *Make sure you rehearse the entrances and exits well. We can't afford a slip-up on stage.*

slow 'down become slower or less energetic; (of a vehicle) decrease speed. *Gerald has slowed down considerably since his heart attack.* □ *The lorry slowed down and stopped at the traffic lights.*

'snap at someone speak sharply to someone. *When I asked her a question, she just snapped at me!*

'snap at something accept something immediately and with enthusiasm. *I would snap at the chance of going to China for a year.*

snap 'out of something   quickly bring oneself out of a bad mood, depression etc. *You're just feeling sorry for yourself. Why don't you snap out of it and think about your future?*

snap something 'up   take or buy something eagerly without hesitation. *This antique clock was a real bargain, so I snapped it up.*

'sneeze at something   reject something; not treat something seriously (usually negative). *A year in research in Silicon Valley? It's an opportunity not to be sneezed at!*

soak something 'up   absorb something; learn something easily and with enthusiasm. *The child is exceptionally gifted. I've never seen a child soak up knowledge so eagerly.* □ *He soaks everything up!*

soften someone 'up   persuade someone by being especially friendly. *I have to soften Dad up. I need another loan.*

sort someone 'out   (informal) punish/deal with/reprimand someone. *If you two don't get this room cleaned up, I'll come over there and sort you out!* □ *The neighbour's boy is extremely cheeky. It's time someone sorted him out.*

sort something 'out   deal with/attend to/put something in order. *Have you sorted out all that trouble you had with the bank yet?*

sound someone 'out (on/about something)   try to find out someone's attitude to something, judgement on something. *He's an executive personnel consultant. We've asked him to sound Coburn out on whether he's likely to accept an offer from us.*

spell something 'out   (informal) state something in very simple terms for someone who has not yet understood. Usually expresses annoyance at someone's stupidity. *He still hasn't understood what you mean. You'll have to spell it out for him.* □ *Do I really have to spell it out for you?*

spin something 'out   make something last a long time. *How do you manage to spin your money out?*

splash 'out on someone/something   spend money lavishly and sometimes carelessly on someone/something. *The Wilsons certainly splashed out on their daughter's wedding!*

square 'up to someone/something   confront bravely or face someone/something. *You'll have to square up to your responsibilities. You can't simply run away from them.*

square 'up with someone   settle a debt with someone. *Have you squared up with Alex for the meal and the petrol?*

square something 'up with someone   settle or clear a matter with someone. *He said he's got a problem to square up with his neighbour.*

'square with someone   be honest and direct with someone. *I'll square with you, James. The board thinks you're too old for the position.*

stamp something 'out   get rid of something; suppress something. *Everything possible should be done to stamp out drug abuse.* □ *There has been an increase in crime in the area. It needs stamping out before it gets out of control.*

stand 'by 1   be present and look on but remain inactive. *When the boy fell off his bicycle and couldn't get up, two women went to help him, but most people* *just stood by.* **2** be present and ready for action when needed. *There are usually a few ambulances standing by at pop festivals.* Note: **a 'stand-by.**

stand 'by someone support and comfort someone through a difficult time. *She went through a difficult time after her illness, but she had good friends who stood by her.*

stand 'down surrender a position, chance etc., usually to the advantage of others. *Johnson was asked to be chairman for the third time, but he stood down in favour of a younger club member.*

stand 'in for someone substitute for someone. *'I didn't know you worked in this department.' 'I don't. I'm just standing in for a colleague.'* Note: **a 'stand-in.** *A stunt man is a stand-in for an actor.*

stand 'out be very noticeable/conspicuous. *Your red pullover stands out well in this photograph.*

stand 'out from something be in favourable contrast with something. *Elizabeth's voice really stands out from the rest of the choir. She should consider singing professionally.*

stand 'up for someone / something give moral support to someone; defend someone/something. *If any rough boys start to bully him, his friend always stands up for him.*

stand 'up to someone face someone; confront someone bravely. *If that big girl hits you, stand up to her and hit her back!*

stand 'up to something **1** resist something. *Some children's toys don't stand up to much knocking about.* **2** bear examination when questioned. *Her story sounds convincing, but I don't think it will stand up to questioning in a court of law.*

step 'in intervene to help or to prevent something happening. *The police had to step in to control an outbreak of rioting.* □ *If my brother hadn't stepped in with a generous loan, we would have closed the business down.*

step something 'up increase something. *The increased export demand will mean stepping production up considerably.* □ *Staff efforts will have to be stepped up, too.*

stick a'round (informal) stay and wait to see what happens, who comes etc. *Tourists outside Buckingham Palace seem to think that if they stick around long enough, they might see a royal coming or going.*

stick 'at something persevere with something. *When he has work to do, he sticks at it until it's finished.*

stick 'out for something be resolute in trying to get something. *The strikers are sticking out for a higher bonus.*

'stick to someone be loyal to someone; remain with someone. *Andrew always sticks to his friend, no matter what happens.*

'stick to something adhere to something, not change it. *Make sure you stick to the same story when questioned a second time.*

stick 'up for someone defend/support someone. *You've got to learn to stick up for yourself, not only for others.*

stir something 'up provoke trouble or something unpleasant. *Laura's always trying to stir up trouble between Kate and Jackie.*

stop 'off break a journey for a short time. *Shall we stop off in Coventry and visit the Harveys?*

stop 'over break a long journey by air, usually for a night. *When we fly to Sydney, we usually stop over in Singapore.* Note: **a 'stopover.**

straighten something 'out put something right; bring something to order. *We've had a bit of trouble at the factory, but the management and the union should be able to straighten it out.*

string someone a'long mislead someone into believing something; not be honest about one's intentions over a period of time. *Lynn doesn't care much for Luke. I have the feeling that she's just stringing him along until she finds someone else.*

sus someone/something 'out (informal) find out hidden information about someone, or about what is going on or being planned without one's knowledge. *He was planning to get me discredited so that he could take my job, but I sussed him out in time.* □ *Atkins wanted to get me taken off the project. Good job I sussed it out before it was too late.*

'swear by something (informal) have a high opinion of something; value/believe in something. *Grandfather swears by rum as the only medicine for a cold.*

switch 'off (informal) stop paying attention or listening because of lack of interest. *The phonology lecture was boring, so I switched off half-way through.*

take someone a'back shock/surprise someone. *The dreadful sight of the accident took me aback.*

take 'after someone resemble, have a similar character or appearance as a parent etc. *Margaret takes after her father in being strong-willed.*

take something 'back withdraw a statement/remark/accusation/criticism etc. to demonstrate that it was unjust or incorrect. *I'm sorry that I called you an opportunist, and I take it all back.*

take something 'down write something down; record something. *The policeman took down the details of the accident and the addresses of the witnesses.*

take someone 'in trick/fool someone. *He's a clever talker but don't let him take you in.* □ *I don't allow myself to be taken in by sales talk.*

take something 'in 1 fully understand something. *This book is difficult to take in, especially when you're tired.* □ *What you say is unbelievable. I need a minute to take it all in!* 2 observe/look at something. *I was too busy taking in the beautiful antique furniture to notice who was in the room.* 3 (in sewing) make narrower. *This dress is too big at the waist. It needs taking in a little.*

take 'in someone give accommodation to someone. *Mrs Lawson is considering taking in students next year. She's taken them in before.*

take 'off 1 (aircraft) leave the ground. *Did the flight take off on time?* Note: **a 'take-off.** *Yes, it was a smooth take-off.* 2 (informal) leave in a hurry. *Janet took off for Toronto as soon as term ended.*

take someone 'off (informal) imitate someone for amusement. *Bob's speciality at parties is taking politicians off.* Note: **a 'take-off.** *His take-offs are hilarious.*

take something 'off 1 remove something. *Take your coat off and sit down.*□ *Who took the knob off the door?.*□ *Why doesn't the government take the tax off unleaded petrol?* 2 remove from service. *Some local trains have been taken off, as there was no demand for them.* 3 lose weight by dieting. *I took off three pounds last week!* 4 take free time from work. *I took a week off in March and I'm taking Easter off, too.*

take someone 'on 1 employ someone. *Is the supermarket taking on any more assistants?*□ *No more workers are being taken on at present.* 2 accept someone as an opponent. *Will you take me on for a game of chess?*

take something 'on accept something; undertake to do something. *I really don't think I can take the work on at the moment. I've got too much to do.*□ *Is she willing to take on the responsibility?*

take 'on something acquire/develop a characteristic. *His writing has taken on a very peculiar style in the past year.*□ *In translation, the word takes on a rather different meaning.*

take someone 'out 1 invite and accompany someone to a place of entertainment/recreation. *Ted takes his mother out every weekend, usually for a ride in the country.* 2 (US, slang) cheat, harm or kill someone. *I shall take Green out the way he took out my sister!*

take something 'out 1 (a contract, licence etc.) pay for, obtain for a fixed time. *You'll have to take out a radio and TV licence.*□ *I've taken out an annual subscription for 'Time'.* 2 (dirt, stains etc.) remove. *I need something that will take out these ink stains.* 3 (in military contexts) eliminate, destroy. *There are reports of allied aircraft having taken out a significant number of enemy tanks.*

take something 'out on someone make someone else suffer unfairly because one is angry, disappointed etc. about something. *I know you're furious about the affair at the office, but you shouldn't take your anger out on your family.*

take something 'over (from someone) come into control or possession of something. *Henry's taken over the running of the family business from his father.* Note: a **'takeover**. *There is talk of a company takeover, which is likely to affect the share prices.*

'take to someone form a liking for someone; be attracted to someone. *I didn't take to our new editor at first, but now we're good friends.*□ *Terry first took to Anne at school, when she was only fifteen.*

'take to something 1 form a liking for something. *How has Scott taken to his new school?* 2 form the habit of something. *If a person once takes to gambling, it's difficult to stop.* □ *My father has taken to playing golf at the weekends.*

take something 'up 1 (sewing) make something shorter. *That skirt's too long – why don't you take it up a bit?* 2 occupy space. *This big bed takes up a lot of room.* 3 discuss/examine something. *That's an issue we ought to take up at the next meeting.* □ *The matter has already been taken up with my Member of Parliament.* 4 accept (an offer etc.). *Do you intend to take up the job offer?* 5 absorb a fluid. *Use blotting paper to take up the ink, not your shirt sleeve!*

take 'up something 1 begin to pursue (hobby, interest, sport). *Patsy has taken up sky-diving at the weekends.* 2 begin duties/work. *When does the new man take up his post?* □ *She takes up her duties as representative for this area next September.* 3 continue (an unfinished narrative). *She took up the story at the point where the thief had just made his get-away on a motorbike.*

take someone 'up on something 1 question someone about something. *Do you mind if I take you up on the question of membership?* □ *Linda took the speaker up on a few points that she didn't agree with.* 2 accept (an offer, challenge etc.). *He said he'd buy me a drink, so I took him up on it and ordered a large brandy.*

take 'up with someone become friends with someone; keep company with someone. *When Derek went to London, he took up with some very strange people in Soho.*

talk someone 'down silence someone by talking as much oneself. *Caroline is good at talking her opponents down.*

talk 'down to someone address someone in a patronizing manner. *The lecturer talks down to his first-year students as if they were children.*

talk someone 'into something persuade someone to agree to something. *The salesman tried to talk me into buying a caravan.* □ *Don't let yourself be talked into doing anything you don't want to do.*

talk someone 'out of something persuade someone not to do something. *I'd like to go camping, but my wife's trying to talk me out of it.*

talk someone 'round persuade someone to do something that he was against. *I was against going to the opera, but Nancy eventually managed to talk me round.*

tell someone 'off reprimand someone. *The manageress told one of the waitresses off for making private telephone calls from the restaurant. But she didn't like being told off in front of the others, so she gave in her notice and walked out.*

'tell on someone 1 have a bad effect on someone. *All this smoking and drinking will tell on his health in later life.* 2 betray something that someone has done wrong (mostly used of children). *Jimmy told on his brother for breaking the vase, so their mother punished them both.*

'think about something 1 consider something. *It's certainly an offer well worth thinking about.* □ *We're thinking about buying a new car before prices go up.* 2 have as one's opinion; judge or assess something. *Would you read through this report and tell me what you think about the style?*

think of something 1 remember something. *I know her face, but I can't think of her name.* 2 give attention to something; consider something. *John would like to have accepted a well-paid job in Alaska, but he had his family to think of, so he refused it.* 3 contemplate as a possibility. *I'd never think of asking someone to lend me so much money!* □ *You know we wouldn't think of going without you!* 4 have as one's opinion; judge something. *What do you think of my new suit?* □ *Tell me what you thought of the concert.* 5 invent/suggest something. *I'm trying to think of a good example to illustrate my point.* □ *Helen says she's thought of a good scheme to make some money.*

think something 'over consider something carefully. *When you've thought things over, you'll probably realize that my advice is sensible.* □ *I made him a good offer, but he said he would have to think it over first.*

think something 'up invent something. *Al's very good at thinking up excuses for not working.* □ *I realized that her story had been thought up on the spur of the moment.*

throw something 'off discard/get rid of something. *Peter can't throw off his annoying habit of staring at people in buses.* □ *I've been trying to throw off a cold for days.*

throw someone 'out cause someone to make an error. *The slightest inaccuracy will throw us out in our calculations.*

throw something 'out dismiss/reject something. *I considered the proposal to be fairly good, but it was thrown out by the Board immediately.*

throw 'out something 1 radiate, produce (heat, light etc.). *This electric fire throws out a lot of heat.* 2 give a casual or indirect hint/warning/ suggestion etc. *He refused to throw out even the slightest hint about his future plans.* □ *The suggestion is brilliant and I'm sure we'll follow it. It was thrown out by Mark, by the way.*

throw someone 'over reject someone; end a relationship with someone. *She threw him over for a tall, dark, handsome Arab.*

throw 'up vomit, be sick. *When I think of all the injustice and intrigue that's going on, it makes me want to throw up!*

throw something 'up abandon something; reject something. *He threw up a promising career in the diplomatic service to run a small farm in Wales.*

tick 'over (informal) live, work etc. quietly without any special or important events, successes etc. *'And how are you these days, Alex?' 'Well, just ticking over, thanks.'*

tie someone 'down restrict someone's actions. *I don't want you to feel tied down by my presence – please go out whenever you like.*

tie 'in with (something) fit/correspond with. *It all ties in very well with what Miriam said, so it must be true.* □ *Her story didn't quite tie in with his. That's why the police were suspicious.* Note: **a 'tie-in.**

tie someone 'up (with work etc., often passive) keep someone occupied or busy. *Organizing this international conference is likely to tie Judith up for the rest of the summer.* □ *I'll ring you from the office, if I'm not too tied up all day.*

tie something 'up 1 complete (organization etc.). *Are all the arrangements for Saturday tied up now?* 2 (money) invest long-term so that it is difficult to withdraw. *He's tied all his money up in stocks and bonds and has no cash to pay his debts with.*

tip someone 'off (informal) inform someone or warn someone of something that is planned (e.g. a crime etc.). *Customs officers had been tipped off that the drugs were due to be smuggled over the border, so they were on special alert.* Note: **a 'tip-off.** *The tax authorities got a tip-off that a certain percentage of the profits was not being declared.*

touch something 'off cause something to start; initiate something. *An incident in the market-place touched off a riot and the police had to intervene.*

□ *The crisis was touched off by a few undiplomatic remarks made by one of the heads of state.*

'touch on/upon something mention something very briefly. *The President only touched on the issue of taxation in his speech.*

touch something 'up improve the appearance of something by means of minor alterations, by painting etc. *The kitchen needs touching up in a few places. We'll put a bit of paint on this afternoon.* □ *Your essay is quite good. Just touch it up a little with a few illustrations and quotations.*

trade something 'in use something in part-payment. *We'd like to trade in our video recorder for a new one with the latest improvements.*

'trade on something take advantage of something. *You'll always find someone who's willing to trade on your generosity and never offer any help in return.*

trip someone 'up deliberately cause someone to show his ignorance, lack of information etc. *In the interview, he tripped me up by asking me what I thought about his book. I later discovered that he's never published one!*

trump 'up something invent a story or false charge against someone. *The lawyer was able to prove that the charge against his client had been trumped up.* □ *You're a fool if you believe such a trumped-up story!*

try something/it 'on (with someone) (informal) attempt to gain an advantage from someone; cheat someone. *The woman tried it on with the policeman by saying she hadn't seen the traffic lights, but it didn't work.* Note: a 'try-on.

tuck 'in start to eat eagerly with appetite. *What a delight to see hungry children tucking in like that!*

turn someone/something 'down reject or refuse someone/something. *We've had to turn down four applicants already, as they didn't have the necessary experience.* □ *His book has been turned down by three publishers.*

turn 'in (informal) go to bed. *It's past midnight. Come on, time to turn in.*

turn someone 'in (informal) hand someone over to the police. *The youth was afraid that the supermarket manager would turn him in for stealing cigarettes.*

turn something 'in 1 hand in/submit something. *Cassey is a hard-working student. She turns in two essays a week.* 2 (informal) abandon something. *David has a part-time job at a garage but he's having to turn it in because they want to replace him with a full-time mechanic.*

turn someone 'off (something) (informal) cause someone to lose interest in something. *I always enjoyed French in school, but the advanced course in literature turned me right off it.* □ *Men with long hair really turn me off!*

turn someone 'on (informal) thrill/delight someone; attract/excite someone sexually. *Rock music really turns me on.* □ *I don't know what Stephanie sees in Earl, but she says nobody turns her on like he does!*

'turn on someone attack someone; criticize someone sharply. *He beat the dog so much that it turned on him.* □ *Please take back that nasty remark! I refuse to be turned on by someone I hardly know!*

turn 'out 1 result. *How did your bread-baking turn out? □ We weren't looking forward to the outing, but it turned out to be really enjoyable.* 2 assemble, appear, attend. *The whole village turned out to watch the procession.* Note: **a 'turn-out.** *There was a good turn-out at the council meeting last night.*

turn someone 'out (of somewhere) make someone leave. *Shhh! You'll get us turned out of the library! □ He was turned out of his lodgings for taking women visitors up to his room.*

turn something 'out 1 empty something. *When you turn out the drawers you'll probably find the letter.* 2 switch something off. *Don't forget to turn out the lights when you leave.*

turn 'out something produce/manufacture something. *The factory turns out bottles. They turn them out at the rate of several thousand per day.*

turn someone/something 'over 1 deliver or hand someone/something over. *His family refused to turn him over to the police. □ Luckily, my brief-case was turned over to the lost property office.* 2 do an amount/volume of business. *The company turned over more than £350 million last year.* Note: **a 'turnover.**

turn 'up arrive, appear; be found. *I waited for twenty minutes, but Sue didn't turn up. □ Has your missing ring turned up yet?*

wade 'through something read/study something that is very long, difficult or boring. *I have some legal documents to wade through before the discussion tomorrow.*

wait 'up (for someone) not go to bed until someone comes home. *Don't wait up for me. I may be very late.*

wake 'up realize the truth of something, become aware of a situation. *I wish Vincent would wake up and see that his so-called friends only want him for his money.*

walk a'way with something win something easily. *Everybody expected Steve Holly to walk away with the Oscar for Best Actor, and he did.*

walk 'out strike, lay down one's work. *There's a strike threatening. Some of the workers walked out today.* Note: **a 'walk-out.** *In these times of serious unemployment, walk-outs are becoming a thing of the past.*

walk 'out on someone/something abandon someone/something. *She treated him badly, but she never thought he'd walk out on her. □ He's walked out on his job, as well as on his wife.*

'want for something need/lack/be without something. *They don't earn much money, but their children want for nothing.*

want 'out (of something) (mainly US, informal) want no further involvement in something, want to stop an activity or situation. *This deal is getting too risky. I want out before it's too late. □ If you want out of this relationship, just say so and leave!*

warm 'up become lively. *We arrived just when the party was beginning to warm up. □ Once Ted warms up, he'll be the life and soul of the party!*

wear 'off lose in attraction, power, interest. *His enthusiasm for the plan seems to have worn off. □ Ben rides his new bicycle every day, but when the novelty has worn off it will be left in the garage.*

wear 'on continue, pass. *The snow will melt as the day wears on.* □ *The evening wore on and his wife still hadn't come home from work.*

wear someone 'out (informal) make someone tired; exhaust someone. *Playing with little children really wears me out.*

wear something 'out make something useless by long or hard wear. *The children have worn their gym shoes out.*

weed someone/something 'out take out unnecessary or unsuitable persons or items from a group etc. *We've got a good set of applicants for the job. It will be difficult to weed them out.* □ *This pile of photographs needs weeding out before we stick any in the album.*

weigh someone 'down (with difficulties, responsibilities, problems etc.) depress someone; make someone sad or worried. *Since Michael was promoted to plant manager at the chemical works, he's been continually weighed down with responsibility.*

weigh someone 'up understand or form an opinion about someone. *'What's your new neighbour like?' 'Strange. We can't weigh him up at all.'*

weigh something 'up consider something carefully before taking action or making a decision; assess points for and against. *'Are you taking the job in Kuwait?' 'Can't say yet. The pros and cons have to be weighed up.'*

whip 'round (informal) 1 collect money given voluntarily from colleagues etc. *Claire's leaving to have her baby next week, so Sheila's whipping round to raise enough for a nice leaving-present.* Note: a **'whip-round.** *Who suggested a whip-round for the boss's birthday?* 2 run/walk quickly. *Whip round to the corner shop and buy a sliced loaf, will you?*

'whistle for something (informal) ask for something without hope of getting it. *I've reminded Trevor three times that he still owes me money, but as far as he's concerned I can whistle for it.*

wind 'down relax. *You'll be able to wind down, now that all the election excitement is over.*

wind something 'up end something. *Let's wind up the meeting. It's getting late.* □ *Oh, that's all over now. The case was wound up a year ago.*

work something 'off 1 get rid of something (e.g. surplus energy, weight). *Bruce is digging the garden. He's trying to work his Sunday lunch off.* 2 repay a debt or loan by working. *I shall have worked my debts off at Joe's garage by Christmas. Then I can start saving my earnings.*

'work on someone try to influence someone by constant persuasion. *Jason has a holiday apartment on Mallorca. I'll work on him to let us have it for a fortnight in July.*

work 'out 1 succeed; develop in a satisfactory way. *Don't despair. Everything will work out all right in the end.* 2 do physical fitness and health training exercises. *After working out at the fitness centre I feel like a new man!* Note: a **'work-out.** *Health conscious people often start the day with an intensive work-out.*

work something 'out 1 calculate something. *Have you worked out what I owe you yet?* 2 devise/construct something. *We must work out a marketing strategy as quickly as possible.* 3 understand/make sense of something. *It's a very strange situation. I can't work it out.*

work 'out at something amount to a sum of money. *The car repairs work out at £165.*

work something 'up 1 stimulate something. *Take a brisk walk to work up a good appetite.* □ *I can't work up any enthusiasm for the essay, I'm afraid.* 2 increase/ build something. *He's worked up a good business over the last five years.*

work 'up to something 1 develop into something. *The film works up to an exciting climax.* 2 prepare to express something (e.g. wish, suggestion). *I didn't know at the time what he was working up to. Then he asked me to move into his flat with him!*

wrap something 'up finalize/complete something. *They're going to wrap up the negotiations this week.* □ *The agreement was wrapped up at the last meeting.*

write someone 'off regard someone as no good. *He was written off by his family as a failure, so they were surprised when he passed all his exams and went to university.*

write something 'off 1 regard (a debt) as a loss. *There seems to be no hope of recovering these debts. I think we can write them off.* 2 regard something as being without value; (a vehicle) not worth repair. *The car was completely written off after the accident.* 3 regard something as a failure. Note: **a 'write-off.** *The new comedy at the Grand Theatre is a complete write-off so don't waste money on tickets.*

write something 'up 1 write a full account of something. *I've got a lot of lecture notes that need writing up.* 2 review (a film, play) for publication. Note: **a 'write-up.** *I've been asked to do a write-up of the play for a local newspaper.*

7 Verbal idioms

argue the toss argue/discuss vigorously, often about something that cannot be changed. *There's no point arguing the toss now. It has already been decided that Jones will be sent to represent the company in Tokyo, not you.*

ask/look for trouble behave/act in a way that is likely to bring trouble or difficulties. (Used mainly in continuous tenses.) *You're asking for trouble if you leave valuables on the front seat of your car.*

bark/be barking up the wrong tree get the wrong idea, make a wrong assumption, accuse the wrong person etc. *If you think it was Penny who gave Mr Evans the wrong information, then you're barking up the wrong tree. She wasn't even here when he rang.*

(not) be born yesterday (not) be easily deceived; be alert to what is happening. *If you think Joe will believe such a stupid story, you're wrong. He wasn't born yesterday.*

be/mean curtains (for someone) (informal) be the end of someone's life, lead to someone's downfall. *I wish Jeff wouldn't drive so fast on his motor bike. If he ever fell off, it would be curtains!*

be a cut above someone/something be better than, be in a higher class than someone/something. *The new assistant seems to be extremely efficient. He's certainly a cut above the last one.*

be dying for something/to do something (informal) be waiting impatiently for something, be looking forward to something very much. *The children are dying for the summer holidays.* □ *I'm simply dying to introduce you to my fiancé. You'll love him!*

be the (absolute) limit (informal) be someone/something that annoys/ exasperates/shocks etc. others intensely. *Well, Pamela really is the limit. I've bought two expensive concert tickets for Saturday, and now she says she's going to someone's party instead!*

be 'new to the game lack experience in an activity, job or situation. *You're still new to the game and have a lot to learn. No one will expect you to become a first-class journalist overnight.*

be no picnic (informal) not be an easy or pleasant experience. *The oral exam was no picnic. The professor asked me some very tricky questions.*

beat about the bush talk indirectly about something; not say directly what you are thinking. *Stop beating about the bush and tell me how much money you want to borrow!*

beat someone at his own game fight back with the same methods, only better. *I wouldn't let Walker cheat me like this. I'd try to beat him at his own game.*

bend/lean/fall over backwards (to do something) try very hard, take great trouble to do something for someone else. *Joanne's a very good-natured girl. She'll bend over backwards to help her friends.*

bite (on) the bullet accept that you cannot avoid something unpleasant and face it with courage. *The bank has refused a further overdraft facility, so we'll have to bite on the bullet and sell the house.*

bite off more than one can chew take on a task that is too difficult; expect too much of oneself. *Martin promised to get his book to the publisher by September, but he's now realized that he's bitten off more than he can chew.*

blot one's copybook do something that spoils one's good record or reputation. *Joan has never failed an exam in her life, but she thinks she'll blot her copybook when she takes her driving test next week.*

blow one's own trumpet praise one's own successes, abilities etc. *Mark's been very successful and he makes sure that everyone knows about it. He's always blowing his own trumpet at the club.*

blow one's top lose one's temper suddenly; become furious. *Sally will blow her top when she sees what's happened to her drawings. I've spilt coffee all over them!*

break the bank win or take all one's/someone's money. *Could you let me have ten pounds over the weekend – or will it break the bank?*

break even make neither a profit nor a loss; get the same amount of money out as you put in. *Don't expect to get rich quick in this business. We'll be lucky to break even in the first three years.*

break fresh/new ground work at/discover something new in an area of knowledge. *Professor Orwell's latest research breaks fresh ground in the study of micro-electronics.*

break ground with something make a start. *We are hoping to break ground with the new office complex within the month.*

break the ice say or do something which relaxes a stiff, tense atmosphere. *The guests don't know each other, but Philip's a wonderful host. He always knows how to break the ice and get people feeling relaxed.*

break the news tell someone news which will affect him personally in a good or bad way. *I've crashed Steven's car – but I haven't broken the news to him yet.*

bring home the bacon (informal) earn the necessary money; obtain the necessary success. *Charles writes books that never seem to get published. It's Elizabeth who brings home the bacon with the agency she runs.*

bring (something) home to someone make someone realize something or see the situation clearly. *A month in prison really brought home to him just how stupid he had been to get involved with criminals.*

bring someone to book make someone explain his actions or conduct. *Whoever is responsible for this damage will certainly be brought to book.*

bring something to light reveal new facts or information. *My conversation with Mark brought to light many things about Sarah that I hadn't realized before.*

burn one's boats/bridges follow a course of action that cannot be reversed or changed later. *Keep your job and your flat. Don't burn your bridges here until you know for sure that you're going to stay in Canada.*

burn the midnight oil work or study until late into the night. *I have some exams in six weeks, so I shall be burning the midnight oil quite often.*

bury the hatchet decide to end hostility, disagreement etc. and become friendly again. *Surely the old quarrel is long forgotten! Why don't George and Harry bury the hatchet at last?*

call someone's bluff invite someone to carry out his threat, prove his claim etc., because you don't believe that he really will. *Ted keeps threatening to resign if we don't do things his way. Next time I shall call his bluff and accept his resignation.*

call the shots (informal) have control of a situation; tell others what to do and how to do it. *Baxter's the big man right now, but he won't be calling the shots much longer if he loses the contract with General Dynamics!*

call a spade a spade speak frankly; name or describe something, a situation etc. in direct, straightforward terms. *Celia is used to calling a spade a spade. If she thinks you're stupid, she'll tell you.*

(not) care/give a damn (informal) not care/be worried at all. *Roger does exactly what he wants when he wants. He doesn't care a damn about what his employer thinks.*

carry the can (for someone) be obliged to accept the responsibility or blame if something goes wrong. *No, I won't support such a risky project this time and end up carrying the can again.*

carry something/it/things (a bit/rather) too far do more than, or continue something beyond, what is necessary or reasonable. *Mrs Robins takes her son to the dentist's every two months. I think that's carrying things a bit too far, don't you?*

carry (some/little/no etc.) weight be of some/little etc. importance/ influence. *I'll try to put in a good word for you with the team captain, but I'm afraid what I say doesn't carry much weight these days.*

catch someone in the act find/catch someone actually doing something wrong or forbidden. *She couldn't deny stealing the money, because she was caught in the act.*

catch someone napping (informal) gain an advantage over someone when he is not paying attention. *We have to incorporate new technologies. We can't afford to be caught napping by our competitors.*

change one's tune change one's opinion, attitude or way of thinking about something. *Richard suggested that we should modernize the house, but he soon changed his tune when he realized how much it would cost!*

clear the air get rid of suspicion or doubts by telling the true facts; make a better personal atmosphere by speaking openly and frankly. *After all these rumours, I need to have a frank talk with Gilbert to clear the air.*

climb/jump/get on the bandwagon (informal) join in with what others are doing because it seems profitable or likely to bring personal or financial gain. *You can see that the future lies in high-tech. It's time to climb on the bandwagon with the competitors, before it's too late.*

clip someone's wings limit someone's power or influence so as to slow down his action or plans. *Dixon has great improvement plans for the department, but the reduced budget will clip his wings considerably.*

come clean admit the truth, confess one's guilt. *He decided to come clean and tell the police that he had given the gang inside information.*

come a cropper (informal) meet with sudden failure or bad luck. *Mike has gambled and won on many occasions, but one of these days he'll come a cropper and lose everything.*

come down to earth return to reality, stop dreaming about plans and ideas that cannot be realized. *Helen had big ideas about a career in the army, but she soon came down to earth when she failed the medical.*

come/go full circle come back to the original position, situation etc. *All my shares have dropped on the Stock Exchange, but I shall simply wait until things come full circle again.*

come in handy (informal) prove to be useful. *Don't throw these old screwdrivers away. They might come in handy.*

come into one's own receive the praise or fame for one's talents, abilities or achievements that one deserves. *Ruth's artistic talent had never been taken seriously, but she came into her own when she went to art school.*

come of age become adult in law, i.e. reach the age of 18 or 21 depending on the country. *When Max comes of age, he'll inherit his father's 55% share of the family business.*

come off second best lose in a competition, argument etc. *Paul isn't very pleased with himself. He hates coming off second best in arguments with his brother.*

come on (too) strong (mainly US, informal) show too much emotion, be too familiar or critical to someone. *I'm sorry I came on too strong. I know I shouldn't have said that – we've only just met.*

come out on top win, gain an advantage, overcome difficulties. *The candidates all spoke pretty well, but Mrs Fraser clearly came out on top with her brilliant argumentation.*

come/get to grips with something get control of a problem; learn how to handle a situation. *It's time Alan got to grips with reality. If his work doesn't improve, he'll lose his job!*

come to terms with someone/something come to an understanding or agreement with someone; learn to accept a situation that cannot be changed and adapt to it. *After years of resentment following the unfair provisions of their father's will, Andrew has finally come to terms with his brother.* □ *It took Penny a long time to come to terms with the fact that her former fiancé left her and married her sister.*

come to the crunch (informal) usually **if/when it comes to the crunch.** When the time to decide/act etc. comes; when the situation reaches its climax. *Nicola is going to have to choose between her boyfriend and her career. When it comes to the crunch, it's my bet that she'll choose her career.*

come un'stuck fail, not materialize (plans, arrangements etc.) *John had big plans to work as a doctor in a Third World country, but when he met Jane and married her, they all came unstuck.*

compare notes exchange thoughts and ideas with another person. *I'd like to know what you think about Drabble's new book. Let's compare notes over coffee.*

cook the books (informal) falsify a firm's accounts or records to one's own advantage, often to take money out unnoticed. *Apparently, he had been cooking the company's books for years to meet his gambling losses.*

cost a bomb/a packet/the earth (informal) cost a lot of money. *Have you seen John's new car? It must have cost a bomb!*

cramp someone's style (informal) restrict or interfere with the way someone likes to do business or conduct his private life; prevent someone from acting freely. *Peter's younger brother is moving into the same flat with him. Poor old Peter – it's sure to cramp his style!*

cross swords (with someone) argue or have a verbal contest with. *I'm not afraid of Jackson. I've crossed swords with him on several occasions, both in and out of court.*

curry favour (with someone) try to win favour by flattery. *It's no use trying to curry favour with Miss Marshall by bringing her flowers. She only appreciates hard work.*

cut the cackle (informal) stop wasting time with unnecessary talk. *Time's short. Can't we just cut the cackle and start on the important issues?*

cut a corner/corners do something in the easiest, quickest, cheapest way etc. *It's not worth cutting corners on this project. We'll have to invest in the necessary hardware, no matter what it costs.*

cut one's losses end an unsatisfactory situation and accept a loss before the losses get even bigger. *He's lost a lot on the low dollar exchange rate, but I advised him to cut his losses and exchange the rest of his money, before the dollar drops even further.*

cut no ice/not cut much ice (with someone) make no impression; have no influence on. *Janice's know-all attitude impresses the trainees, but it cuts no ice with the supervisor.*

deliver the goods (informal) produce the expected results, high standards etc.; do what is asked within the time. *Don't make promises until you know for sure that you can deliver the goods.*

dig one's own grave (informal) make difficulties for oneself, engineer one's own misfortune. *If you go into partnership with Robson, you'll be digging your own grave. He's simply not reliable.*

do a bunk (informal) disappear; leave unexpectedly telling no one where one is going. *Apparently, he had lots of personal debts and was in trouble with the tax authorities, so he did a bunk overnight and hasn't been heard of since.*

do all 'right for oneself (informal) make a successful life, career, business etc. *Apparently, Charlotte's doing all right for herself. She's got a boutique in Edinburgh.*

do as/what one is told conform; obey instructions etc. *Raymond thought that he would be able to change everything once he got into Parliament, but he soon realized that even in Westminster one has to do as one is told.*

do one's bit take one's share of the responsibility, work, costs etc. *If we all do our bit, we'll soon have the place cleaned up again.*

do/try one's damnedest (to do something) (informal) put one's greatest energy and effort into something. *Max tried his damnedest to get into the team, but he just wasn't good enough.*

do the dirty on someone (informal) play a mean trick on someone, betray someone. *Trevor did the dirty on Robin by telling the board of directors that it was he who had given the unconditional guarantees.*

do (someone/something) (some/no/a lot of etc.) good help/be good for one's health etc; improve an unsatisfactory situation. *A week's rest would do you a lot of good.* □ *I felt like complaining to the bank manager, but I knew that it wouldn't do any good.*

do one's homework (informal) obtain the necessary facts or information beforehand, be well-informed and prepared for questions etc. *You know all the latest figures. I can see you've been doing your homework.*

do the honours act as host or hostess. *Who's going to do the honours and open the champagne?*

do one's level best (to do something) try as hard as possible. *Alex says he'll do his level best to get us a good price for the old car.*

do one's nut (informal) lose one's temper, become very angry. *The headmaster will do his nut when he finds out that someone has let the air out of his car tyres!*

do the right thing act in a wise or morally correct way. *I hope we did the right thing in telling Judith the truth about Oliver. She had the right to know.*

do the sights visit all the things worth seeing in a town. *You need more than two or three days to do the sights in London.*

do the spadework do preliminary, basic or necessary work before the most important work can be done. *There's a lot of spadework to be done before we can discuss the actual chapter contents of the book.*

do one's stuff (informal) perform; do what one is expected to do as well as one can do it. *You've had all the help we can give you, so now it's up to you to do your stuff on the day and pass the exam.*

do the trick/job serve the purpose, be the correct solution to a problem. *You see, a bit of oil did the trick. The door doesn't squeak at all now.*

do wonders/miracles (with something) produce excellent or unexpected results. *Ed will come round and repair your washing-machine. He can do wonders with a set of tools!*

draw a blank not get what one wants, not find what one is looking for. *Kate was obviously waiting for someone to offer to lend her money, but she drew a blank.*

draw in one's horns spend less money, be satisfied with less. *If Father loses his job, we shall certainly have to draw in our horns. No more expensive clothes and holidays!*

drive a hard bargain be hard or egoistic in doing business; be strong-willed in asserting one's wishes etc. *Peters is usually fair in business dealings, but he certainly knows how to drive a hard bargain.*

drop a brick/clanger (informal) say or do something that is tactless, causes embarrassment etc. *Valerie really dropped a clanger when she asked Bob why his wife wasn't with him.*

drop names mention influential names in one's conversation in order to impress on others that one knows such people. *If you want to widen your* *clientele, try dropping a few names – it always works with potential customers.* Note: **name-dropping**. *Cynthia is a dreadful snob. She can't hold a simple conversation without name-dropping.*

earn one's keep be useful and helpful enough to compensate for the cost of one's stay at someone's home. *During his three weeks with us Roger certainly earned his keep. He helped in the house every day.*

(not) entertain the idea/thought/suggestion etc. refuse to consider the idea etc. *The children suggested taking a camping holiday this year, but their parents wouldn't entertain the idea.*

fall into one's/someone's lap be easily obtained without trouble or effort. *When Jane came to live in Colchester she had no trouble getting either a job or a flat. Everything just fell into her lap.*

fall/come short of something be less or worse than one expects, hopes or requires. *We had been looking forward to the new comedy at the Queen's Theatre, but it fell short of our expectations.*

feel the pinch feel an unpleasant change in one's standard of living because one has less money than before. *Because of the steep rise in prices over the past months, people living on small pensions are feeling the pinch.*

fight a losing battle try hard without much chance of success because circumstances are against one. *The medical profession is still fighting a losing battle against cancer.*

fight shy of (doing) something avoid (doing) something because it is unpleasant. *Michael always fights shy of taking difficult decisions. He prefers to leave the responsibility to others.*

fill/fit the bill be suitable; serve the intended purpose. *If you're looking for a bright, cheery T-shirt this one in red, yellow and orange should fill the bill.*

find/get one's bearings adjust/adapt to a new situation, position or place. *When I walked out of the hotel lift it took me a while to find my bearings. All the corridors looked the same.* Note also: **lose one's bearings**.

flex one's muscles show one's power or influence as a warning to others. *The new headmaster has introduced a few changes that aren't very popular with the staff. He's obviously flexing his muscles.*

fly off the handle (informal) become angry with someone; lose one's temper suddenly. *I'm sorry. It wasn't your fault. I shouldn't have flown off the handle like that.*

follow in someone's footsteps show the same interests, talents or ability as a parent/relative or as one's predecessor. *Jenny's father was a professional artist and it looks as if she's following in his footsteps. Her paintings are superb.*

follow suit do the same as someone else has just done. *When the City Bank lowered interest rates, all the other banks soon followed suit.*

get/be above oneself act in a conceited or arrogant way; be self-opinionated. *I admit that George is a good tennis-player, but he often gets above himself and tells others how to play.*

get cracking/weaving (informal) act, move or work quickly. *It will take you longer than you think to paint the fence, so you'd better get cracking.*

get down to brass tacks (informal) stop generalizing and discuss practical or essential details. *In theory the plan sounds good. But when you get down to brass tacks, it's too difficult to put into practice.*

get down to business begin serious discussion of a matter after a period of general or social talk. *It's 7.30, so I suggest we get down to business. What's the first point on your list, Janet?*

get even (with someone) take revenge (on someone); pay someone back for some harm he has done. *Terry blamed Ken for the accident that cost him his job, and he swore he would get even with him one day.*

get a grip on something get a situation under control. *If the government doesn't get a grip on inflation soon, the country's economy will suffer.*

get a grip/hold on oneself get oneself or one's emotions under control. *After the dreadful accident, Jim said he would never drive a car again, but he soon got a grip on himself.*

get/come in on the ground floor (informal) become involved in a plan or project (often with the prospect of financial gain) from the start. *When the company goes public I want to get in on the ground floor, so I've applied for a thousand shares.*

get into one's stride give one's usual or best performance again after a time of inactivity or after a change of circumstances. *Because of an injury, he hadn't played tennis for three months. But once he was back in action, he soon got into his stride.*

get knotted/lost/stuffed (slang, often an exclamation) go away! no, I won't! Expresses annoyance with someone or strong refusal to do something. *'Sorry to bother you but...' 'Get knotted, Roy! You can see I'm busy.'* □ *Jenkins asked me to clear away the mess but I told him to get stuffed. It wasn't me who made it.*

get a move on (informal) be fast; hurry to do something. *We ought to get a move on. The concert starts in half an hour.*

get (someone) nowhere (informal) (cause someone to) make no progress or fail to achieve an aim. *I've been studying this diagram all morning, but I'm getting nowhere. It simply doesn't make sense.* □ *All this talk will get us nowhere. We'll have to act.* Note also: **not get (someone) anywhere.** *Just talking about dieting won't get you anywhere.*

get (something) off the ground (cause something to) start, develop or function successfully, e.g. a plan or project. *Janet has this great idea of publishing a technical magazine for children, but she doubts that she'll ever get the plan off the ground.*

get on someone's nerves irritate or annoy someone. *I do wish Adrian wouldn't sing to himself all the time. It gets on my nerves when I'm trying to read.*

get on top of someone/something 1 (with **someone**) become too much for someone to handle, e.g. work or worry. *Work's been getting on top of me lately. I think I need a holiday.* 2 (with **something**) take control of a task; handle something successfully or complete the worst part of something. *The extension to the house has caused a lot of dirt and upset, but thankfully we've got on top of it now.*

get one's act together (informal) organize oneself/one's actions or a situation satisfactorily. *It's time Joe got his act together at last and did something worthwhile with his life.* Note also: **get it together.**

get one's cards (slang)/**the sack** (informal) be dismissed from one's job; be made redundant. *Paul got his cards for being rude to a customer.* Also: **give someone his cards/the sack.**

get one's own back (informal) get one's revenge. *Sam played a rather nasty trick on Jerry but Jerry's determined to get his own back.*

get one's skates on (informal) hurry. *If you want to come to the cinema with us, you'd better get your skates on. We're leaving in five minutes.*

get oneself together regain control of one's emotions. *Pat's been crying. Just give her a moment to get herself together. She'll be all right.*

get out of bed (on) the wrong side (informal) be bad-tempered or in a bad mood all day. *Bill obviously got out of bed on the wrong side. He's been grumpy all day.*

get something straight make a matter or situation clear to someone; clear up a misunderstanding. *Let's get this straight. It's my car and I shall decide who I lend it to, not you.*

get the better of someone overcome someone; defeat or gain an advantage over someone physically or in an argument etc. *Excitement and curiosity got the better of him so he opened the birthday present two days before his birthday.* □ *I'm not surprised that Barry soon got the better of Tim in the fight. He's a year older and much bigger.*

get the chop (slang) be dismissed from one's job; be rejected, closed down or discontinued. *I wouldn't worry if I were you. If anyone gets the chop it will be the new man.* Also: **give someone ~** *A few restaurants were given the chop by the Department of Health because their kitchens did not come up to the required standards of hygiene.*

get the feel of something become used to (doing) something that requires physical movement or skill. *Skiing isn't as easy as it looks, but you should get the feel of it within a few days.*

get/lose the hang of something find out or understand how best to do something that requires physical or mental ability/lose this ability, e.g. through lack of practice. *Robert's been struggling with algebra problems. He still hasn't got the hang of them.* □ *There are a few things that you never really lose the hang of, once you've learnt them. For example, driving a car or typing.*

get the message (informal) understand or realize what someone wants one to understand or realize. *When Jack asked me for some money a second time, I pretended not to hear. I think he got the message because he didn't ask again.*

get the picture clear understand the situation correctly. *Now let me get the picture clear. You're going to be away from the 21st to the 28th of June and from the 7th to the 13th of July. Is that right?*

get the push (slang) be dismissed from one's job; be rejected in a relationship. *He used to play in an orchestra, but he soon got the push because he stopped going to rehearsals.* Also: **give someone ~.** *She soon gave him the push when she found out that he had been involved in a robbery.*

get the wind up (informal) become afraid. *They were about to break into the house but when a burglar alarm went off unexpectedly they got the wind up and ran away.* Also: **put the wind up someone.** *The burglar alarm put the wind up them.*

'**get there** (informal) complete a task slowly; achieve one's aim with patience and perseverance. *'How's the work on the new dictionary coming along?' 'Quite well, thanks. We're getting there.'*

get to/reach/make first base (with something) (mainly US, informal) reach or complete the first important stage of a plan or project. *I doubt that John will ever reach first base with his plan to make a film. He hasn't even done any research.*

get/come to grips with something begin to tackle a problem or deal with a situation successfully. *It's time Peter got to grips with reality. He still thinks school is just a place to meet one's friends.*

get to the bottom of something find out the reason for or the answer to a puzzling situation. *John has been acting very strangely recently. His parents don't know what's wrong, but they are determined to get to the bottom of it.*

get wind of something receive some news or information (secretly or by chance) which one is not supposed to know. *Make sure that Jack doesn't get wind of the plan. If he does it will spoil the surprise for him.*

get/be wise to someone/something become/be aware of what someone is doing or planning; realize the reason for someone's actions. *Ben often said he felt sick in school and asked to be excused. But the teacher soon got wise to him, because it was always before the maths lesson.*

get someone wrong (informal) misunderstand someone's reasons for doing or saying something. *Don't get me wrong on this. I'm not rejecting your idea because I don't like it. I just don't think it's practicable.*

get something/it wrong (informal) be mistaken about the facts of something; fail to understand a situation properly. *The newspaper article has got it wrong. That wasn't how the accident happened at all.*

give someone the creeps (informal) make someone feel afraid, nervous or ill at ease. *Please don't talk about the murder case. It gives me the creeps every time I think about it.* □ *That man gives me the creeps. It's the way he looks at people.*

give someone his due admit something positive about someone, e.g. that someone has some good qualities or good reasons for doing something. *Harry may be lazy and sometimes unreliable, but to give him his due, he is always willing to help.*

give someone an/the edge (over/on someone) give someone an advantage (over someone else). *She's written TV scripts before, so her experience naturally gives her the edge over newcomers to television writing.* Also: **have (got) an/the edge (over/on someone).**

give the 'game/show away (informal) reveal or betray secret intentions or plans. *We were planning to take Mother on a surprise holiday to Spain, but unfortunately she found the booking form, so that gave the game away.*

give someone hell (informal) give someone a very difficult or painful time. *The pain in my back really gave me hell for three days.*

give someone a (good) run for his money (informal) provide someone with a strong challenge; make competition difficult for someone. *Williams expects to win the tennis tournament. I suppose he will, but all the competitors are determined to give him a good run for his money.*

give someone the slip (informal) escape from someone, often by using a trick. *A young boy had been stealing apples from the farmer's orchard. The farmer caught him, but the boy was able to give him the slip.*

give someone to understand that ... lead someone to believe something by not making the situation clear. *I was given to understand that I should be offered the job of club treasurer, not secretary. There was no mention of Jack wanting to be treasurer as well.*

give something a try try to do something even if success is doubtful, e.g. because one has never done it before. *I've never skied before, but I'm willing to give it a try.* □ *Dick says German is too difficult to learn in a few months, but he hasn't even given it a try.*

give vent to something express one's feelings freely, especially anger. *I couldn't restrain my anger any longer. I simply had to give vent to it.*

give someone/something the (full/whole) works (informal) do or provide everything possible. *We're redecorating the house – new tiles in the bathroom and kitchen, new wallpaper and carpets throughout. We're giving it the full works.*

go begging not be wanted; be unclaimed. *If those sandwiches are going begging, we'd better finish them.*

go by the board (plans, arrangements etc.) be discontinued or abandoned. *The car broke down and couldn't be repaired for ten days, so the holiday arrangements had to go by the board.*

go down a bomb (slang) be extremely well received (e.g. a performance). *Their nightclub act used to go down a bomb with the audience.*

go down well/badly etc. (with someone) be praised, well received or welcomed/be criticized etc. *The new train set went down very well with the children. They were thrilled.* □ *His suggestion went down badly with the club members. No one wanted to pay higher membership fees.*

go downhill deteriorate in quality or standards. *We stayed at this hotel four years ago, but it's certainly gone downhill since then.*

go great guns (informal) (used in continuous tenses) do something with great energy or effort, usually successfully. *Sue was going great guns on the tennis court. She's improved a lot since the last time I saw her play.*

go halves (with someone) agree to pay half each of the total cost. *Bob paid for the meal for both families and Ken went halves with him later.*

go haywire (informal) stop functioning properly; become confused or out of control. *The printer's gone haywire. It's churning out paper with nothing on it!*

go off at half cock (informal) do or say something before the time is right; (a plan, arrangements etc.) fail because badly prepared or started too early. *Don't say anything to Williams. There's no point going off at half cock before we are sure of our facts and have a strong argument against him.*

go/fly off at a tangent suddenly leave the topic of discussion and talk about or do something completely different. *His talk was good, but half way through he went off at a tangent and consequently the audience became restless.*

go phut stop functioning; break down or collapse. *The electric kettle won't work. First there was a funny smell, then it just went phut.*

go places (informal) 1 visit and get to know many foreign countries. *Apparently Helen has really been places. She tells some incredible stories about her adventures.* 2 become very successful in one's career. *Barbara worked for a small newspaper, but she really started to go places when she joined a TV station. Now she's got her own foreign news programme.*

go public (a company) issue shares on the Stock Exchange for the public to buy. *For years Littletons was a small private company. Then they invested and expanded and finally went public two years ago.*

go spare (slang) become excessively angry or worried. *When you tell Father that you're leaving university to become a pop singer he'll go spare.*

go straight (informal) (a criminal) abandon crime and lead an honest life. *When he came out of prison he swore he would go straight, but nobody would give him a job.*

go to hell (informal) (often an exclamation) used to show strong rejection of someone, his demands, suggestions etc. *Jack wanted to borrow my car again. Last time he borrowed it he smashed a headlight, so I told him to go to hell.*

go to pieces deteriorate (e.g. one's health or state of mind); lose one's self-control. *After the shock of the accident, he just went to pieces. He didn't know what had happened or where he was.*

go to pot (informal) go to ruin. *After his wife's death, Mr Palmer let the house go to pot.*

go to town (on something) (informal) make a supreme and successful effort with something, often to provide enjoyment for others. *Liz really went to town on the buffet. All the guests said the food was excellent.*

go to the wall be ruined; be in a hopeless situation. *Several small companies always go to the wall in a time of recession.*

go the whole hog do something thoroughly; exhaust all possibilities. *If you're buying a new dress, why don't you go the whole hog and buy coat, shoes and handbag as well?*

gum up the works (informal) stop progress; delay or ruin an activity. *John was making good progress with his book, but then his computer broke down, so that really gummed up the works.*

hang fire be delayed; be awaiting completion. *Our plans for the extension to the house are hanging fire until the builder comes out of hospital.*

have (oneself) a ball (informal) thoroughly enjoy oneself; have a very good time. *The garden party was a great success. The children especially had themselves a ball.*

not have (got) a clue (about something) (informal) have no idea about something; understand or know nothing. *I don't speak Spanish, so I'm afraid I haven't got a clue what he's telling us.*

have a go/crack/bash (at something) (informal) try (to do) something.
I'm going to have a go at repairing the car myself. □ *I've never tried to hang wallpaper before, but I'm willing to have a crack at it.*

have (got) a nerve (informal) be extremely bold in one's demands or treatment of others. *She's got a nerve – wanting to borrow more money when she hasn't paid back the ten pounds she owes me yet.* Also: **have (got) the nerve (to do something)** (informal). *She had the nerve to tell me that I wasn't bringing my children up properly.*

have been a'round (informal) have gained much experience of a worldly or social nature; have been to many places, had many social relationships etc. *'What do you know about Charles Fraser?' 'Quite a bit. He's certainly been around.'*

have (got) something coming to one (informal) be about to experience something pleasant or very often unpleasant which one does not suspect. *Jane's got a nice surprise coming to her when she gets home. There's a letter telling her that she's won first prize in a competition.* □ *He's got a shock coming to him when he finds out that he's bottom of the class in the French test.*

have (got) designs on/upon someone/something (informal) be very interested in and want to become friendly with someone of the opposite sex; secretly want and plan to get or win something (e.g. someone's job). *Paul has been promised the part of Macbeth but Harry has designs on it, too. So Paul will have to watch out.*

have (got) everything/a lot going for one (informal) have everything/a lot in one's favour (e.g. good opportunites or prospects). *I don't understand why Jack wants to go to live in Canada when he's got everything going for him in this country.*

have (got) (the) first refusal be given the chance to buy something before others. *Joe might be selling his car and if he does, I've got first refusal.* Also: **give someone (the) first refusal.**

have 'had a few (informal) have drunk enough or too much alcohol. *Brian's rather quiet usually, but when he's had a few he becomes very chatty.*

have (got) mixed feelings about someone/(doing) something not have clear feelings about someone/something; see positive and negative aspects. *Janet has mixed feelings about leaving home. On the one hand she wants to go to college, but on the other hand she'll miss her parents and her friends very much.*

have (got) money to burn (informal) have a lot of money that one spends unnecessarily. *'Why does Peter need two cars?' 'He doesn't, but he's always had money to burn.'*

have (got) no business doing something (informal) have no right to do something because it is not one's concern. *What are you looking for in Father's briefcase? You've got no business going through his papers like that.*

have (got) no/not much/more/less call for something have no need of or no use/demand for something. *'How about a new lawn-mower, sir?' 'No thanks, I've got no call for one. I haven't got a garden.'* Also: **there's no/ not much etc. call for someone/something.** *If everyone could repair their own cars, there would be less call for good car mechanics.*

have (got) no call/not much/more/less call to do something have no reason to do something; have no justification for doing something. *I've got no call to complain at all. The builders have done an excellent job.* Also: **there's no etc. call to do something.** *All right, I can hear you. There's no call to shout!*

have no truck with someone/something (informal) have no dealings with someone/something; not be concerned with someone/something. *The students from the engineering faculty have no truck with the art students from the college next door.*

have (got) something on the go (informal) be busy with something; have something planned. *'Gina is giving a talk on Greece for the local Archaeology Society next week.' 'I'm not surprised. She always has something on the go.'*

have a/one's say (in something) state one's opinion. *We should ask Grandfather what he thinks about us buying a caravan. You know he likes to have his say in everything.*

have (got) something/nothing/not much etc. to say for oneself (often used in the negative) be able to excuse or explain one's actions or behaviour. *When the teacher asked Jimmy why he hadn't done his homework again, he didn't have much to say for himself.*

have (got) the guts (to do something) (informal) (often used in the negative) have the necessary courage or strength of character. *'Why did Bob let himself get involved in a break-in?' 'I suppose it was because he didn't have the guts to say No.'*

have (got) the hots for someone (slang) be very infatuated with or interested in someone of the opposite sex. *He's got the hots for you. Surely you must have noticed!*

have (got) to do with/be to do with someone/something be concerned with someone/something. *What are you talking about? Has it got to do with me again?* □ *Jeff wants to talk to you. It's to do with looking after the house while they're on holiday.*

have (got) something up one's sleeve (informal) have some secret information; have something planned secretly. *Barry's looking pleased about something. I expect he's got a surprise up his sleeve again.*

have (got) one's wits about one be bright and alert; know exactly what is happening, what one is doing etc. *Susan always has her wits about her when she's playing chess. She never misses a good move.*

have (got) one's 'work cut out (informal) have a difficult job or task to face. *'I'm looking after the neighbours' children this week.' 'All four of them? Well, you've certainly got your work cut out.'*

hit the headlines become a main subject of newspaper and media interest. *I see the royals have hit the headlines again this morning. Another baby for the Princess.*

hit the jackpot have unexpected success with something which often brings money. *I think the group have really hit the jackpot this time. Their new record is already in the charts.*

hit the road (mainly US, informal) start a road journey. *If you want to be in Detroit by lunchtime, we ought to hit the road by 7.30 at the latest.*

hit the roof/ceiling (informal) become angry suddenly. *Mother hit the roof when I told her I didn't want to go to university.*

hold down a job keep a job for a long time. *Roger can't hold down a job for longer than three months. He's too careless and lazy.*

hold the fort (informal) take charge of or look after something in someone's absence. *We have to go to Bristol unexpectedly, but Mother will be at home holding the fort until we get back.*

hold one's own maintain one's position or achievement level in spite of difficulty or opposition. *Barbara is able to hold her own in any argument.* □ *Foreign competition is very tough. We may not be able to hold our own in the market for much longer.*

hold water (informal) (often used in the negative) be able to withstand investigation or testing. *He knew that his alibi didn't hold water. He couldn't prove to the police that he had been in bed asleep.*

jog someone's memory remind someone of something; help someone to remember or recall someone/something. *Don't forget the appointment. Put a note near the telephone to jog your memory.*

jump the gun (informal) do something before the right or permitted time; be too hasty. *'A baby already? They've only been married a few months. That's what I call jumping the gun.'*

jump the queue go to the front of a queue unfairly; not wait in line until it is one's turn. *That man jumped the queue. It wasn't his turn to pay.*

keep someone company accompany someone somewhere or stay with someone for a long or short period of time. *'I'm going to the theatre on Saturday.' 'Do you mind if I keep you company? I haven't been to the theatre for ages.'*

keep/lose one's cool (informal) keep/lose control of one's anger or patience etc. *That man made me so furious. How did you manage to keep your cool?*

keep something dark (from someone) keep something hidden; not tell or show someone something. *Charles won a lot of money, but he tried to keep it dark from his friends because he knew they would want to borrow from him.* Also: **keep someone in the dark (about something)**. *Charles kept us all in the dark about his win.*

keep one's distance not come/get too close to someone either physically, emotionally or socially. *The people next door moved in over a year ago, but we hardly know them. They keep their distance.*

keep in touch (with someone) continue to visit or have written or telephone contact with someone. *When the Parkers moved to Cornwall, they said they would keep in touch, but unfortunately we've had no news of them.*

keep on the right side of someone (informal) remain in someone's favour; not annoy or disappoint someone. *You had better keep on the right side of your father, or he'll cut your pocket money.*

keep oneself to oneself not have many social contacts; prefer to do things alone. *Roger ought to go out more and make some friends. I think he keeps himself to himself too much.*

keep open house welcome visitors at any time without previous invitation. *Jill and Brian keep open house. I'm sure they won't mind letting you stay the night when you're in London.*

keep pace with someone/something make progress as fast as another person; be as good or as fast as someone. *You'll have to work harder if you want to keep pace with the rest of the pupils.*

keep someone posted continue to give someone the latest information or news. *There's no more news about Jack at the moment, but I'll keep you posted.*

keep tabs on someone (informal) follow someone's movements and activities. *Ruth thinks that her son may be getting into bad company. But it's difficult keeping tabs on a nineteen-year-old.*

keep a tight/loose rein on someone/something exercise strict control/little control over someone/something. *If you want to save money, you'll have to keep a tighter rein on your spending.*

keep up appearances continue to make a good impression in public in order to hide what one does not wish others to know. *It's difficult to keep up appearances for long when you lose your job and have little money.*

keep up with the Joneses compete with one's neighbours and friends in material standards; want to possess the same material goods as others. *It used to be a new car. Now it's a personal computer and a sauna if you want to keep up with the Joneses.*

kick up a fuss/row (about something) (informal) create or cause trouble, an unpleasant argument etc. *I'm sorry I forgot to phone you, but I don't think it's anything to kick up a fuss about.*

know better (than to do something) be more sensible or wiser. *You're ten years old. You should know better than to let a small child play with a fragile toy.*

know something inside 'out/backwards know something very well. *Thomas has been learning his part for the school play in a month's time. He knows it inside out already.*

know one's onions/stuff (informal) know one's subject or how to do something very well. *When it comes to car repairs, David certainly knows his onions.*

know/learn the ropes (informal) know/learn how something works or how something is usually done. *Miss Robertson is new to the school, so she doesn't know the ropes yet. Show her round and tell her all about us, Sarah.*

know the score (informal) assess the situation or state of affairs correctly. *Mark, you know the score. Do you think we should accept Ben's offer or not?*

know where one is/one stands (with someone) know what someone else wants from you; know one's exact position with someone. *There's one good thing about Maggie. She says what she thinks. You always know where you stand with her.*

not know whether one is coming or going (informal) be disorganized or confused because one has too much work or too many things to attend to. *I have so much work to do at present that I don't know whether I'm coming or going.*

labour the point emphasize something by continually repeating it or further explaining it. *All right, Jeff. You have made it perfectly clear why you don't want to help Jim. There's no need to labour the point.*

laugh up one's sleeve (informal) be secretly amused or pleased about something. *Two of the boys had been nasty to Jimmy, so he laughed up his sleeve when they both failed the maths test.*

lay down the law (informal) say something with an authoritative tone; tell others what has to be done. *Father loves to lay down the law on political issues. He thinks he could run the country better than the Prime Minister.*

lead someone a dance (informal) cause trouble or difficulties for someone by being evasive/elusive, e.g. by changing one's mind often or by moving from place to place. *The suspect knew that the police were following him and he certainly led them a dance before he was arrested.*

leave the arena (informal) stop competing; withdraw one's candidacy. *Fuller has decided to leave the arena and not stand as Conservative candidate after all.*

leave someone cold (informal) not interest someone; not stimulate someone's feelings; leave someone indifferent. *I'm sorry, but Jeff's bad luck story leaves me cold. It was all his own fault.*

leave one's mark (on something/someone) have a lasting influence on someone/something; affect someone recognizably. *John lived in America for twenty years before returning to England and the American way of life has certainly left its mark on him.*

leave someone/something standing (informal) be far superior to someone/something. *Kate is by far the best pupil in mathematics. She leaves all the others standing.*

leave someone to his own devices leave someone to manage a situation or solve a problem without help. *For a child to become independent, you have to leave him to his own devices now and again.*

leave well a'lone leave the situation as it is; not interfere or try to change something. *Bill and Tony have had a major disagreement. I'd like to talk to them about it, but I suppose it's best to leave well alone.*

lend itself to something be particularly suitable for something. *The novel would lend itself very well to a TV mini-series.*

let oneself go 1 be uninhibited in the expression of one's joy/pleasure etc.; not restrain one's feelings. *Brian really let himself go at Mike's party. He was singing, dancing and telling jokes and generally having a good time.* 2 neglect one's appearance or allow one's general attitude to life/work to deteriorate. *Andrew hardly ever shaves or changes his clothes these days. Why is he letting himself go like that?* □ *Father let himself go after Mother's death. For a year he didn't care about anything or anybody.*

let something go let the condition of something deteriorate. *The garden next door is in a terrible state. The neighbours have just let it go.*

let someone off the hook (informal) free someone from punishment or obligation to do something. *It's my turn to wash the dishes, but Dad said he would let me off the hook today because I have a lot of homework.*

let off steam (informal) expend surplus energy; relax tension. *'Why is Dad shouting at everyone today?' 'Don't worry. He's just letting off steam.'*

lie low hide and wait. *The police found no trace of the escaped convict. He's obviously lying low somewhere until he thinks it is safe.*

not/never look back continue to be successful or prosperous; never regret one's past course of action. *Since David completed a course in computer science at the Open University he's never looked back.*

look daggers at someone (informal) look at someone very angrily because of something he has just said or done. *When Peter looked daggers at me, I realized that my remark must have embarrassed him in front of his guests.*

look on the 'cheerful/dark etc. side take an optimistic/pessimistic view of a problem or difficulty. *Let's look on the cheerful side, shall we? The situation may not be as serious as we think.*

lose one's grip gradually lose one's control or understanding of something. *When Grandfather realized that he was beginning to lose his grip, he sold his car and began using public transport.*

lose one's nerve lose one's self-control; become afraid and panic. *I like driving on quiet roads, but I soon lose my nerve in heavy city traffic.*

lose the thread of something (e.g. of an argument or explanation) fail to follow or understand something to the end. *We lost the thread of his argument because he didn't express himself clearly enough.*

lose one's touch lose one's skill or ability at a particular task. *He used to be an excellent barrister, but because he lost a prominent murder case he felt that he was losing his touch.*

make a bolt for something/it (informal) suddenly run fast, e.g. to safety or in order to escape from danger or captivity. *When we saw the bull charging towards us, we had to make a bolt for the stone wall at one end of the field.*

make a bomb (slang) earn a lot of money from a business. *Fred's making a bomb with his video shop.*

make a change (from something) be a welcome alternative to one's routine. *Let's drive to the coast at the weekend. It would make a nice change.*

make a dash for something/it (informal) suddenly run fast in order to be in time for something, e.g. to catch a train. *The bus is just leaving. If we make a dash for it, we might be able to jump on.*

make a go of (doing) something (informal) make a success of (doing) something. *Robin has opened a café in the High Street. He's hoping that he will make a go of it.*

make a meal of something (informal) prolong an activity, e.g. because one is enjoying it or because one thinks it is more important than it is. *Don's been washing and polishing his car for two hours. He always makes a meal of it.*

make a mess/hash of something (informal) spoil or mismanage something; do something wrong or badly. *I'm afraid we made a mess of tiling the kitchen. It's more difficult than it looks.* □ *The index to the book was very long and I made a hash of it at first.*

make a mountain out of a molehill treat something as being more difficult or more serious etc. than it is. *Ron's remark wasn't meant to insult you. You're making a mountain out of a molehill.*

make a move (informal) leave; start a task etc. *It's been a lovely evening, but we really ought to make a move. It's late.*

make a name for oneself become known for one's accomplishments. *Maxwell made a name for himself as a physicist at an early age.*

make a scene (informal) argue loudly in public. *Two hotel guests were making a scene in the hotel lobby. It was most embarrassing for the manager.*

make amends (to someone) (for something) compensate for damage, injury, insult, wrongdoing etc. *The youth was obviously sorry that he had stolen the money and was willing to make amends.*

make oneself at home act with as much freedom as if one were at home. *I do hope you'll enjoy your stay with us. Please make yourselves at home.*

make do (with something) (informal) manage or be satisfied with something although it may be inferior in some way. *Peter's school trousers are too short for him, but he'll have to make do with them until the end of term.*

make the grade (informal) attain the required standard. *Peter would like to go to university, but his teachers don't think he'll make the grade.*

make (little/no etc.) headway make progress. *I've been trying to order these piles of papers but I'm not making much headway at present.*

make heavy weather of (doing) something (informal) find something difficult or troublesome. *David's trying to put up a shelf. I thought it was a simple job, but he seems to be making heavy weather of it.*

make light of something make something appear to be less serious or less difficult than it is. *A heart attack is always serious. Father shouldn't make light of it as he does.*

make mincemeat of someone/something (informal) easily defeat; show one's superiority over someone either physically or verbally. *Forbes made mincemeat of Fuller in the TV debate. He brought forward a much better argument.*

make one's presence felt use one's authority, power or strong personality to enforce one's will. *The children are getting rather boisterous. It's time we adults made our presence felt.*

make oneself scarce (informal) go away or keep out of sight so as not to be discovered or because it is tactful to do so. *When the headmaster appeared, the boys who had broken the window quickly made themselves scarce.*

make something stick (informal) prove something, e.g. an accusation or criminal charge; make others believe something said about or against someone, even if it is a lie. *It's one thing accusing Roberts of blackmail, but it's another making it stick in a court of law.*

mean business be serious or resolute in one's intentions. *We thought*

Patrick was joking when he talked of taking the matter to court, but he means business. He has already contacted his lawyer.

meet someone half-way   compromise with someone; come to a mutual agreement. *I won't buy you a new bicycle but I'll meet you half-way. You put in your savings and I'll pay the rest.*

meet one's match   encounter or be in competition with someone who has equal abilities. *Bill has had no difficulty beating all the other players in the chess tournament, but I think he's met his match in Charlotte.*

mind one's own business   not interfere in the affairs of others. *Pat asked me how much I earned, so I told her to mind her own business.*

miss the boat   miss a favourable opportunity; be too late to gain an advantage. *It's too late to send in an application form now. The closing date was the 30th of September. You've missed the boat, I'm afraid.*

nip something in the bud   put a stop to something undesirable at the outset, i.e. before it can develop into a problem. *We caught our thirteen-year-old smoking, so we decided to nip it in the bud there and then.*

pack one's bags   (informal) leave because one is dissatisfied or annoyed. *She didn't like the job, so after three months she packed her bags.*

pass the buck   pass the responsibility to someone else. *Don't try to pass the buck, Simon. It was your decision and yours alone, so now it's your responsibility.*

pick holes in something   criticize something or find fault with something unnecessarily. *It's easy to pick holes in our method, but can you suggest a better way of doing it?*

pick a quarrel/fight   try to begin a quarrel. *A man at the bar was trying to pick a quarrel by saying insulting things about foreigners, so we left.*

pick up the pieces   put right damage that has been done; put a confused state of affairs into good order again. *After a strike it takes weeks to pick up the pieces and get production back to normal again.*

pip someone at the post   defeat someone by a small margin or at the last moment. *Opinion polls showed the Labour candidate to be leading, but on election day he was pipped at the post by the Conservative candidate.*

play ball (with someone)   (informal) co-operate; comply with someone's wishes, sometimes unwillingly. *If Briggs won't play ball and give us the information, we'll have to find someone else who will.*

play one's cards well/right/badly etc.   (informal) act wisely or cleverly so as to gain an advantage from a situation. *If David plays his cards right, he can become editor of the newspaper within two years.*

play havoc with something   ruin something; put something at risk (e.g. one's health). *Cathy works too hard and doesn't get enough sleep. She's playing havoc with her health.*

play the game/by the rules   (informal) act fairly according to the rules. *Trevor, you've got to play the game. You can't promise to do something and then pretend you know nothing about it.*

play second fiddle to someone   be second in importance to someone. *Matthew always felt that he played second fiddle to his younger brother who was more intelligent and more successful than he was.*

play straight (with someone) (informal) behave honestly and fairly towards someone. *Can we rely on Williams? Is he playing straight or is he trying to cheat us?*

play with fire involve oneself in a risky or dangerous situation. *Judith's negotiating with two publishers at the same time for the same book. She's playing with fire.*

pull out all the stops (informal) use all one's resources or influence to achieve one's aim; spare no effort or energy. *Robert needs a large amount of money as soon as possible and he's pulling out all the stops to get it.*

pull the plug on someone (slang) damage someone's success, reputation, career prospects etc. *The higher you climb up the ladder of success, the more rivals you have who are likely to pull the plug on you.*

pull one's punches (informal) attack or criticize less severely than one could. (Often used in the negative.) *He said my novel showed promise. He liked the style and the story-line, and he wasn't pulling his punches just to be kind.*

pull rank (on someone) use one's superior position or rank to gain advantages or to secure privileges. *He's a Member of Parliament and he often pulls rank to get what he wants.*

pull one's socks up (informal) improve one's achievements by working harder; make a greater effort. *You'll have to pull your socks up and practise more if you intend to enter for the piano competition.*

pull (a few/the etc.) strings (informal) use one's personal influence or good connections in order to gain advantages for oneself or for others. *I've applied for a job at the hospital. Hugh knows someone on the hospital board so he's going to pull a few strings for me.*

pull one's weight do one's share of the work; contribute as much as others. *We'll never get the work finished if Ron doesn't pull his weight.*

push one's luck (informal) rely too much on continuing good luck. *You're pushing your luck, Frank. You've backed the winning horse twice, but you can't expect to win a third time.*

put down roots settle in a place. *I think Michael intends putting down roots here. He's looking for a job and a house.*

put one's (own) house in order organize one's own affairs or personal situation properly before criticizing that of others. *Before you tell me how to run my life, I would advise you to put your own house in order.*

put in an appearance (informal) attend a social function for a short time because one feels an obligation to do so. *I don't want to go to the club party, but as chairman I feel I ought to put in an appearance.*

put someone in the picture (informal) inform someone of the details of a situation. *Who are Jones and Fellows? What have they got to do with our plan? Would someone please put me in the picture?*

put someone in his (proper) place (informal) correct or criticize someone who has become over-confident. *One of the pupils was becoming increasingly aggressive until the teacher decided to put him in his place.*

put someone/something in the shade (informal) be far superior to someone/something else. *The winning song put all the others in the shade.*

put something on the map (informal) make something known to the public; give something a name. *It was the new product that put the company on the map. No one had ever heard of them before.*

put one's oar in (informal) interfere in or try to influence someone's personal affairs. *I admit that I did put my oar in, but in the end it was Frank's own decision to move here.*

put someone off the scent mislead someone, e.g. by giving him wrong information. *The murderer managed to put the police off the scent by incriminating someone else.*

put on airs behave in a self-important manner to impress others. *Roger certainly put on airs in the television interview. He gave the impression of being arrogant and self-opinionated.*

put someone on his guard warn someone that he must be careful. *Rumours that he was to be overthrown put the President on his guard.*

put/set someone on a pedestal (informal) treat someone as though he were far superior in moral or personal qualities, knowledge or ability etc. *The students tend to put their professor on a pedestal. They accept everything she says without question.*

put out (one's) feelers (informal) test what someone's reaction to something may be, e.g. by listening to opinions and asking careful questions. *Don't ask Graham outright if he's prepared to support your campaign. Put out feelers first. Talk to his friends and co-workers.*

put paid to something (informal) end or spoil something totally. *My neighbour's lawn-mower and his noisy children soon put paid to my quiet Saturday afternoon in the garden.*

put a 'spoke in someone's wheel (informal) hinder or prevent someone from making progress; cause an obstruction to someone's plan. *The government grant for our research project should be approved within the month, unless anyone puts a spoke in our wheel.*

put the boot in (slang) kick someone when he is already down; attack or treat someone unfairly. *First the landlord put up the rent. Then he really put the boot in by selling the property and turning the family out.*

put the frighteners on someone (slang) frighten someone into doing or not doing something. *Someone's trying to put the frighteners on us with anonymous phone calls so that we won't tell the police what we know.*

put/set the record straight correct wrong information or beliefs. *Just to set the record straight, it was my brother who smashed the car, not me.*

put the screws on someone (slang) pressure someone into doing or not doing something, often with physical force. *When the gang realized that one of their members was withholding information, they put the screws on him to tell them what he knew.*

put one's money on someone/something (informal) be confident that someone will be successful or that something will happen etc. *I'm putting my money on David. Chris plays just as well, but in a tournament David has the stronger nerves. □ Labour will win the next election. You can put your money on it.*

put the skids under someone (slang) make someone hurry; cause someone difficulty or unpleasantness. *Someone in Ken's department is trying to put the skids under him. He's had a lot of problems recently that he didn't cause.*

put the tin lid on something (informal) end or ruin an activity or plan etc. *Jack had plans to go skiing, but he broke his leg a week before, so that put the tin lid on his holiday.*

put one's 'thinking cap on (informal) try to think of a solution or consider ideas. *It isn't an easy problem to solve. We'll have to put our thinking caps on.*

put someone through his paces test someone's capabilities, see what someone can do, e.g. in a new job. *The idea of the seminar is to put the junior teachers through their paces.*

put someone through the mill put someone through an unpleasant experience, e.g. by thorough testing or through severe disciplinary measures. *They certainly put me through the mill at the oral examination. They asked some extremely tricky questions.*

raise hell (informal) create a great disturbance; protest or complain loudly and angrily. *My father raised hell when I told him that I had decided to spend all my savings on a motor bike.*

raise the roof (informal) make a lot of noise or disturbance, e.g. by clapping, laughing, shouting angrily etc. *The audience loved the comedian at the theatre last night. They really raised the roof.*

rest on one's laurels enjoy a period of inactivity or rest as a reward for some achievement. *I've finished the translation at last, but I can't afford to rest on my laurels because I have another one to do before Friday.*

ring a (familiar/faint etc.) bell seem familiar; remind one vaguely of someone/something. *Her name rings a bell. I've probably read one of her novels at some time.*

rise to the occasion cope with a situation adequately, even if one was not expected to do so. *When the guest speaker fell ill Mary was asked to give a talk at short notice. Everyone agreed that she rose to the occasion very well.*

rock the boat (informal) cause upset or disturbance which spoils a pleasant event or satisfactory situation etc. *We were all happy with the progress of our work until Murray rocked the boat by persuading some of us to do it differently.*

roll up one's sleeves (informal) prepare oneself to start working. *If your teacher wants the French essay written by tomorrow, it's time you rolled up your sleeves.*

rule the roost (informal) be in control; dominate or direct others. *It's Mum who rules the roost in our house, but she always asks Dad what he thinks.*

run in the family (a physical feature, a talent, character trait etc.) recur and thus become characteristic of the family through different generations. *The children are all very musical, as are the parents and grandparents. It runs in the family.*

run riot behave in an uncontrollable manner. *When the teacher went into the classroom the children were running riot, throwing books and running over the desks.*

run the gauntlet (of someone/something) endure (usually justified) attack or criticism. *A major pharmaceutical concern is still running the gauntlet after one of its most popular drugs was taken off the market.*

run true to form act as one is expected to, according to one's usual behaviour; happen as expected. *The firm is running true to form again. Delivery is six weeks late.*

save one's/someone's bacon (informal) manage to save oneself or someone else from danger, failure, criticism, punishment etc. *The teacher knew that it was Tom who had torn the book, and the boy managed to save his bacon by admitting it straightaway.*

save one's breath (informal) not waste one's time talking because it has no effect on one's listeners. *No one is listening to your advice, so you might just as well save your breath.*

say one's piece (informal) say to others what one has planned or intended to say; state one's opinion or thoughts to others. *Not now, Jim. You'll have the chance to say your piece later at the meeting.*

see fit (to do something) consider it correct, advisable or advantageous to do something. *Mr Perry wouldn't sign our petition. He obviously doesn't see fit to support our cause.*

see someone/something in a different/better etc. light see someone/something from a different point of view; change one's opinion about someone/something. *A long talk with Kate's teacher helped us to see our child in a different light.*

see life experience different aspects of life, people and countries. *He joined the army to see life, but he spent two years at a training camp near his home town.*

see reason/sense realize what is a reasonable or sensible course of action after thinking carefully about one's situation or after taking advice. *Our talk helped John to see reason. He has decided to apply for a place at college now.*

see the light (informal) be converted in one's way of thinking; realize one is wrong. *Some of the men wanted to strike but when the union leader explained that the time was wrong they saw the light.*

see the sights visit buildings or places worth seeing in a city or country. *We spent a wonderful week in Venice and Florence seeing the sights.*

see the world travel around the world; work or live in different countries. *As a technical sales consultant for a multi-national company he had plenty of opportunity to see the world.*

sell oneself short be too modest in one's assessment of oneself, one's abilities and experience; undervalue oneself. *I've warned Barbara not to sell herself short at the interview tomorrow.*

send someone about his business send someone away; stop someone from interfering in things that do not concern him. *A pupil was trying to* *listen in on a private conversation in the staff room, but the headmistress soon sent him about his business.*

send someone packing (informal) tell someone to go away; dismiss someone from his job, often hastily or in anger. *If he comes here again asking for money, send him packing!*

serve someone right (informal) be a just punishment for something one has done. *It will serve you right if your toys get broken. You shouldn't leave them lying around for people to step on.*

set one's sights on something aim at having/doing something. *She's set her sights on becoming the first lady president of the USA.*

set/start/get the 'ball rolling (informal) set something in motion, e.g. an activity, a conversation etc. *It was a junior reporter who set the ball rolling. He suspected a cover-up story and informed the editor, who then ordered a full investigation.* Note also: **keep the ball rolling.**

set the pace fix the speed, rate or standard which all others try to follow; take the lead in a competitive situation. *The good pupils usually set the pace in a mixed ability class.* □ *We are expecting our new designs to set the pace in fashion for the coming winter season.*

set the scene for something prepare others to expect something. *Compromise on both sides had set the scene for peaceful and constructive talks between the two nations.*

settle a score (with someone) (informal) take one's revenge (on someone) for harm etc. done to one in the past. *When Brewster came out of prison he said he had a score to settle with the man who had put him there.*

show one's true colours (informal) reveal one's true (usually bad) character, intentions or plans etc. *We thought Ed was our friend, but he showed his true colours when we needed his help and he didn't give it.*

sit on the fence (informal) stay neutral and not take sides (e.g. in an argument); be undecided which of two opposite courses of action to take. *No decision has been taken about the building of the new airport. The authorities are still sitting on the fence.*

sit tight wait patiently and see what happens; stay in one place and do nothing. *When the air traffic controllers were on strike we had no choice but to sit tight at the airport and wait.*

speak for itself/themselves something needs no further comment because it is clear. *The new teaching method is a great success. The results speak for themselves.*

speak volumes (for someone/something) (informal) show clearly the nature of something; give enough evidence of something. *The fact that the team won every game of the season speaks volumes for their new trainer.*

spill the beans (informal) tell a secret or let out information or news before one should do so. *The father showed the children the present for their mother's birthday and asked them not to spill the beans.*

spread one's wings develop one's activities or interests further. *After his successful novel he's thinking of spreading his wings and writing for television as well.*

stand a (fair/good/poor etc.) chance (of something) have fair etc.

prospects of doing or achieving something. *With such good exam results she stands an excellent chance of getting a place at university.*

stand/hold one's ground maintain or defend one's position, e.g. in an argument. *Whatever you do, make sure you stand your ground in the discussion. We can't afford a change of policy.*

stand on ceremony pay too much attention to correct rules of behaviour and etiquette; be too formal. *Don't stand on ceremony with him just because he has a title. He's no different from the rest of us.*

stand the pace be able to maintain the fixed speed, rate or level of achievement etc. of others. *I was put in a Spanish class with intermediate students, but as a beginner I couldn't stand the pace.*

stand to gain/win/lose etc. (something) be in a position to or be likely to gain something etc. *If he makes a mistake now he stands to lose a lot of money.*

stay put remain in the same place; not move. *These dictionaries have to stay put. They are for reference and not for borrowing.*

stay/survive/last the course continue with an activity or a competition etc. until the end. *Louise is finding the hospital training very strenuous. She's not sure that she'll be able to stay the course.*

steal the show receive more attention, applause etc. than anyone else. *Don't let Mark steal the show when it was you who did all the work. You prepared the talk, so why not give it yourself?*

steer clear of someone/something avoid someone/something because of the difficulties, danger, unpleasantness etc. that may be involved. *If I were you, I would steer clear of fatty and spicy foods until your stomach's better.*

stew in one's own juice (informal) suffer the consequences of one's own foolish actions without help from others. *David has no one to play with today. It's his own fault for quarrelling with his friends and it will do him good to stew in his own juice.*

stick to one's guns (informal) be firm and resolute; not be influenced in one's point of view. *If Mary thinks she's right, she'll stick to her guns no matter what anyone else tells her.*

stop/stick at nothing do everything necessary to accomplish one's aim, even if it is dishonest, unscrupulous or dangerous etc. *Don't trust Wilson. He's the sort of person who'll stick at nothing to get what he wants.*

strike lucky be lucky in finding what one is looking for or what one needs. *I struck lucky in the winter sales. I was looking for a coat and found just what I wanted.*

sugar/sweeten the pill make something that is unpleasant seem more pleasant. *Some airlines are putting up their prices, but to sugar the pill they are offering an improved in-flight service.*

suit someone (right) down to the ground (arrangements, plans etc.) suit someone perfectly. *The tour includes a lot of visits to museums, which will suit Beth down to the ground. Looking round museums is her favourite pastime.*

sweep/brush something under the carpet (informal) hide or forget something that one prefers not to remember because it is shameful or may cause trouble etc. *It's a political scandal and the opposition won't let the government simply sweep it under the carpet.*

swim/go with/against the tide/current conform/not conform in one's opinions or actions to general tendencies; do/not do what everyone else is doing. *In politics it's sometimes wiser to swim with the tide than to take an individual course.*

take a dim/poor view of someone/something (informal) disapprove of or be disappointed in someone's behaviour or actions; disapprove of something. *Granny will take a dim view of your not going to see her on her birthday.*

take a hint understand what is meant or stated indirectly (e.g. a suggestion or advice) and act accordingly. *All right, David, I can take a hint. That big yawn meant that you're tired and you want me to leave.*

take a joke not be offended by something said or done teasingly or for fun at one's expense. *I can take a joke, but I don't think that putting salt in my coffee instead of sugar is very funny.*

take a leaf out of someone's book follow someone's good example. *Peter's working hard at school, but unfortunately I can't say the same for his sister. I wish she would take a leaf out of Peter's book.*

take/have a 'rain check (on/for something) (US, informal) postpone accepting something until a later time. *'Come on. I'll buy you lunch.' 'Thanks, not today, but I'll take a rain check on it.'*

take/get a rise out of someone (informal) mock or make fun of someone, usually with the intention to hurt. *I remember that some pupils in my class used to take a rise out of me because I was small and fat.*

take advantage of someone use someone's weakness to get what one wants. *A lot of door-to-door salesmen take advantage of old people and sell them things that they don't need.*

take advantage of something make use of or get benefit from the opportunities/facilities that are available. *A lot of students on the course took advantage of the language laboratory facilities in their free time.*

take something amiss misunderstand someone's intentions and be offended or insulted. *I didn't have time to ask Mrs Bates in when she called this morning. I hope she didn't take it amiss.*

take something as read regard something as being known or understood even if it is not expressly stated. *You will all have heard why Mr Baxter can't be with us today, so we'll take it as read and start the meeting.*

take someone/something by storm make a great impression or impact on someone/something. *The latest designs from Italy have taken the fashion world by storm.*

take someone 'down a peg (or two) (informal) lower someone's pride because he has been acting over-confidently. *The new assistant walks round the building as if he owns the place, telling people how to do their jobs. He needs taking down a peg.*

take someone for a ride (informal) cheat someone, often in money matters. *Don't buy a second-hand TV from Sam. He'll probably take you for a ride and sell you one that's faulty.*

take one's 'hat off to someone (informal) admire someone's achievements. *They adopted a 13-year-old and did an excellent job of bringing him up. I have to take my hat off to them.*

take something in one's stride deal with a problem or difficulty calmly and without much effort. *When Susan changed schools she found that she was behind in a few subjects, but she took it all in her stride and soon caught up on the work.*

take its toll (of something) cause a lot of harm or damage. *He's worked outside in all kinds of weather all his life and now it seems to be taking its toll of his health.*

not take kindly to someone/something resent or not welcome someone/something. *Bob won't take kindly to Andrew's words of advice. He doesn't like people interfering and telling him what to do.*

take leave of one's senses act in an irrational, unwise or unfitting manner. *He's spent all his redundancy pay on a Rolls Royce! He must have taken leave of his senses.*

take something lying down (informal) accept criticism, unfair treatment etc. without objection. *That's slander! Dodson can't expect me to take this lying down. I shall see my lawyer immediately.*

not take no for an answer (informal) refuse to accept someone's rejection, refusal or objection to something. *I've told her twice that I can't lend her my car but she still keeps asking. She simply won't take no for an answer.*

take one's pick (informal) choose from several possibilities. *You can have any one of these books for just £1, so take your pick.*

take pot luck (informal) take a chance; accept whatever one gets without knowing in advance whether it is good or bad. *When you go abroad as an au pair you usually have to take pot luck with the family you get.*

take shape become or look real; materialize. *The book is beginning to take shape. She's already drafted two or three chapters.*

take sides (with someone) defend or support one of two people in an argument etc. *I know John and I aren't the best of friends, but I didn't expect him to take sides with my biggest rival.*

take some/a lot of doing (informal) be difficult to realize, accomplish or put into practice. *Building up a business out of nothing wasn't easy. It took a lot of doing.*

take (the) (necessary/appropriate etc.) steps (to do something) take necessary or suitable action in order to achieve something. *Several cases of stealing had been reported, so the headmistress took necessary steps to put an end to it.*

take the biscuit (informal) be the best example of some usually negative characteristic. *I've often had difficult pupils to deal with, but for laziness young Smith really takes the biscuit.*

take the floor stand up and address an audience. *Everyone had been looking forward to Jane's speech, so we all clapped when she was asked to take the floor.*

take the lid off something (informal) reveal information that was previously secret or confidential. *Yesterday the Prime Minister took the lid off her plans for a cabinet shake-up.*

take the plunge (informal) stop hesitating and finally do something planned. *Sharon has been thinking about going to work in the States. At last she's taken the plunge and has applied for a visa and work permit.*

take the rap (for someone/something) (slang) take punishment for a mistake or crime whether one is guilty or not. *I'm going to tell Mr Hollings that it wasn't my mistake and that I know who broke his window. I'm not going to take the rap for Charlie Adams.*

take the rough with the smooth (informal) accept and be prepared to deal with the bad as well as the good. *As an actor you can be a success one day and forgotten the next. You have to be prepared to take the rough with the smooth.*

take the 'wind out of someone's sails (informal) put a sudden and surprising end to someone's over-confidence. *Trevor used to boast about being the best player in the chess club until a new member – a boy of fifteen – beat him. That certainly took the wind out of his sails!*

take someone/something to bits/pieces skilfully criticize and destroy someone's character, conduct or argument. *I didn't have a chance in the debate. Peter is such a clever talker and he simply took me to pieces.*

take someone to task (for something) reprimand or criticize someone for a mistake, failure, bad work etc. *It's the first mistake I've made and I didn't expect to be taken to task for it. Is Mrs Murphy always so intolerant?*

take someone to the cleaners (slang) cheat someone out of a lot of money; cause someone to spend a lot of money on one. *She's thirty years younger than him and has no serious intentions. We've warned him that she'll take him to the cleaners.*

take someone under one's wing protect, help, care for or guide someone. *Barry seems to have taken the new pupil under his wing. He's introducing him to his friends and showing him around the school.*

talk through (the top of) one's hat (informal) talk foolishly or ignorantly. *What he said was nonsense. He was talking through his hat again.*

teach someone a lesson make someone improve his behaviour by punishment or by an unpleasant experience. *You were teasing the cat again and this time she scratched you. That will teach you a lesson!*

tell someone where to get 'off (informal) criticize someone strongly; tell someone what you think of him/his behaviour etc. *The next time she comes in here poking her nose into my personal affairs, I shall tell her where to get off!*

think better of something reconsider and decide not to do something. *I almost asked Susan to the party, but I thought better of it and didn't say anything. I don't think she would want to come.*

(not) think twice about doing something do something immediately without pausing to consider it. *If I had the chance of going to Australia I wouldn't think twice about it.*

throw a fit (informal) become extremely angry. *Mother will throw a fit when she sees what I've done to her car.*

throw a party (for someone) organize a party or celebration. *We're throwing a party for Ken on Saturday to celebrate his return from Nigeria.*

throw one's 'hat into the ring signal one's will to compete or become a candidate in an election etc. *So far there is no Liberal candidate for the constituency. Political observers are wondering who's going to throw his hat into the ring.*

throw in the towel (informal) admit defeat or failure and give up trying; lose one's will to try. *He's failed his driving test three times and I have the feeling that he's going to throw in the towel.*

throw someone off (his) balance confuse or shock someone so that he does not know how to react. *I was expecting a transfer to Glasgow, but the news that I am to be sent to China completely threw me off my balance.*

throw the book (of rules) at someone (informal) reprimand someone for not having done something the correct or official way. *This time he threw the book at me for not showing him the report before I sent it to head office. Usually he doesn't want the trouble of having to read them.*

throw one's weight about/around use one's authority or superior position in an arrogant way. *If Barnes starts throwing his weight around in here again, I'll ask him to leave. He may be chairman of the council but in my pub he's just a customer.*

tighten one's belt (informal) spend less money at a time of financial difficulty. *When Mother lost her job we all had to tighten our belts and manage on Father's small wage.*

tip the balance/scales settle a matter that was previously undecided. *The fact that Miller was willing to travel abroad tipped the scales in his favour. The other applicant was just as suitable but he wanted a home-based job.*

touch base (with someone) (US, informal) make contact with someone. *Hello, Pete! I wanted to touch base with you before I return to the States, so here I am.*

toy with an idea think about an idea but not really have serious intentions of putting it into practice. *Betty has been toying with the idea of joining the army, but I don't think she will.*

turn over a new leaf completely change one's behaviour or views for the better; improve oneself and start again. *Since Ted came out of prison he has turned over a new leaf. He's determined to lead a better life.*

turn the corner pass or overcome the most dangerous, difficult or critical part of something. *Father was critically ill after the heart attack, but he's turned the corner now.*

turn the tables (on someone) reverse the situation so that one's rival/opponent loses his advantage and becomes the weaker etc. *Roger once refused to help Mike financially, so when the tables were turned after Roger had lost all his money, Mike didn't help him.*

turn up/out trumps (informal) be a reliable friend to someone at a time of trouble. *You once turned up trumps for me when I needed support, so I shall do the same for you now.*

upset the 'applecart spoil a plan that was well organized; spoil someone's progress. *There are six jobs to do and six helpers to do them, so if anyone else volunteers, say no, or it will upset the applecart.*

wait one's turn wait until it is one's turn to do something. *You can't make an appointment with the doctor on Fridays. You just go to his surgery and wait your turn.*

not want to know (informal) not be interested in and not want to be concerned with someone's situation; ignore someone's difficulties. *If you're out of work and down on your luck most of your former friends just don't want to know.*

wash one's dirty linen in public (informal) reveal private or family secrets, scandals etc. publicly. *We must not allow this matter to be taken to court. The last thing we want to do is to wash our dirty linen in public.*

watch/mind one's step (informal) be careful in one's actions or behaviour so as not to make a mistake or get into trouble or danger. *The robbers are likely to be armed, so you had better tell the men to watch their step, constable.*

weather/ride the storm survive a crisis; overcome difficulties. *Industry has been badly hit by the recession. Several small firms are still trying to weather the storm.*

wipe the floor with someone (informal) triumph over someone; beat or defeat someone easily. *What a terrible game! Our players hadn't got a chance. The visiting team wiped the floor with them.*

wipe the slate 'clean put right what is wrong and begin again; forget past mistakes, arguments, trouble or crimes. *Smith and Walker had been rivals for years, but when Smith's daughter married Walker's son they decided to wipe the slate clean and become friends.*

work/do wonders/miracles have a very beneficial effect; bring improvement or very good results. *You need a rest and some fresh air. A weekend by the sea would do wonders.* □ *This new cream is supposed to work miracles on your skin.*

8 Idioms from special subjects

This chapter presents idioms, terms and expressions from special subjects for easy learning and reference. It groups together idioms and phrases which are typically used in the following situations: **banking; business; buying and selling; health, illness, death; motoring; politics and government; the Stock Exchange; telephoning; travel; work and industrial relations.**

Banking

You **open/close a 'bank account.** You **pay money 'in** and **draw money 'out.** If you have **a 'current/cheque account** (US **a 'checking account**) you can pay in and draw out as you wish. If you have **a de'posit account** (GB only) or **a 'savings account** (GB/US) you receive interest on that money. In order to withdraw from such an account, you usually have to **give notice (of withdrawal).** A **'joint account** is one that can be used by two or more people, e.g. husband and wife. If there is money in your current account you are **in the black.** If you owe money to the bank because your account is overdrawn you are **in the red.**

You **pay in cash/by cheque/on credit (by credit card).** You can **charge something to** a credit card, e.g. American Express, Access, Visa.

When you **write/make out a cheque (to someone)** for an amount of money, you are the **drawer.** If the **cheque bounces** (informal) you have not got enough money in the account to cover payment of the cheque. The cheque is then returned to the payee marked **R/D (return to drawer).** **An open cheque** can be cashed at a bank by the payee. **A crossed cheque** (with two parallel lines printed or drawn on it) can be paid into the payee's account only, i.e. it is safe. **A 'bearer cheque** has the word 'bearer' written on it. It can be cashed by anyone who has it and is therefore not safe. **A blank cheque** is a signed cheque without an amount written on it. Usually, the amount to be paid is not known at the time of writing out the cheque and is filled in by the payee later. **A post-dated cheque** has a future date on it. This ensures that the cheque cannot be cashed until there is enough money in the drawer's account to cover the amount on the cheque.

A standing order is an order to the bank to pay the same amount regularly to the same payee, e.g. one's rent, subscriptions.

If you need to borrow from the bank you **take out a loan.** If you need a very large sum in order to buy a house you **take out a mortgage.**

Business

A business **runs at a profit** or **runs at a loss**, i.e. it makes or loses money. If a business makes neither a profit nor a loss it **breaks even**. You **open (up)/set up a business** or you **go into business**. You **close 'down a business/go out of business**.

A single person who **runs a business** is **a sole trader**. If a private company decides to offer shares in the company to the general public, the company is said to **go 'public**. One company may **take 'over** another company, i.e. take control or ownership. Note the noun: **a 'takeover**. The directors of a company are known as **the board**. A **'board meeting** is thus a meeting of the directors. **A sleeping partner** (US **a silent partner**) is a person who provides a percentage of the capital of a business but who does not play a part in its management.

We say that a company's finances are **in good/bad shape**. If a company cannot pay its debts it must **go into liquidation**. We also say that this company **is wound 'up**, i.e. ceases to exist. If a private person cannot pay his debts he is said to **go/be bankrupt** or go **'bust** (informal).

You **do business** with someone. You **bring/pull 'off a (business) deal**, i.e. complete a deal successfully. Someone may **pull a fast deal** (informal), i.e. deal unfairly. **Sharp practice(s)** means dishonest business dealings. If you **talk business** or **talk shop** (informal), you talk about business.

Buying and selling

Before you buy something you may **shop a'round**, i.e. compare prices at different shops. If you **go 'window-shopping** you only look at the goods in the shop windows, you do not go inside or buy. If you **buy in bulk** you buy in large quantities at a cheaper price. If you **buy something 'in**, you make a special order/purchase of something so that it is in stock. You may buy goods/clothes etc. **at/in the sales**, i.e. at special times of the year when goods are reduced in price for approximately two weeks, in order to clear old stock. We say **the sales are 'on/over**.

You may **shop with (a particular shop)**, i.e. buy regularly from a particular shop. An article may be **a good/bad buy**, i.e. well worth/not worth the money paid. You may **take goods on approval**, i.e. buy goods that you can return soon after the purchase date if you are not satisfied. You may **buy something on hire purchase**, i.e. pay in weekly or monthly instalments. This is also called buying **on (the) HP** (informal) or **on the never(-'never)** (informal). You can **pay cash** or **pay by cheque/credit card**. You may **run up an account/bill (with a shop/firm)**, i.e. buy goods **on credit**. If you are allowed to do this regularly you can **open an account** with the shop. The shop will **charge goods to your account**. To **settle an account** is to pay a bill.

Shops may sometimes sell **seconds**, i.e. goods which have a small flaw or defect or which are shop-soiled. A shop may **sell something** 'off, i.e. sell the remaining stock of an article cheaply. A shop may **sell** 'out of something, i.e. have nothing left of a particular article. If an article **sells like** 'hot cakes it is **in demand**, i.e. it sells very well. A shop may **sell cut** 'price, i.e. below the normal price of other shops. If an article is **in stock** it is actually in the shop to sell. If it is temporarily **out of stock** it is not there and must be ordered. We also say the shop **is** 'out of something.

In order to attract customers, supermarkets often sell an article at a very low price. This is called **a** 'loss leader because the supermarket **makes a loss** on this article. When advertising an article **hard sell** methods may be used, i.e. a forceful, aggressive, insistent technique. A **soft sell** approach is more subtle, based on indirect suggestion. Some supermarkets and petrol stations give their customers 'trading stamps for the amount spent. Customers collect these stamps and can exchange them for goods or cash.

The 'lower end of the market refers to consumers who buy cheap goods. Note the adjective: 'down-market. The 'upper end of the market means the consumers who buy expensive goods. Note the adjective: 'up-market.

A shopkeeper/supermarket etc. may **put prices** 'up and occasionally **bring prices** 'down. A shopkeeper may **knock money** 'off an article, i.e. sell it for less than the price on the label, when the article has a slight defect, for example.

An amount/bill/invoice which has not been paid is called **an outstanding amount** etc. **Bad debts** are customers' debts which are not expected to be paid, i.e. a loss for the shopkeeper.

A 'shop-lifter is a person who steals from shops while pretending to be a customer, i.e. during business hours. A shop-lifter hides goods on his person and does not pay for them at the counter/cash-desk or **(supermarket)** 'check-out, i.e. the place where one pays and can pack/wrap one's goods before leaving.

A small business may **be run on a** 'shoe-string, i.e. with very low maintenance costs. A shopkeeper or owner of a business may **do a** 'roaring trade, be raking/coining it 'in (informal), **be making a bomb/a packet/a pile/a fortune** (informal), i.e. make high profits.

You may **put something up for sale/auction**, i.e. offer it for sale/auction (e.g. a house, a painting). The item is then said to **be up for sale/auction**. To **bring something under the hammer** is to sell it by auction. Goods or property **come under the hammer**. An item can **fetch a price** or **go for a price**. *The house fetched/went for £73,500.* An item may **go for a song**, i.e. very cheaply, under its true value. To **sell someone** 'up means to sell someone's goods or property forcibly as payment for bad debts.

Health, illness, death

If a person is in good health he may be described in the following ways: he **is/looks the picture of health**; he **feels on top of the world**; he **has never felt better**; he **is fighting fit**; he **is in pretty good shape**; he **is (feeling) above par**.

If a person is not feeling well he may be described thus: he **is not feeling himself**; he **is not feeling (quite) up to the mark**; he **is feeling (rather/somewhat) under the weather**; he **is (feeling) (somewhat/ rather/a bit etc.) below par**; he **is not feeling so hot**.

If a person is seriously ill one may say: he **is in bad/poor shape**; he **is in a bad way** (informal). If a person becomes worse/better we say that he **has taken a turn for the worse/better**.

When a person becomes ill we use the following idioms:

fall/be taken ill (with something) *She fell ill with/was taken ill with influenza last week.* US usage is **get sick**. *Getting sick away from home is usually very unpleasant.*

go/come down with something *He went down with gastric flu last week. I hope I'm not going to come down with it too!*

get/catch/contract a disease *He caught malaria when he was in the tropics.*

Note that **ill** is GB usage, **sick** is US usage. In GB usage **be sick** means *vomit, throw 'up*. A person who vomits **cannot keep anything 'down**. In US usage, **be sick** means simply *be ill*, e.g. with flu. If a person is forced to stay in bed or at home because of an illness, a broken leg etc., he **is laid 'up with** the illness.

If a person is very ill, he may **go into/be taken to hospital** (US **be hospitalized**). In hospital, the doctors may **run some tests**.

When a person is recovering from an illness we say: he **is on the mend**; he **is over the worst**; he **is picking 'up**; he **is getting 'over it**; he **is doing well**; he **is improving by the day** (i.e. every day).

If you **catch a cold** you are ill with a cold. If you manage to **throw 'off/ fight 'off a cold** (or minor illness) you do not become ill with a cold etc.

In Britain and America body temperature is measured in degrees Fahrenheit. Normal body temperature is 98.6 (ninety-eight point six). When the body temperature is too high we use the idiom **run/be running/have a (slight/high) temperature**. The doctor **takes someone's temperature**.

When a person is exhausted we can use the following: he **is/looks/feels worn 'out/all 'in**, he **has 'had it**. When a person is pale and tired, due to overwork, illness, weakness etc. he **is/looks/feels washed 'out/run 'down**.

When a person is critically ill we say he **is on the critical/danger list**, he **may not 'make it/make the night/pull 'through/come 'through it**, it

is touch and go (with him). Such patients are usually **in intensive care/in the intensive care unit,** i.e. are in a special care unit under continuous observation by the nursing staff.

The most simple way of talking about **death** is to use the verb **die** and the adjective **dead.** However, several idioms are also used:

pass a'way (formal) *Mr Henderson passed away peacefully in the night.*

depart this life (formal, church language).

kick the bucket; 'snuff it; peg 'out (informal, humorous) *The old chap kicked the bucket/snuffed it before he had chance to make his will.* □ *Don't worry about me! I've no intention of pegging out just yet!*

Motoring

If your car is new it is not good to **rev up the engine** too much (US **gun the motor**), i.e. increase the speed of revolutions of the engine by accelerating too fast.

In order to **drive 'off** you must **put the car in gear.** You drive off **in first** or **in bottom (gear),** then you **change ('up) into second/third (gear)** or **go/move into second (gear)** etc. When you drive fast you are **in fourth/ fifth/top (gear).** When you **change 'down** you are in a lower gear. If the car **is not in gear** it will not move: you are **in neutral (gear).** To drive backwards, you must be **in reverse (gear).** You **put the car into reverse.**

When you drive faster you **speed 'up/get 'speed up.** This is also expressed by **put one's 'foot down** (i.e. on the accelerator). When you reduce speed you **slow 'down.** If another vehicle **has the right of 'way,** i.e. is allowed to move before you, you must **give 'way** (US **yield**). If you have to stop suddenly you may **jam on the brakes,** i.e. suddenly use the brakes to full capacity. This may be necessary if another vehicle **cuts 'in** in front of you, i.e. drives in front without warning.

When you stop a vehicle you **pull 'up/pull 'in/pull into the side/pull off the road.** A stopping-place at the side of a road (not in a town) is **a 'lay-by** (US **a 'pull-in**). You **pull 'out** when you move into the traffic or when you overtake another vehicle. When you reverse a car you **back ('in/ out/up).** *You can back in here and park in this yard.* □ *When you back out of the garage, just be careful!* □ *Come on, you can back up a little bit more. There's enough room.* When you drive forwards very slowly and carefully, e.g. when parking, you **nose 'in/out/up.** You **bear right/left** when following a road that branches to the right/left. You **take a right/left (turn)** when you **turn 'off** to the right/left at a crossroads or junction.

A bad driver may **hog the road,** i.e. drive slowly in the middle, not allowing cars behind to pass. He is **a 'road-hog.**

On the **motorway** (US **super highway/freeway/expressway**) you can use **the 'slow/inside lane** or **the 'fast/outside lane.** On a wide road there may be **three-** or even **four-lane traffic. A dual 'carriageway**

(US **a divided 'highway**) is a fast road with two lanes in each direction. **A 'trunk road** (GB) is a main road. **A 'bypass** is a wide road passing around a town or an area of heavy traffic. **A 'flyover** (US **'overpass**) is a road or bridge which crosses above another road. **A 'bottleneck** is a narrower part of a wide road where the traffic is held up. Where two roads come together to form one, the traffic from the minor road must **filter 'in**, i.e. move carefully into the main stream of traffic.

When the roads are busy you may be **caught/stuck/held 'up in a 'traffic jam**. This happens in **the 'rush-hour** or **at 'peak periods**, i.e. when the traffic is at its heaviest in the morning and in the evening.

If you drive too fast and **break the 'speed limit** you will **get a ticket (for speeding)** (informal), i.e. a police fine. If you park your vehicle in an unauthorized place, you may **get a 'parking ticket**.

You go to a **'filling/ petrol station** (US **'gas station**) to **fill 'up (with petrol/gas)**. A driver may ask the attendant to **fill her 'up** (i.e. the car/ tank).

A big accident where many cars have **run 'into** each other is called **a 'pile-up**. If you **have a smash** you have quite a bad accident with another vehicle. If you **have a knock/bump** there is only a little damage. A car can **smash/knock/bump/run/back into** another vehicle. If you **hit an oncoming car**, i.e. an approaching car, you **have a 'head-on collision**. If your vehicle is very badly damaged and cannot be repaired, you **write the car 'off** (US you **total the car**). The car is a **'write-off** (US **is totalled**).

A car may **do/average 25 (miles) to the gallon**, i.e. can travel 25 miles (on average) using one gallon of petrol. The driver can **get 25 to the gallon**. If a car is economical we can say it **gets very good mileage**. We say a car **has done** (i.e. driven) **5000 (miles)**.

You **run a car**, i.e. you own and use it. The costs are called **the 'running costs**.

Politics and government

The following expressions are relevant to politics and government in Great Britain.

The Commons is the House of Commons or Lower House of Parliament. **The Lords** is the House of Lords or Upper House of Parliament. It has limited power.

A member of the Commons is called **an MP** (Member of Parliament). An MP represents a constituency, the voters of which elect him to Parliament. At a general election, a candidate can **win/lose a/his seat**. An MP is said to have **a safe seat** if the electorate always votes for the party that he represents, i.e. always Conservative/Labour/Liberal etc. by tradition. The MP holding the seat for a particular constituency is called **the sitting member**.

If the Prime Minister thinks that the chances for re-election are good he may decide to **go to the country** before the end of his term of office, i.e. call a general election. The political party which governs the country is said to **hold office/be in office** or **be in power**.

A candidate for political office **stands/runs for election/office**. The candidate who gets the most votes is said to **get 'in** (informal). A **'by-election** is an election which has to be held in a single constituency while a government is in office, usually because of an MP's death or resignation.

Shadow means 'in opposition'. Thus, the **Shadow Cabinet** is the group of ministers of the parliamentary opposition, i.e. the party which is not in power. Other examples are: **Shadow Foreign Secretary, Shadow Chancellor,** etc.

The first introductory speech made in the House by a new MP is called **a maiden speech. The Speaker** is the officer in the Commons who directs the debates and keeps order. MPs who are not ministers, i.e. do not hold office, are known as **the back-benchers** because they sit on the back bench(es) furthest away from the Speaker's chair. The **front-benchers** are the more important members who **hold office**, i.e. are ministers. They sit on the front bench(es) nearest to the Speaker's chair.

In order to become law, a bill (a draft of an **Act of Parliament**) must **pass through the first/second/third reading** in the Commons, i.e. it must be presented, discussed and amended three times. If the **bill is adopted/passed**, i.e. accepted by the Commons at the third reading, it is **sent 'up** to the Lords (or **sent 'down** to the Commons if it was introduced by the Lords). When the bill is passed, it is said to have been **put through the Commons/Lords**. The **bill goes 'through**. If a bill is not accepted, it is said to have been **thrown 'out/defeated/rejected**.

The Stock Exchange

The financial and commercial part of London including the Stock Exchange and the banks is referred to as **the City**. A **'City man** is therefore a man who is engaged in commerce, banking or finance in the City. **'Wall Street** is the American money market.

A **'falling market** or a **'bear market** means that share prices are dropping. A **'strong market** or a **'bull market** means that share prices are rising. When shares **are looking 'up** their value is increasing after a period of low value. If shares **touch 'bottom** they fall very low indeed and they **bottom 'out** if they stay very low for a long time. Shares are **at par** when they sell at their nominal value, i.e. original price. Shares are also either **above par** or **below par**. If the price of shares does not **go 'up** or **go 'down** it **stays 'put**.

'Blue chips are industrial shares which are considered a safe investment because the companies are of good financial standing. **Gilt-edged stocks/securities** are safe securities etc. usually issued by the government.

Telephoning

Other idiomatic expressions for **telephone someone** are:

ring someone ('up), give someone a ring (all GB only). *Ring me when you arrive, will you?* □ *I'll give you a ring around lunchtime.*

give someone a buzz (informal). *I'm sorry, I have to dash now, but give me a buzz later, will you?*

phone someone ('up). *I tried to phone you at the office, but you weren't there.*

make a call (to a place), call someone, call someone 'up (mainly US), **give someone a call.** *I want to make a call to the States, please.* □ *I've been trying to call her all day. She just isn't at home.*

You telephone someone **on his/her 'private line/'business line**. You **make a 'private/business call**. If you **reverse charges/make a reverse 'charge call** (GB) the cost of the call is charged to the person you telephone. In US usage you **call col'lect** or **make a col'lect call**. If you make a long distance **'personal call (US person-to-'person call)** with the operator's help, you wish to speak to a specific person only and no other person. There is no charge for the call if the person named is not there. In the US you can make a long distance **station-to-'station call**, i.e. you will speak to any person who **answers the phone**. In GB long distance calls are also called **'trunk calls**.

When you telephone someone you **get 'through**, i.e. get a connection. If it is an operator-assisted call, the operator may say **'you're through'** (GB), i.e. *'you are connected'*. In US usage this means *'you are finished, the time you paid for is up'*.

If you do not **get 'through** it may be because **the line is engaged** (US **the number is busy**), i.e. someone is already speaking on that number. The operator may **put you 'through** (US **connect you**). You may **be cut 'off**, i.e. the line is interrupted and the connection is lost. The telephone may be **out of order**, i.e. not working because of a technical fault. You may have **a poor/bad line**, i.e. you cannot hear well because of interference on the line. You may have **a crossed line**, i.e. you can hear other people talking in the background. The line may **go dead**, i.e. the connection may be lost.

If you have no time to speak when the telephone rings, you may not **take the call**. If you cannot speak to the caller immediately the caller must **hold the line, hold** (US) or **hold 'on** i.e. wait. The call may be **put on hold**. When you end a call you **hang 'up** or you **ring 'off** (GB only), i.e. you replace the receiver. If you wish to call someone again later, you can **ring (someone) 'back** (GB only), **get 'back to someone** (mainly US), or **phone/call (someone) 'back**. If you are expecting another important call and wish to keep the line free you have to **clear the line** or **get the caller off the line**.

The expression **be on the phone** has different meanings. 1 have a private telephone line. *Are the Jacksons on the phone yet?* □ *You can't ring Dorothy because she isn't on the phone.* 2 be waiting on the line to speak to someone.

Mr Powell is on the phone for you. 3 be speaking on the telephone at the moment. *I'm afraid Betty's on the phone at the moment, but I can take a message for her.*

If your phone number is not in the telephone directory/phone book (because you wish it to remain private) you have **an ex-di'rectory number** (GB)/**an unlisted number** (US).

Travel

You **go on holiday** (GB)/**vacation** (US) **by air/by train/by car** etc. You **go on a journey/trip/excursion/outing/'sight-seeing tour**. You **see/do the sights** with a guide if you **go on a conducted/guided tour**. You **go on/take a cruise**, i.e. on a passenger ship. You **go on a world trip/on a round-the-world tour**. If you **do a round trip** you travel around a country and return to your starting point. If you **go touring** you travel around a country or countries by car or coach. You may **take a short break (holiday)**, i.e. for 3 or 4 days only. A **'package holiday** is a holiday booked through a travel agent which includes travel, accommodation, meals and often excursions.

You **set 'off on a journey**. You may **break the journey**, i.e. stop somewhere for a short time or for some hours, you may **travel non-'stop** or **travel 'through**. You **stop 'off/over (at/in a place)**, i.e. break the journey. You may **stay the night/stay 'overnight/make an overnight stop** somewhere. You may **put 'up at a hotel**, i.e. sleep and eat there. You **make a reservation/booking** if you reserve a room in advance, i.e. by letter or telephone.

You **travel/go/book first etc. class**. If you fly you have to **check 'in** at the airport and **weigh 'in** (your luggage). When you leave or enter a country you have to **go through customs**. You may book **a do'mestic flight** (i.e. inland) which is usually also **a 'scheduled flight** (with an airline working on a regular schedule). A cheap flight booked for tourists on most holiday tours is **a 'charter flight. An 'APEX flight** is a scheduled 'advance purchase excursion' flight at a reduced rate.

Work and industrial relations

When you want a job you **send in an application (form)** or you **apply for a job.** You might also send **a curriculum vitae (CV)**, i.e. a written summary of your education and work experience with dates, employers' names etc. You may be asked to **go for interview**. You may **get an offer**, you may **be turned 'down**, i.e. rejected, or you may **be put on the 'short list/be shortlisted**, i.e. receive special consideration for the job together with two or three other candidates.

You may receive **on-the-job training** (US **hands-on training**), i.e. you are trained by the company's staff during working time. You may **work in the field**, i.e. outside the company, not in an office, often travelling from place to place. Your job may include several 'fringe benefits, i.e. extra advantages such as a company car, luncheon vouchers etc. These extras are also called **perks** (short for 'perquisites'). You may **work nine to five** (i.e. the usual office hours in Britain) or you may have **flexitime**, i.e. flexible working hours, starting and finishing work earlier or later according to personal choice.

If you are **on the board** you are a director of a company. A **white-collar worker** does an office job. A **blue-collar worker** is a manual worker, e.g. in a factory. Manual workers who work on the production line are **the shop 'floor/shop-floor workers/on the shop floor**. A **shop 'steward** is a person chosen by his fellow workers to represent them in their trade union. **A closed 'shop** is a place of work (factory, firm, workshop) or a trade or profession which is only open to members of a particular trade union.

A worker may **work/do overtime**, i.e. work longer than the usual hours for extra pay. He may **be on double 'time**, i.e. receive double the hourly payment for working at inconvenient times, e.g. Sundays, at night, public holidays etc. This is called **working unsocial hours**. If a worker is **on 'piecework** he receives payment for the number of pieces produced, not for the length of time he works. A worker may **do 'shift-work/work shifts/be on shifts**. A shift is usually an 8-hour working period. A worker may **be on the 'day-shift/be on days** or **be on the 'night-shift/be on nights**. When a worker finishes work, he **knocks 'off** (informal). *When is knocking-off time?*

Workers in a factory must **clock 'on** when they arrive and **clock 'off/out** when they leave, by punching a ticket in a machine which prints the time. These times are recorded by an automatic clocking-in machine.

If you want to have a personal wage/salary increase, you **put in for a rise** (GB)/**raise** (US). A group of workers **makes a 'wage-claim**. If the employer does not want to increase wages there may be a **'pay dispute**, eventually leading to a strike. Usually, however, the union officials and the management will **enter into negotiations** to discuss ways of resolving the conflict. Negotiation by the union on behalf of the workers is called **collective 'bargaining**.

There are various forms of worker protest. A trade union can **order a work-to-'rule**. The workers are then **on a work-to-'rule**, i.e. they follow strictly the rules which are laid down for the job, which leads to a considerable slowing down in the pace of work. Workers may **go slow/be on a go-'slow**, i.e. they work very slowly and do not do overtime. If this happens in a public service, e.g. the postal system, deliveries will be delayed by several days. The workers may **stage a sit-'in/a sit-down 'strike** in a factory etc., i.e. they stay in the factory and refuse to move until their demands are considered by the employers. If the workers **strike/go on strike/come 'out (on strike)** they refuse to work. They can strike for higher wages, better working conditions etc. A **wild-cat strike** is an unofficial strike which does not have the support of the union.

A worker who refuses to strike is **a strike breaker, a blackleg** (slang) or **a scab** (slang). Note the verb: **to blackleg. A picket** is a group of striking workers who gather outside their place of work to prevent others going to work – often by force. They **form a 'picket-line** (verb: **to picket**). **The hard core** of the strikers is the central controlling group which is most extreme. When strikers refuse to handle goods, materials, a cargo etc. they **black the cargo** etc.

The workers may agree to **go to arbitration,** i.e. have their claims judged by an independent arbitrator appointed by the government. There may also be **a 'lock-out.** The employers lock the workers out and refuse to let them enter their place of work until they agree to accept the proposed conditions and pay.

An employer may **fire someone** or **give someone the sack/the push** (informal), i.e. dismiss a worker from employment. An employer may **lay workers 'off,** i.e. dismiss them from work temporarily because there is not enough work for them. A worker is **laid 'off.** Note the noun: **a 'lay-off.** Alternatively, a worker may **be (put) on short time,** i.e. work fewer days than usual. Thus a worker may **be on/work a three-day week.** If his work is no longer needed, e.g. because the factory has to close, a worker **is made redundant.** Redundant workers may **sign 'on** (informal), i.e. register as unemployed and receive money weekly from the state. The worker is then **on the dole** (informal) receiving **'dole money** (informal). A worker will then **sign 'off** as soon as he finds work.

9 Idioms with key words from special categories

Animals

badger someone persuade someone to do what one wants by harassing and bothering him, often with repeated questions. *The police badgered the suspect with question after question until eventually he told them what they wanted to know.*

make a beast/pig of oneself eat large quantities of food, leaving little for others. *Henry loves buffet lunches, so I expect he'll make a beast of himself again!*

an eager beaver someone who works hard, busily and with enthusiasm, and who is eager to start the task in hand. *'I've packed my suitcase already.' 'You are an eager beaver. You're not going on holiday until the end of next week'.*

a busy bee a busy, active person who moves quickly from task to task. *Jenny's a real busy bee today. She's been rushing around all morning.*

have a 'bee in one's bonnet (about something) be continually occupied with, or obsessed by, one idea or thing. *Sarah has a bee in her bonnet about only eating health foods. Wherever she's invited, she takes her own things to eat.*

make a 'bee-line for something hurry towards something, taking the quickest and most direct way. *When we arrived at the hotel, the children made a bee-line for the swimming-pool.*

the bee's knees (informal) the best, the most desirable. *I know Phil is quite good-looking, but I wish he wouldn't admire himself in the mirror so much. He obviously thinks he's the bee's knees!*

a bird in the hand (is worth two in the bush) (proverb) it is better to be content with what one has or could easily get than to take the risk of trying to get more and in the end have nothing. *If I were you I would accept John's offer for your car. If you wait for a better one John may change his mind. Remember, a bird in the hand ...*

an 'early bird someone who gets up early in the morning, or who starts work earlier than others. *Father's always been an early bird. He gets up at six o'clock every morning – even on Sundays.*

a 'home bird someone who prefers to spend his social and free time at home. *Isabel always says 'some other time' when I ask her out. Doesn't she like me or is she just a home bird?*

a 'lone bird/wolf someone who prefers his own company or who has little social contact with others. *Harry has been a real lone bird since he lost his wife in a plane crash. He never accepts our invitations to dinner.*

an odd bird/fish an eccentric person whose behaviour or way of life is regarded as strange. *The old chap who lives in the little hut on the beach seems to be a real odd bird.*

a rare bird   someone or something of a kind that one seldom sees. *You are a rare bird in these parts! I haven't seen you here for at least five years.*

birds of a feather (flock together)   (proverb) people of similar character or interests will be found in each other's company. *It isn't surprising that Max and David are good friends. They both look after their own interests and, as we all know, birds of a feather flock together.*

a bird's-eye view (of something)   1 a good overall view or survey (of a thing, place etc.). *If we climb the tower, we'll have a bird's-eye view of the town.* 2 a brief survey of a subject, area of knowledge etc. *I need a book that gives a bird's-eye view of modern European sculpture.*

bug someone   (mainly US, informal) annoy, irritate, bother someone. *Joe keeps bugging me about letting him take my car next week. I must have told him ten times that he can't have it.*

take the bull by the horns   decide to face a problem or difficulty instead of avoiding it. *She decided to take the bull by the horns and tell her boss that she wasn't prepared to do overtime so often without extra pay.*

have butterflies in one's stomach   feel physical discomfort in one's stomach because of nervousness. *I'm expecting an important letter. I get butterflies in my stomach waiting for the postman every morning.*

a 'cat nap   a short sleep taken during the day. *You've got half an hour before choir practice. Why don't you take a cat nap if you're tired?*

lead a cat-and-'dog life   lead a life of constant quarrelling. *The couple in the flat above lead a real cat-and-dog life. I can hear them shouting at each other day and night.*

let the 'cat out of the bag   reveal a secret, often unknowingly or unintentionally. *We were planning a surprise party for Margaret, but she walked in on our discussion, so of course that rather let the cat out of the bag.*

not be/have (enough) room to swing a cat   be/have very little physical room to move about. *But you can't possibly live and work in this tiny flat. There isn't enough room to swing a cat.*

not have (got)/stand a cat in 'hell's chance (of doing something)   have no chance at all, be in a hopeless position. *Faced with such tough competition, Billy doesn't stand a cat in hell's chance of winning the art prize.*

play cat and 'mouse with someone, play a cat-and-'mouse game   keep someone in suspense and uncertainty, play with someone's feelings. *I have the feeling that Mandy is playing cat and mouse with William. She doesn't really want him but she won't let him go.*

put/set the 'cat among the pigeons   say or do something which causes trouble, disturbance or argument. *We had worked out a precise schedule for the work. Then Bill put the cat among the pigeons by saying he might take that week off.*

when the cat's away (the mice will play)   (proverb) when the person in authority is not present, people will do things they cannot do when he is there. *'The teacher was called out in the maths lesson, so the pupils did nothing for twenty minutes.' 'Well, what do you expect? When the cat's away the mice will play.'*

rain/pour cats and dogs rain very heavily. *'Shall we go?' 'Not just yet. It's raining cats and dogs at the moment.'*

be no chicken (informal) be no longer young. *'How old is Mrs Griffin?' 'Well, she's no chicken, that's for sure.'*

'chicken feed a very small or insufficient amount of money or payment (especially in comparison with larger amounts). *Government grants for education are chicken feed compared with the sums spent on defence.*

chicken 'out (of doing something) (informal) stop participating in a plan or activity because one is afraid, especially when it becomes dangerous or too difficult. *I'm not convinced that David is fully prepared to risk half his capital on this deal. It wouldn't surprise me if he didn't chicken out before long.*

count one's chickens (before they hatch) be over-optimistic or over-confident about something in the future. *'Iris is planning how to spend her first salary cheque before she even gets the job!' 'That's typical of Iris – counting her chickens again'.*

a cock-and-'bull story a story, explanation or excuse that is hard to believe; an exaggerated account of events. *Sam was late again this morning. This time he had some cock-and-bull story about having to take a woman with her poodle to see a vet!*

wait till the 'cows come home wait for a long time (referring to something that is never likely to happen). *If you're waiting for John to pay you back the five pounds, you can wait till the cows come home. He has a way of forgetting these things.*

crocodile tears insincere tears for effect only. *'Sylvia seemed very upset at her father-in-law's funeral.' 'No, they were crocodile tears. She never liked the old man.'*

'dog ears folded down corners on the pages of a book. Adjective: **dog-eared**. *This library book must be good. It's dog-eared, so it's obviously been borrowed plenty of times.*

a dog in the manger someone who selfishly prevents others from using, enjoying or profiting from something even though he cannot use or enjoy it himself. *Uncle Stan is a real dog in the manger with his weekend house. He doesn't use it himself any more, but he never offers it to other members of the family.*

dog tired very tired. *The doctor's been on call all night. He must be dog tired but he's still taking surgery this morning.*

every dog has his/its day (proverb) every person will have success or luck at some time. *'Jack was disappointed that he wasn't asked to be on the committee this year either.' 'Well, his time will come. Every dog has its day.'*

give a dog a bad name (and hang him) (proverb) if enough bad things are said about a person they will ruin his reputation even though they may not be true. *Jim has a criminal record, so unfortunately he was the obvious suspect in the recent theft. Give a dog a bad name...*

top dog the person, country etc. that is considered to be the most powerful, influential or superior. *Why should one country want to be top dog over the rest of the world?*

you can't teach an old dog new tricks (proverb) people sometimes refuse to accept changes and innovations because they are used to doing things the old way. *My father refuses to use a computer to do his accounts. He says you can't teach an old dog new tricks.*

a 'dog's life a life of dull routine or with many worries and troubles, with little opportunity for pleasure or freedom. *Being unemployed with little chance of getting work is a dog's life.*

lead/give someone a 'dog's life make life continually difficult and unpleasant for someone. *Maude leads Herbert a dog's life – he does all the housework and shopping after work because she's always at some party or social function.*

barking dogs seldom bite (proverb) people who lose their temper and shout are often harmless and are not to be feared. Note also: **his bark is worse than his bite.** *Tom was too nervous to ask for his ball back when it fell into our grumpy neighbour's garden but I reassured him that barking dogs seldom bite.*

go to the dogs slowly decline into a very bad state or condition, often economically (a country, business, building etc.). *When Mark inherited a lot of money, he went abroad somewhere and just let his business here go to the dogs.*

let sleeping dogs 'lie not interfere with something that is satisfactory; avoid mentioning a subject/event that could cause trouble. *Don't ever mention the subject of Uncle Ben's first wife when Julia's here. It's best to let sleeping dogs lie.*

donkey's years a very long time. *At first I didn't recognize Sam Smith when he stopped me in the street, because I hadn't seen him for donkey's years.*

do the 'donkey work do the most routine, unpleasant or least important part of a task or job of work, often the part involving manual labour. *Don't offer to help Bob. He'll sit back and let you do all the donkey work.*

a lame duck a person or enterprise (often a business) that is not a success and that has to be helped. *Helen's boutique started off very well, but after the initial enthusiasm it seems to be developing into something of a lame duck.*

a sitting duck a person or object in a vulnerable position that is easy to attack or injure. *Jones had stated several times that the government would not devalue the pound, so when they did, Jones was a sitting duck. He had to resign.*

a cold fish someone who is little moved by emotions, who is regarded as being hard and unfeeling. *Harold said nothing at all when I told him about Sally's misfortune. He's a real cold fish.*

a fish out of water someone who feels uncomfortable in unfamiliar surroundings or company. *I didn't know anyone at the party and felt like a fish out of water among all Jane's art college friends.*

have 'other fish to fry have other things to do or more important matters to attend to. *Stuart and Nigel wanted me to join them for a drink, but as I had an appointment with my bank manager about a loan, I told them that I had other fish to fry.*

there are plenty more fish in the sea (saying) there are other people/ things to choose from. *Laura was unhappy that Andrew had gone off with another girl. I told her to cheer up, that there were plenty more fish in the sea.*

a fly in the ointment a difficulty or something unpleasant which prevents or spoils total satisfaction or enjoyment. *After the exams, we had a great celebration party. The only fly in the ointment was that Patrick hadn't passed.*

not harm/hurt a fly said of a person or animal that is especially gentle and good-natured. *Grandfather's often grumpy and short-tempered, but he wouldn't hurt a fly.*

there are no flies on 'someone (informal) he is very alert and clever, not easy to deceive. *'How's the new secretary?' 'Fantastic, she's running the office already. There are no flies on Miss Evans!'*

can't/won't say boo to a goose said of someone who is very timid or quiet (usually by nature). *When Diane first came here she couldn't say boo to a goose, but she's now one of our most critical and independent teachers.*

cook someone's goose spoil someone's plans, chances of success etc., often intentionally. *Lawson was trying to take away one of our best customers by undercutting our prices. But then his suppliers couldn't guarantee delivery, so that cooked his goose!*

a wild 'goose chase a search, investigation etc. that has no chance of success. *I think Ted's sent me on a wild goose chase looking for his pipe. I bet it's in his pocket.*

a 'guinea pig someone who is used in an experiment. *We want to try out a new language teaching method, so we need some volunteer guinea pigs.*

a 'hen party/night a social evening for women only where men are not invited, often held before a wedding. *'I hear Sue has invited you and John over on Saturday.' 'No, just me – it's another of Sue's famous hen parties!'*

back the wrong horse support the wrong person. *Simon backed the wrong horse from the start. He favoured Hart but it was Robins who won the election.*

a 'dark horse 1 a person who does not talk much to others about his plans, activities, feelings etc. *Asquith didn't tell any of the office staff why he had been absent for a month, but then he's always been a dark horse.*
2 a person who has greater abilities than he shows or than people are aware of. *I didn't know Pat could play the piano. Just listen. She's a real dark horse!*

horse about/around play or act in a wild or noisy manner. *Okay, you boys! Stop horsing around and get your homework finished.* Note also: **horseplay.** *The horseplay soon stopped when the manager walked in.*

(straight) from the horse's mouth (used to describe news or information) directly from the person who knows most about a matter or who has the authority to give information about a matter. *'Are you sure that all office staff are getting a 5% rise?' 'Yes. I got it straight from the horse's mouth. The managing director himself told me.'*

change horses in mid-stream change one's views and attitude half-way through something; change sides. *Don't count on Alf's support. He says he's with you now, but he often changes horses in mid-stream.*

hold one's horses be patient; wait or slow down; consider one's actions more carefully (often imperative, used as a request or as a warning to wait). *Darling, just hold your horses with this guest-list. If we invite all these people to the wedding, we won't have enough money to buy the ring.*

(it's) horses for courses things should be used for the purpose for which they are intended; certain jobs should only be done by persons having the necessary skill and knowledge. *Tell Tom I'm sorry I can't let him do the job. This time it's strictly horses for courses. We need a qualified heating engineer, not a plumber.*

look a gift-horse in the mouth show dissatisfaction or find fault with a gift, an offer of help etc. Usually used with a negative. *'Jim hasn't matched the wallpaper very well in a few places.' 'Well, he did decorate the room free of charge, and you know that you should never look a gift-horse in the mouth.'*

be 'up with the lark get up very early in the morning. *We'll have to be up with the lark tomorrow morning. The flight leaves at 8.15.*

a/leopard cannot change his spots (saying) one cannot change one's basic character or temperament. *I've tried again and again to persuade Pete to come out to the pub and enjoy himself for a change, but a leopard cannot change his spots – he always refuses.*

the lion's share (of something) the largest and best part. *The father died without leaving a will, and since one of the sons was abroad at the time, the other simply took the lion's share of the property for himself.*

'monkey business/tricks dishonest, fraudulent behaviour. *The tax office had a lot of questions about Frank's declared profits. They obviously thought there was some monkey business going on.*

make a pig's ear (out) of something make a mess of something, do it very badly. *Don't ask Ken Williams to decorate your living-room. He may be cheap, but he made a real pig's ear of our bedroom.*

someone's pigeon (informal) someone's responsibility, concern etc. *'Jeff's having money problems and I think he expects me to help him out.' 'Well, that's certainly not your pigeon. You're his ex-wife now.'*

rat (on someone) (slang) betray someone to the police or to some person in authority. *Simpson was confident that his part in the robbery would never be discovered, but one of the other three robbers ratted on him when they were arrested.*

the 'rat race the frantic, competitive struggle to be better than others, e.g. in business, social prestige, professional status. *Many young people refuse to join the rat race of modern society and become drop-outs, living a simple life on some remote island.*

smell a rat (informal) detect something suspicious; sense that something is wrong. *The children had planned to play a trick on the teacher, but because the class was so quiet and attentive he smelt a rat.*

at a snail's pace very slowly, e.g. working, driving. *You'll never get the essay written on time at this rate! You're going at a snail's pace!*

a snake in the grass an insincere friend who is secretly harmful or dangerous to one. *There was always something superficial about Paula's* *friendship, but I never thought she would run off with my husband! She was just a snake in the grass.*

a 'stag party/night a social evening to which only men are invited or where only men are present, usually held before a wedding. (See also **hen party.**) *Remember, no wives! It's strictly a stag party!*

one swallow doesn't make a summer (proverb) one fact or occurrence only does not prove a rule, as it may be an exception. *The group's first rock concert was a success, but they know that one swallow doesn't make a summer so they're not being over-optimistic for the present.*

talk turkey (informal) talk seriously and frankly with someone. *'I thought we were meeting to talk turkey, but you've brought your wife with you.' 'Yes, I consult her on all business matters, so I want her to approve the deal.'*

have a 'whale of a time enjoy oneself very much. *Billy invited ten children to his birthday party. They had a whale of a time and it took me hours to clean up the mess.*

a wolf in sheep's clothing someone who pretends to be friendly in order to hide selfish or bad intentions. *Be wary of George Blackburn. Although he's always offering to help I have the feeling that he may be a wolf in sheep's clothing.*

keep the 'wolf from the door earn/have enough money to provide for oneself and one's family. *In areas of high unemployment, thousands are fighting to keep the wolf from the door.*

Colours

black

be in the black have money in one's bank account, be in credit. (See also **be in the red.**) *I've paid off my overdraft and it's a good feeling to be in the black again.*

black and blue having bruises on the body after an accident, fight etc. *Poor Liz took a few falls on her skiing holiday – she's black and blue!*

a black day (for someone/something) an unhappy day when something bad or sad happens. *The day of the Channel ferry disaster was certainly a black day for all the families concerned.*

black ice ice that is almost invisible on roads and therefore very dangerous. *There was a whole series of traffic accidents on the bridge due to black ice.*

a 'black list a list of persons who are considered to be dangerous/ undesirable/disloyal etc. *He knows that his name is on the black list, so he may try to enter the country using a false passport.* Note: **'blacklist someone.** *He was blacklisted by the immigration authorities.*

a black look a look of anger, dislike, resentment etc. *When I remarked that some people let the others do all the work, Paul obviously thought I meant him, because he gave me a black look.*

a black mark a mental or written record of someone's misconduct, failure, etc. that counts against him. *Jackson failed to finalize an important contract in Chicago. He wasn't asked to resign but it was certainly a black mark against him.*

a/the black sheep (of the family) a person whose conduct is considered to be a disgrace to the family or the group. *Alex started taking drugs at college, failed his exams and has been jobless for the past three years. He's certainly the black sheep of the Spencer family.*

a blackout 1 loss of electric light due to power failure. 2 a temporary loss of consciousness or memory. *I must have had a blackout after the accident. I can't remember how I got out of the car.* Note the verb: **black 'out**. *She blacked out. She can't remember anything about the accident.*

a blackspot a place on a road where accidents often happen; a problem area, e.g. with high unemployment, crime, violence etc. *There was a good documentary on television last night about the blackspots of the industrial North.*

in someone's black books out of favour with someone. *I think I'll keep out of the boss's way today. I'm in her bad books for upsetting a client.*

in black and white in writing or in print. Often used to state that something is legally binding. *He promised me a film contract in Hollywood but I'll only believe it when I see it in black and white.*

not as/so black as one/it is painted not as bad as people generally say or believe. *Most of the laboratory staff say that Professor Murray is very difficult to work with, but I don't think he's half as black as he's painted.*

blue

(have) blue blood be royal or aristocratic in origin. Adjective: **blue-blooded**. *Scott is trying to trace his ancestry. His mother told him that generations ago there was blue blood in the family.*

a blue-collar worker/job etc. a manual or factory worker, i.e. not an office worker. (See also **white-collar worker**.) *It isn't only the blue-collar workers who have been hit by unemployment. There are no office jobs either.*

a/the blue-eyed boy a man or boy who is somebody's favourite and with whom he can find no fault. *Brian was always jealous of his younger brother, because he knew that Tim was their mother's blue-eyed boy.*

a blue film/movie etc. an obscene or pornographic film/movie etc. *There has been a considerable rise in the production of blue movies since video recorders came on the market.*

a bolt from the blue a sudden (usually unpleasant) surprise or shock. *The news of her brother's illness came like a bolt from the blue, as she had spoken to him on the phone only the day before.*

disappear/vanish/go off into the blue go away suddenly, unexpectedly and without trace. *Do you remember Walter Smith, the fellow who vanished into the blue with half a million of the firm's money?*

in a blue funk (informal) very worried, in a state of fear about what may happen. *William is talking about resigning. I know what's wrong with him! He's in a blue funk because he thinks he'll be asked to leave, so he wants to resign before they ask him.*

once in a blue moon very rarely. *'Do you still go to art exhibitions?' 'Only once in a blue moon, I'm afraid. No time any more.'*

out of the blue suddenly, unexpectedly (typically **appear/turn up/say/ask** ~). *Rosalind's ex-husband has turned up again out of the blue, saying he wants her to give him a second chance.* □ *I met him purely by chance in a pub, and after a few drinks he offered me a job as his right-hand man. Just like that! Completely out of the blue!*

scream/cry blue murder (informal) shout loudly and emotionally in disagreement; protest; make a lot of fuss. *If the management doesn't agree to the union's proposals this time, the workers will start to scream blue murder!*

till one is blue in the face continuously or exhaustively but without results (with verbs such as **talk, argue**). *I've talked to Jim till I'm blue in the face about smoking, but he has no intention of giving up.*

a true blue (GB) a loyal Conservative with traditional views and values. *We all know how Simon will vote in the election. He's always been a true blue.*

green

be green (informal) be too trusting, naïve and easily deceived through lack of experience; be inexperienced or new to something. Note: **as green as grass**. *When I joined this company as a junior clerk ten years ago, I was as green as grass. But I've learnt a lot since then.*

a green belt an area of fields and woodlands around a town. *The planning committee is firmly opposed to any building in the green belt.*

give someone/get the green light give/get approval or permission to start doing something. *The budget has been approved, so we've got the green light to order the new scientific equipment for the department.*

green with envy (often **be/go/turn/make someone** ~) extremely envious of someone or something. *When Kathy hears that the boss is going to make you her personal assistant and not her, she'll be green with envy!*

have (got) green fingers be good at gardening, looking after plants etc. *Madge can get anything to grow – she's really got green fingers!*

grey

go/turn grey become grey-haired. *When Wilson heard that 55% of his company's shares had been bought up by his rival, he turned grey overnight.*

grey matter one's brain, intelligence, powers of reasoning etc. *I've got a mathematical problem for you to use your grey matter on.*

red

be/go/turn as red as a beetroot go red in the face with embarrassment or anger. *The teacher paid Janice a compliment on her essay and she turned as red as a beetroot.*

be in the red have no money in one's bank account, owe money to the bank. (See also **be in the black**.) *Bill can't handle money. He's been in the red as long as I've known him.*

(catch someone/be caught) red-handed in the act of doing something secretive or criminal. *I caught young Jimmy and his friend red-handed smoking behind the garden shed.*

the red carpet a sign of special welcome or attention for an important visitor. Usually **put/lay out (down)/roll out** ∼. *Our rich Uncle Herbert is coming to visit us tomorrow from the States. We haven't seen him for years, so Mum will be rolling out the red carpet.* Note: **the red-carpet treatment**. *There's a Japanese trade delegation expected tomorrow and the boss is giving them the full red-carpet treatment.*

a red herring an unimportant or irrelevant matter which is introduced into a discussion to divert attention from the main subject, the truth etc. *Make sure Matthews answers all our complaints at the meeting. Don't let him confuse you with any red herrings.*

a red letter day an important or joyful occasion which one looks forward to or remembers with pleasure. *The day we moved into our newly built house was a red letter day for the whole family.*

red tape official, bureaucratic formalities and procedure which slow down people and processes. *I hate applying for visas. For some countries there's so much red tape involved.* Note: **cut the red tape**. *I think that a lot of the official red tape could be cut so that we could get our contracts out more quickly.*

see red suddenly become very angry, lose one's temper. *When Mother saw the mess that Peter's friends had made in the living-room, she simply saw red and threw them all out.*

white

as white as a sheet/ghost very pale because of fear, shock, illness etc. Usually with **be/go/turn/look**. *When Terry read the telegram he went as white as a sheet.*

white coffee coffee with milk or cream. *For breakfast I always have two slices of toast and white coffee.*

a white-collar worker/job etc. a non-manual worker, e.g. office worker/professional or business work etc. (See also **blue-collar worker**.) *For years Bill was a mechanic, but he was given a white-collar job when his health trouble started.*

a (little) white lie a lie which does no harm and is more polite than the truth, usually told to spare someone's feelings or for convenience. *I don't want to go to Steve's party, so I'll tell him I won't be in town until late on that evening. A little white lie is better than hurting his feelings.*

Numbers, size, measurement

number

a back number 1 an earlier issue of a publication or newspaper.
2 a person, company etc. that is no longer regarded as important, that no
longer has influence or power; no longer of public interest or of personal
interest to someone. *Paul Crawford? No, he's no longer on the board of
directors. He's been a back number for years.*

number 'one oneself. Usually **look after/take care of/think about ~**.
*Max is very selfish. With him, it's look after number one and let the rest of the
world go to hell!*

the/one's number 'one the head person, one's direct boss etc. *My
number one is in Japan for three weeks, so I'm in charge until he gets back.*

Number 'Ten 10 Downing Street in London, address and official
residence of the Prime Minister (GB). *It would seem that Mrs Thatcher is
at Number Ten for a further period of office.*

one's (lucky) 'number comes up one is lucky, has good fortune, wins
money (in a game of chance etc.). *I've promised my family that when my
number comes up we'll go on a long holiday.*

one's 'number is up (informal) something bad will happen, e.g. one will
die, be severely punished, suffer etc. *When the rest of the gang find out that
it was Ted who told the police about the burglary, his number will be up!*

one's number two the next person in charge; one's immediate
subordinate. *Mr Walker couldn't attend to our order personally, but his
number two looked after us.*

one's opposite number the person who occupies the same position or
has the same function as oneself in another group, company,
government, organization etc. *I headed the British team and worked closely
together with my opposite number from the Japanese team.*

one

at 'one time at a time in the past. *At one time I used to play tennis quite a lot.
Now I go jogging instead – it's cheaper.*

back to square 'one back to where one started, because of lack of
success, change of circumstances etc. *The construction plans were very near
completion, but then the customer changed his mind on some major aspects. So
now it's back to square one.*

be at 'one with someone be in harmony, share the same view as
someone. *Ed and Sheila are never at one with each other, no matter what the
subject of discussion is.*

be/get one 'up on someone (informal) have/gain an advantage over
someone; be ahead of someone because one knows more than someone
else etc. *You'll be one up on the rest of us if you know the answer to this
problem!*

for 'one thing . . . for one reason (among other reasons). *I really don't
think we should go on holiday this year. For one thing, we can't afford it.*

a 'great one for something a great enthusiast for something. *My grandfather was a great one for horse-racing. He used to take me with him to the track every week when I was a boy.*

have 'one over the 'eight have too much to drink. *As soon as John arrived, it was obvious that he had already had one over the eight.*

I/you/someone etc. for 'one to take at least one example (of a person). *I don't think many people will be able to come on that date. I for one will be in Madrid.*

(all) in one, (all) rolled (up) in/into one combined. *Since Harry's wife died, he's been mother and father rolled up into one for his children.*

it's all one (to me/him etc.) it's all the same, it makes no difference, I don't mind. *'Shall we go to the coast or to the country?' 'It's all one to me – as long as we go somewhere!'*

my/his etc./the 'one and 'only (used for emphasis) the only/sole person or thing. *Please don't lose it. The book's out of print and that's my one and only copy.*

a new one on 'me etc. (informal) something surprising, that one did not know before. *'Did you know that Jenkins used to be in the army before he came to work here?' 'No! Really? That's certainly a new one on me!'*

one and the same exactly the same. Used for emphasis. *I suddenly realized that the woman I had spoken to on the telephone and the woman now addressing me must be one and the same person.*

one by one individually, one at a time, each one separately. *First he addressed the applicants as a group, then he spoke to them one by one.*

one fine day at some time in the very distant future. Said about something that one believes is not likely to happen. *'Ian's 43 now. Do you think he'll ever get married?' 'He might – one fine day.'*

one for the road (informal) one last drink before one sets off home or starts a car journey. *'How about one for the road?' 'No, thanks, I never drink more than one beer when I'm driving.'*

'one good turn deserves another (saying) if a person has received help from someone, it is fair and natural to help him in return. *Of course I'll lend you my car. You helped me to paint the fence, and one good turn deserves another.*

one 'hell/heck of a + noun (informal). Used to emphasize that what follows is superlative of its kind, i.e. very good/bad/difficult etc. *We had one hell of a time at Joe's party. □ That sure is one hell of a story!*

one in the eye for someone (informal) something unpleasant etc. that is deserved, e.g. a nasty shock/surprise etc. *Terry had been scheming to get promotion for months, so it was one in the eye for him when Brian was made head of department instead!*

one in a 'thousand/'million a person with excellent personal qualities who is rarely found. *I couldn't have managed without my neighbour when I was ill. She's one in a thousand.*

a one-night stand 1 a musical performance for one night only. *When on tour, many performers find the strain of one-night stands difficult to endure.*

2 a casual sexual relationship for one night only. *The thought that this chance meeting might turn out to be just another one-night stand stopped him taking further interest in the girl at the bar.*

one of the 'boys a person who is fully integrated and accepted into a social or work group and is not treated as an outsider. *When Alfred started work at the factory, some of the workers gave him a hard time. It took months before he became one of the boys.*

'one of these days soon; before long. *Harry drives too fast in my opinion. One of these days he'll end up in hospital.*

one of those 'days a difficult day on which nothing goes right. *Today was just one of those days. I lost my keys, broke three cups and forgot a dental appointment!*

(just) one of those 'things (saying) something (usually unfortunate and regrettable) that is unavoidable and must be accepted. *These days, leaving school and not being able to get a job is unfortunately just one of those things.*

one or two a few, a small number. *I'll come along later. There are still one or two things that I have to do in the garden.*

the one that got a'way (informal) a missed opportunity or something that escaped; some person/thing with which one experienced failure in the past, but which one has not forgotten. *'Do you remember Pat Jones from our college days?' 'Of course I do. She wouldn't have anything to do with you. She was the one that got away, so to speak!'*

one too many too much alcohol. *No more drinks for Jim! He looks as if he's had one too many already!*

pull a 'fast one (on someone) (informal) cheat (someone); put someone at a disadvantage. *Just watch out for Ken Robinson. He'll pull a fast one on you if you give him half a chance!*

a 'quick one a single alcoholic drink taken before one does something else. *Have you got time for a quick one before you go home?*

two

be in two minds (about something) be undecided. *Jenny says she's still in two minds about going to Jeff's engagement party. On the one hand, she wants to show him there are no hard feelings, but on the other, her presence might embarrass Mary.*

cut both/two 'ways be capable of having two opposite effects, results etc. *Vanessa unreasonably said that she didn't want Paul going off in the evenings with his friends. But that cuts two ways – Paul now expects Vanessa to give up her evening classes to stay at home with him.*

for 'two pins (informal) without much persuading, very nearly. *Roger was very rude to us again. For two pins I could have hit him on the nose.*

have (got) two strings/a second string to one's bow have a second/alternative choice, skill etc., a second course of action available to one in case the first one fails. *When Patrick became a professional tennis-player, he also opened up a sports shop so that he would have two strings to his bow.*

in 'two shakes (of a lamb's tail) (informal) very quickly and without difficulty. *You needn't change your jacket, I'll sew the button on for you. I'll have it done in two shakes!*

kill 'two birds with 'one stone (saying) achieve two aims with only one effort/action. *'Andy's in Sheila's office.' 'Good, I need to speak to them both, so I can kill two birds with one stone.'*

put two and two together make a correct guess, deduct something from the information/facts known. *If you're not at home and not at work, Liz will put two and two together and guess that you're here.*

there are no two ways a'bout it (saying) there is no alternative, no other way to think or act. *There are no two ways about it. If the bank is demanding immediate repayment of the overdraft, you'll have to sell your shares.*

'two bites of/at the cherry (usually get/have/be given ∼) two chances/attempts at doing something. *Gilbert was given his own department once, but he failed to show the necessary managerial skills. And one thing is certain – he won't be given two bites at the cherry.*

'two can play at 'that game (saying) (informal) said as a threat. You can also treat someone in the same offensive way as he has treated you. *So Lydia's purposely withholding information from me, is she? Well, two can play at that game!* Note also: a game that 'two can play.

'two heads are better than 'one (saying) it is better to solve problems, look for solutions, ideas etc. with another person rather than alone. *How about working together on these designs? Two heads are better than one!*

two/ten a 'penny very common; in large supply and easily obtainable, therefore of little value. *Routine jobs like that are two a penny, so don't worry about not getting it.*

two 'wrongs don't make a 'right (saying) you cannot justify your own wrong action by saying that someone else did the same to you. *'If Terry doesn't know the facts, I don't think I'll tell him. He once withheld some information from me.' 'But two wrongs don't make a right.'*

'two's company, ('three's a crowd) (saying) it is better and more tactful to leave two people together than to impose one's presence as a third. *'Would you like to come to the cinema with my new girl-friend and me?' 'Thanks for asking, but no. Two's company!'*

three etc.

three cheers for someone! an expression of praise, approval or enthusiasm for something someone has done well. *'Now three cheers for our competition winner! Hip, hip!' 'Hurray!' 'Hip, hip!' 'Hurray!' 'Hip, hip!' 'Hurray!'*

the three Rs the three basic and essential skills one first learns at school: reading, (w)riting and (a)rithmetic. *Primary education concentrates on the three Rs as the basis for learning all other subjects.*

on all fours on one's hands and knees. *The children love to have Uncle Albert on all fours playing donkey with them.*

at sixes and sevens in a state of confusion, muddle, disorder. *We moved into the house last week, but I'm afraid everything is still at sixes and sevens.*

it's six of one and half a dozen of the other (saying) it is the same in both cases; there is little difference between two things, situations etc. *If you buy a camera in Hong Kong and have to pay customs duty on it, it's just as expensive as buying one here. As I see it, it's six of one and half a dozen of the other.*

knock someone for six (informal) 1 defeat an opponent completely in any kind of competition or rivalry. *'Who do you think will win the tennis finals?' 'Walters. He should knock Johnson for six!'* 2 have a strong emotional effect on someone. *The bad news really knocked him for six.*

six feet under (humorous) dead and buried. *'Old Sam Gates! He's been six feet under for twenty years now!'*

six of the best corporal punishment; six blows with a cane. *Parents were very strict two generations ago. When Grandfather was a boy, it was six of the best for doing practically nothing at all!*

a nine days' 'wonder someone/something that attracts a lot of attention, publicity etc. for a short time only and is then forgotten. *She was an actress who made one brilliant film and then just disappeared. A real nine days' wonder.*

'nine times out of 'ten almost always; in most cases. *Judith thinks she knows everything about computers and doesn't hesitate to let everyone know. The trouble is, nine times out of ten, she's right!*

a nine-to-'five job/attitude/mentality etc. a routine job in an office, shop etc; a way of thinking/attitude to life that reflects routine. *Being a doctor is very hard work, but at least you don't develop a nine-to-five mentality.*

on cloud 'nine (informal) very happy; in excellent spirits. *Felicity has been offered a contract with a modelling agency in New York, so of course she's on cloud nine.*

a stitch in 'time (saves 'nine) (saying) any kind of damage, mistake etc. should be repaired or corrected at once in order to prevent it getting worse. *My car is showing the first signs of rust so I'm going to have it rust-proofed at the garage. I believe in a stitch in time.*

dressed up to the 'nines dressed in one's best clothes. *It was quite a formal occasion. Everyone was dressed up to the nines.*

ten to one very likely. *It's four o'clock already. Ten to one, Paul will be late again.*

talk nineteen to the 'dozen talk quickly without pause for a long time. *Aunt Madge is coming this afternoon. She talks nineteen to the dozen and usually exhausts us all!*

forty winks a short sleep during the day (not usually in bed). *Father was tired after lunch, so he's just taking forty winks in his chair.*

a hundred to 'one shot/chance a guess not likely to be right; a small chance not likely to bring success. *'Paula has just disappeared. No one knows where she is.' 'Well, I suppose it's a hundred to one shot, but what about ringing Scott in San Francisco to see if she's flown over this week instead of next?'*

a 'hundred/thousand/million and one very/too many (things to do, places to go, people to see etc.). Used to indicate that one is very busy. *'Why don't you come out to supper with us this evening?' 'Sorry. I'd love to, but I have a thousand and one things to attend to at home.'*

size

cut someone/something down to 'size show someone to be less important, capable etc. than he leads people to believe; show that a matter is not as important, difficult etc. as is generally believed. *Charles has become very arrogant since he was asked to give a radio interview. He needs cutting down to size.* □ *I don't think the problem is all that serious really, once it's cut down to size by comparing statistics.*

that's about the 'size of it (informal) that's a fair description of the situation, problem, matter etc. *So that's about the size of it. Now I've told you what the problem is, perhaps you can help us.*

try it/this/that for 'size! try something to see if it suits you, pleases you etc. *Jill's not really settled in her new job. I think she's just trying it for size until something more exciting turns up.* □ *'What are you doing sitting in the boss's chair?' 'Just trying it for size!'* Also used humorously. *Now try this for size! It's our most expensive 12-cylinder model!*

inch

'every inch a + noun thoroughly; through and through. *Richard has excellent manners. He's every inch a gentleman.*

give someone an 'inch and he will take a 'mile (saying) if you yield partly to someone's wishes, e.g. allow someone more freedom, a small advantage etc., he will take advantage and want even more. *We allowed the children to stay out until nine o'clock, but if you give them an inch they'll take a mile. It's half past nine and they're not home yet.*

not budge/give/yield an 'inch not budge/give/yield at all, not one little bit. *We need a compromise if we are going to solve this matter amicably, but Peters is sticking to his point of view. He won't yield an inch.* □ *The window is stuck. I've been tugging at it for ages, but it won't give an inch.*

within an 'inch of doing something be very close to doing something. *I was within an inch of being killed today. Some idiot on a motorbike didn't see me crossing the road!*

mile

be 'miles away be day-dreaming; be thinking of something else instead of concentrating on the present situation. *'James, I asked you if you'd like some tea. Didn't you hear me?' 'Oh, I'm sorry, June, I was miles away.'*

a 'miss is as good as a 'mile (saying) even if one only just fails, the effect is the same as if one has failed badly. *Peter needed 60% to pass the exam, and he had 58%, so he failed by just 2%. But a miss is as good as a mile.*

run a 'mile go away quickly in order to avoid someone or something unpleasant. *When I mentioned the washing-up, everyone seemed to run a mile.* □ *She's terrified of snakes. She'd run a mile if she ever saw one.*

see something a 'mile off see or understand something that is very clear/obvious. *Derek is crazy about Vanessa. He's never told anyone, but you can see it a mile off.*

stand/stick out a 'mile be easy to notice or differentiate. *Mark is extremely talented. His paintings stick out a mile from those of the rest of the class.*

talk a 'mile a 'minute chatter continuously and rapidly. *Most men would say that women talk a lot, but Harry beats the lot. He can talk a mile a minute.*

Parts of the body

arm

cost someone an arm and a leg (informal) cost someone a great deal of money. *It must have cost Fred an arm and a leg to send all three children to private schools.*

give one's right arm (usually with **would**) be willing/prepared to make a great sacrifice in order to do/get something. *Most of the pupils in my class would give their right arm to have a car of their own.*

keep/hold someone at arm's length avoid becoming too friendly with someone; keep someone at a distance. *The new man is one of those over-friendly types. Everybody's trying to keep him at arm's length.*

a shot in the arm something (often money) that has the short-term effect of stimulating and reviving a situation; something that does a person good. *If our company gets the Russian order, it will be a real shot in the arm for us.* □ *I feel so much better after hearing the exciting news. That's just the shot in the arm that I needed!*

twist someone's arm gently persuade someone to do something (i.e. without using physical force or unfair methods). Often used humorously. *'Would you like another piece of cream cake?' 'Well, if you twisted my arm I suppose I could eat another piece.'*

with open arms willingly, with enthusiasm. Usually **welcome/receive/ accept something** ~. *Thank you so much for the brochures. Bob will welcome them with open arms.*

back

behind someone's back when someone is not present or not informed; without someone's knowledge or approval. *The matter was discussed behind my back. I had no say in it.*

break the back of something (a piece/job of work etc.) complete the hardest/worst/largest part of it. *It's a very big garden to plan, but we hope to break the back of the work before the cold weather starts.*

get/put someone's back up (informal) make someone angry. *Mandy is so tiresome these days. She gets my back up every time I see her!*

get off someone's back (informal) leave someone in peace, stop annoying someone. *Look, just get off my back, will you! I've got work to do.*

have one's back to/against the wall be in a difficult position where one is forced to defend oneself. *Steve's got his back to the wall with everyone against him. He'll fight in any way he can to save his good name.*

pat oneself on the back congratulate oneself, feel pleased with oneself. *That's an excellent piece of work, Mary. You can certainly pat yourself on the back.*

put one's back into something work very hard at something, mentally or physically. *If you really put your back into it, you'd have the work finished in no time!*

see the back of something get rid of someone/something that is tiresome, unpleasant etc. *If we work hard all next week, we'll soon see the back of this job.* □ *I'll be glad to see the back of Mrs Hawkins. She loves wasting my time!*

stab someone in the back be disloyal to a friend when he does not expect it. *Don't trust Charles. He's the sort of person who's likely to stab you in the back when it suits him.*

turn one's back on someone refuse help when it is needed. *I've never liked Susan very much, but I can't turn my back on her when she's in trouble.*

have no backbone have a weak will or character without drive or fighting spirit. *Jeremy has no backbone! If he had, he wouldn't let the company manager treat him like that!*

blood

be after/be out for/want (someone's) blood want revenge; want to punish someone severely. *Where's Clive? Jacobs is after his blood for undercutting prices.*

be in someone's blood be born with a particular natural aptitude/talent or inherit it by nature. *Horses are in his blood. He's an excellent horseman, like his father.*

blood is thicker than water (saying) family ties are stronger than ties of friendship in spite of family quarrels. *Although he had no contact with his son for thirty years, he left much more money to him than to his housekeeper. It seems that blood's thicker than water after all.*

get someone's blood up make someone very angry. *What a nasty thing to say. That's the sort of remark that really gets my blood up.*

in cold blood in a calculated and deliberate way; calmly and without feeling. *How can I remain her friend after she lied to me like that in cold blood?*

like getting blood from/out of a stone expresses that something is hopeless or impossible. Often used when trying to get something from someone who is unwilling to give it. *Gerald has owed me fifty pounds for over a year now. I've asked him for it on several occasions, but it's like trying to get blood out of a stone.*

new blood someone new to an organization, job of work etc. who is expected to bring new ideas, innovations etc. *This company has been run in the same way for over twenty years. What it needs is some new blood.*

one's blood boils, it makes one's blood boil one becomes very angry. *It makes my blood boil to think that he's taken all the praise for my work!*

one's blood runs cold/freezes, it makes one's blood run cold one feels sudden distress, fear or horror. *The pictures of the massacre made my blood run cold.*

bone

a bone of contention a subject of constant argument or disagreement. *Trade unions are a bone of contention in our family. My father says they have too much power and I don't think they have enough.*

bone idle extremely lazy by nature. *He's intelligent enough to do the job but he won't because he's bone idle.*

bone 'up on something study a subject or an area of interest hard; learn all about something. *You ought to bone up on differential calculus before the exam. There's sure to be a question on it.*

have (got) a bone to pick (with someone) have something to complain about, a reason for displeasure. *Where's Janet? I've got a bone to pick with her. She gave me some wrong information.*

make no bones about (doing) something do or say something frankly, without hesitation or pretence, although it may not be pleasant. *I'll make no bones about it – I think Pearson would make a better job of being chairman than you.*

near the bone/knuckle (a joke, song, remark) offensive; likely to hurt someone's feelings because it is vulgar, indecent, too personal or painful. Often **too/rather/a bit** ~. *When Ken's had a drink or two, he starts singing songs that are a bit near the bone – I'm warning you!*

the bare bones (of something) a bare outline, the essential or main facts of a matter. *I'm not interested in the details, just give me the bare bones.*

brain

have (got) someone/something on the brain think repeatedly or constantly about someone/something. *Kate met a boy called Gordon in the lift and she's had him on the brain ever since. She talks of nothing else!*

one's 'brain-child one's own (usually clever) invention or idea for which one wishes to claim credit. *If this suggestion is put into practice, let it be remembered that it was Henry's brain-child, not the boss's!*

the 'brain drain the loss of a country's best-qualified academics, usually scientists, to another country which pays them more money for their work. *The brain drain of the sixties certainly made Britain less competitive in the field of technology.*

pick someone's brains(s) find out what someone knows/thinks about something by asking questions. *John, I need to pick your brain about computer software before the meeting.*

rack one's brain(s) (about something) think very hard to find a solution to a problem or to remember something. *I've been racking my brains all day to remember the name of the agency that Sheila recommended.*

have a brainwave have a sudden good idea/thought/suggestion; think of a solution to a problem suddenly or unexpectedly. *Read out the clue to the crossword once again. I've just had a brainwave. I think I know the answer!*

chest

get something off one's chest say/admit something (usually unpleasant) that one has wanted to say for a long time. *Tell him it was your fault. You'll feel a lot better when you've got it off your chest.*

play/hold/keep one's cards close to one's chest not reveal information about one's activities, plans, intentions. *Philips says nothing about progress on the X37 project. He's playing his cards close to his chest this time.*

ear

be out on one's ear (informal) be thrown out or dismissed at short notice from a job etc. usually through one's own fault. *If the new mechanic can't do a simple repair job better than this, he'll soon be out on his ear!*

play by ear play an instrument without music, from memory. *Catherine's very musical. She plays everything by ear.*

play it by ear act according to the situation, i.e. without a definite plan; do/say what seems best at the time. *'Have you prepared what you're going to say at the interview tomorrow?' 'No. I'll just play it by ear this time.'*

turn a deaf ear to something deliberately ignore something unwelcome, e.g. criticism, complaints, by pretending not to have heard it. *I told Mark to stop parking his car in front of our drive, but he just turned a deaf ear to it.*

be all ears listen attentively and with keen interest to news or information that may be to one's advantage. *Howard was all ears when I told him that I had some complimentary theatre tickets for Saturday evening.*

be up to one's ears (in something) (e.g. work, problems) be extremely busy, totally immersed in work etc. *I would help you at any other time, but at the moment I'm up to my ears in work.*

fall on deaf ears (advice, a request etc.) be ignored. *I asked the women in my office to smoke outside because of my cough, but my request fell on deaf ears.*

keep one's ear(s) (close) to the ground listen for and gather information about what is happening and what is likely to happen. *When you're at the conference, remember to keep your ears close to the ground. Perhaps you can find out what our competitors are planning.*

wet behind the ears naïve and inexperienced, usually because of one's youth, immaturity or lack of knowledge. *In your first job, older colleagues automatically think you're still wet behind the ears and seldom take you seriously.*

elbow

at one's/someone's elbow near to one, close by. *When doing translation work, it's imperative to have a good dictionary at one's elbow.* □ *I don't need you at my elbow telling me how to do my job, thank you!*

'**elbow grease** physical effort which one puts into a task. *If you want to get that mud off your car, you'll have to put a bit more elbow grease into it.*

'**elbow room** enough room to move freely; enough freedom of action or enough opportunity to use one's abilities and follow one's interests. *Working on the tight budget of a university physics department doesn't give you much elbow room.*

eye

cast/run an/one's eye over something look quickly over something. *Would you cast an eye over these designs and tell me what you think?*

catch someone's eye attract someone's attention, make someone notice. *If you could catch the waiter's eye, I'd like some more wine.*

easy on the eye pleasant to look at. *I love your colour scheme in this room. It's very easy on the eye.*

have (got) an eye for something (e.g. fashion, colour, talent) be a good judge of it, have a good sense of appreciation for it. *Kate's apartment is very attractive. She obviously has an eye for colour and furnishings.*

have (got) one's eye on something/someone want; wish to buy/ possess. *Don's got his eye on a Volvo 740 Turbo. □ Larry had his eye on our new assistant, but she told him that she's not interested.*

have (got) an eye to/on/for the main chance look out for an opportunity to further one's own interests, e.g. further one's career, make money, improve one's situation etc. *Simon has found favour with the managing director's wife. He's obviously got an eye to the main chance.*

keep an eye on something/someone observe continually and carefully; look after something/someone in someone's absence. *Maureen had to go to the doctor's, so I kept an eye on the children for her. □ Would you like us to keep an eye on your house when you're on holiday?*

see eye to eye (with someone) (on something) have the same opinion; agree. *There are a few matters that Pat and I don't see eye to eye on, but we agree basically on most things.*

a smack in the eye a sudden and unexpected setback, loss, defeat, sudden failure etc. *The Conservatives are calling an early election because they are expecting to win. It will be a real smack in the eye if they don't!*

there's more to something/someone than meets the eye a situation/ person etc. is more complex than it/he appears on the surface. *Bob's bank manager wants to see him. Bob says that it's about a trivial matter but I think there's more to it than meets the eye. □ Sally seems to be a very quiet, timid kind of girl, but I bet there's more to her than meets the eye.*

turn a blind eye to something ignore the existence of something; pretend not to be aware of something. *The boss knows that we often waste time chatting, but she just turns a blind eye to it.*

with an eye to (doing) something with a special intention or aim. *They bought a big house, with an eye to letting rooms to students later on.*

eyeball to eyeball (used of two people) close together, e.g. in a fight, in conversation. *I didn't say much to Clive on the telephone – it's best to talk about the matter eyeball to eyeball.*

be/become/seem all eyes look attentively and keenly, usually at something pleasant. *The children were all eyes when I brought in the birthday cake with six candles.*

be up to the/one's eyes/eyeballs (in something) (e.g. work, problems) be extremely busy, totally immersed in work etc. *I stopped in at Mary's, but I didn't stay long as she was obviously up to the eyeballs.*

before/under someone's (very) eyes in someone's presence; with someone watching. Used for emphasis. *Just imagine, she took the money out of the cash-register before my very eyes and never said a word!*

cannot/can hardly take one's eyes off someone/something be physically attracted to someone; find something delightful to look at. *The painting is so beautiful. I can hardly take my eyes off it. □ Roger saw this lovely Chinese girl in a restaurant. He couldn't take his eyes off her all through the meal.*

cry one's eyes out cry very much. *Little Susie cried her eyes out when her pet hamster died.*

do something with one's eyes closed do something very easily, without any effort or trouble. *The new photocopier is easy to work. When you've done it once, you can do it with your eyes closed.*

eyes down! (informal) prepare to look and listen with your full attention. *And now, ladies and gentlemen, it's eyes down for the most spectacular magician of all times – Mr Marvel!*

go into something with one's eyes open start something although one is fully aware of the difficulties involved, of what the results may be etc. *We all warned Paula against buying such an old house so she went into it with her eyes open.*

have (got) eyes in the back of one's head be very alert; see and notice everything going on around one. *Our teacher knows everything that's going on in the classroom. She must have eyes in the back of her head!*

have never set eyes on someone/something used to emphasize that one has never seen someone/something. *'Did you know the man who stopped to give you a lift?' 'No, I had never set eyes on him before!'*

keep one's eyes skinned/peeled watch carefully, remain alert. *Keep your eyes peeled for Jacobs. I don't want him to come in and find me looking in his papers.*

make eyes at someone show interest (usually not serious) in a member of the opposite sex by looking at him/her in an inviting way. *Pete doesn't remember how much he paid for the things he bought because he was too busy making eyes at the shop assistant.*

only have eyes for someone/something be attracted to one person only; want to have or be interested in one thing only. *Since Eleonor met Mark, she's only had eyes for him. □ Trevor needs a new car. The trouble is, he only has eyes for the new Porsche!*

open someone's eyes make someone realize the truth (usually unpleasant) about someone or something. *Janet wouldn't believe that Ted was seeing another girl, so it really opened her eyes when she saw him with her in a bistro.*

pull the 'wool over someone's eyes deceive someone by lying about one's true intentions, motives or actions. *You've managed to pull the wool over many people's eyes, but it won't work with me. I know you too well.*

face

be staring someone in the face be very obvious or clearly noticeable, but often not noticed by the person concerned. *Can't you see? He's in love with you! It's staring you in the face!*

blow up in someone's face (used of a plan, arrangement etc.) fail; be destroyed by some unexpected and unwelcome event or situation. *The deal just blew up in my face. Simpson reneged on all we had previously agreed on.*

face to face (two people) together, person to person, in each other's presence. *The atmosphere was tense when the two rival leaders came face to face.*

face the music meet criticism, punishment etc.; deal with an unpleasant situation. *He was in big trouble with the tax authorities and his business was on the rocks, so he simply disappeared rather than face the music.*

fly in the face of someone/something disregard, defy or oppose rashly something that is generally accepted (e.g. an opinion, a decision, facts). *She's the sort of woman who opposes everything on principle and loves to fly in the face of convention.*

have egg on one's face (informal) be seen as/shown to be foolish. *At the Annual General Meeting, the Chairman quoted last year's sales figures by mistake and didn't even realize it. He certainly had egg on his face!*

in the face of something (e.g. difficulties, danger) in the presence of, confronted by. *Father taught us to remain calm in the face of danger, but it isn't always easy.*

keep a straight face not laugh even though one finds something very funny; hide one's amusement. *I could hardly keep a straight face when Father's spectacles fell off the end of his nose in the middle of his speech.*

laugh on the other side of one's face lose one's reason for laughter because of a nasty surprise etc. *John was amused when he heard that the TV company is sending Tom to the Middle East and not him. But he'll laugh on the other side of his face when he finds out that he's being sent to Belfast.*

let's face it let's be truthful/admit the truth to ourselves. *We all know that Williams is difficult to work with and some of us would be happier without him, but let's face it, he's the best man for the job.*

lose face be humiliated; lose the respect of others. *One of the worst things that can happen to a political leader is for him to lose face.*

on the face of it as it appears to be according to the facts that are available. *On the face of it, it would seem that the market research was successful, but has it really answered the essential questions?*

put a bold/brave face on it hide one's worry by pretending that nothing is wrong; show courage in times of difficulty. *'How is Linda coping after her divorce?' 'Well, she feels terribly lonely and depressed, but she manages to put a brave face on it most of the time.'*

show one's face appear, come, be present. *After all the trouble you have caused, I don't know how you dare show your face here again!*

a slap in the face a sudden and unexpected rejection, defeat, disappointment etc. *Jessica was sure that she would be asked to represent the company at the conference, so it was a real slap in the face for her when Patricia was asked to go.*

finger

get/pull one's finger out (informal) stop being lazy and start making an effort. *Tell Joe to get his finger out and help us with this machine instead of looking on and telling us how not to repair it!*

have (got) a finger in every pie be involved in many activities, concerned with many matters, often for personal gain. *Jim's on the board of three companies, chairman of the local planning committee, and a school governor. He makes sure he's got a finger in every pie.*

have (got)/keep one's finger on the pulse (of something) have an up-to-date knowledge of something; keep well informed. *If you want to know what's happening on the social scene, ask Jan. She has her finger on the pulse and can tell you who's going to be where.*

lay a finger on someone get hold of someone, usually with intent to hurt physically. (Usually as a warning.) *Don't you dare lay a finger on him! Fight with boys of your own size!*

lay/put one's finger on something define, identify or discover something, e.g. what is wrong or the reason for it. *There's something about Wilson that makes me suspect that he's not telling the truth, but I can't quite put my finger on what it is.*

point the finger at someone (informal) accuse, betray or inform on someone, e.g. a criminal. *The police would never have caught the murderer, if a former accomplice hadn't pointed the finger at him.*

twist someone round one's (little) finger have someone under one's influence; manipulate someone. *I expect Dad will let Peter borrow the car again on Sunday. He can twist him round his little finger.*

all fingers and thumbs clumsy with one's hands, often because of nervousness or lack of concentration. *I'm sorry I spilled your coffee. I'm all fingers and thumbs this morning because I've got a job interview after lunch.*

get one's fingers burnt suffer harm, especially financially, by being too rash, careless or trusting. *David is going into partnership with a man he hardly knows. If he's not careful, he's likely to get his fingers burnt!*

keep one's fingers crossed (for someone) hope/wish for luck with a problem or difficulty. *'I'm taking my driving test this afternoon.' 'Oh, good! I'll keep my fingers crossed for you.'*

work one's fingers to the bone work very hard manually for a long period of time, usually because one needs the money. *Since her husband died, Mrs Smith has worked her fingers to the bone to provide for her four children.*

have (got) something at one's fingertips have a thorough knowledge of a subject or familiarity with a skill. *I've never seen anyone use a computer as efficiently as Marion. She's certainly got it at her fingertips.*

foot, feet

the boot is on the other foot the position or situation is now reversed (usually in favour of the speaker). *When I was in need of a job, I asked Wilfred to help me and he refused. Now the boot's on the other foot. He needs a job and has asked me for help.*

foot the bill pay, often unwillingly or for another person. *In the middle of the meal, Joe got a phone-call and left in a rush, leaving me to foot the bill!*

get/start off on the right/wrong foot make a good/bad start with someone/something (e.g. a relationship). *I'm sorry for that silly remark. I hardly know you, and I don't want us to get off on the wrong foot.*

have (got) a foot in both camps be involved with two activities, groups etc. with differing or opposing aims or ideas at the same time. *Jill can't make up her mind which political group to join, so at the moment she still has a foot in both camps.*

have (got) a/one's foot in the door have secured an introduction or have made oneself known to some person, group etc. *Stone is trying to get a business contract with General Computers. According to his secretary, he's already got his foot in the door.*

my foot! certainly not! Expression of disagreement, e.g. with a speaker's statement. *Paul said he was working yesterday evening so he couldn't come. Working my foot! Janet saw him with a girl in a disco!*

put/set a foot wrong act unwisely; make a mistake. *Be very careful how you handle the situation when they ask for delivery dates. We mustn't set a foot wrong, or we'll lose the order.*

put one's best foot forward do one's best, work one's fastest etc. *If Patrick wants to pass his exam, he'll have to put his best foot forward. There are only three weeks to go.*

put one's foot down insist on something; be firm in an objection or protest; assert oneself. *The children were getting out of control, until the teacher put his foot down and made them all sit in their places.*

put one's foot in it say or do something foolish, tactless, embarrassing, offensive etc.; blunder. *I put my foot in it when I said I didn't like Joan's new painting. Uncle Norman had given it to her and he was sitting beside me.*

set foot in/on somewhere visit or go to a place/building etc. *Barbara hated Blackpool. She said she wouldn't be sorry if she never set foot in the place again.*

fall/land on one's feet get out of a difficult or unpleasant situation by being lucky. *Don't worry about Ken. He may have lost his job, but he'll probably get something even better. Ken always falls on his feet!*

feel/find one's feet begin to show one's abilities or become self-confident. *The new girl seems very bright. I'm sure she'll be an asset to the firm, once she's found her feet.*

get cold feet stop something or withdraw from something (e.g. a plan) because one becomes afraid of the consequences. *The planned burglary never took place. Fred's accomplice got cold feet and Fred couldn't do it on his own.*

get (back) on one's feet recover after a period of difficulty, failure, financial worry etc. *Mark was very kind to Jill and the children. He helped her a lot after her divorce, until she got back on her feet.*

have (got) both/one's feet on the ground be a sensible, realistic, practical person. *I like Tom. He's no dreamer. He's got both feet firmly on the ground.*

pull the carpet/rug (out) from under someone's feet stop giving one's help or support suddenly and unexpectedly. *Our research project is funded by private industry. If any of the companies involved decide to pull the rug from under our feet, we can't possibly continue.*

run/rush someone off his/her feet overwork, cause to work at speed. *It was hectic in the office today. Mr Parsons rushed us all off our feet.* Note also: **be rushed off one's feet.** *The hospital is under-staffed. The nurses are always rushed off their feet.*

stand on one's own (two) feet be self-supporting and independent; be able to defend or look after oneself without help. *Don't worry so much about Betty. At 19, she's perfectly able to stand on her own two feet.*

hair

keep your hair on! calm down, don't get angry. *I'm sorry I broke the vase. But keep your hair on! It isn't the end of the world!*

let one's hair down relax, enjoy oneself, have a carefree time after being formal and correct in behaviour. *The conference is over now and it all went very well. So you can let your hair down and relax.*

make someone's hair curl/stand on end frighten/horrify someone. *My uncle is a detective with the Criminal Investigation Department. Some of the crimes he tells me about make my hair stand on end!*

not turn a hair not show fear; remain calm in the face of danger or shock. *When Barry was accosted by three youths with a knife, he didn't turn a hair.*

by/within a hair's breadth by/within a very short distance or a very small amount. *I came within a hair's breadth of being killed this morning. I ran across the road behind a bus.*

split hairs talk or argue about irrelevant or unimportant differences or details. *Let's not argue about whether we sold eleven million two hundred thousand newspapers or eleven million three hundred thousand. That's splitting hairs. The fact is, we haven't sold enough!*

hand

at first hand directly. *'Who gave you that information about David?' 'I got it at first hand. David told me himself.'*

at hand near, close by. *I haven't got the books at hand, but I can get them for you by this afternoon.*

be hand in glove with someone be in close co-operation or relationship with someone; be working towards the same aim etc. *Apparently, the American and British secret services were hand in glove on the latest espionage case.*

bound/tied hand and foot be unable/powerless to act. *I'm afraid there's nothing I can do to help you. I'm bound hand and foot by the bank's rules.*

cap in hand humble; in a humble manner. *He had a strong disagreement with the boss and gave in his notice. The next morning, he went back cap in hand and asked for his job back.*

come the heavy hand (with someone) criticize strongly; blame or threaten. *You needn't come the heavy hand with me! You're just as much to blame for this mess as I am!*

a dab hand (at something) a person who is clever/skilled at some job/ task or experienced in some situation. *Ron is quite a dab hand at repairing electrical things. Let him have a look at your spin-drier.*

eat/feed out of someone's hand(s) be under someone's influence; submit to his wishes willingly. *The boys love their new teacher. She has them eating out of her hand already and they do whatever she tells them.*

force someone's hand force someone to act, make a decision etc. more quickly than he may be willing to. *Couldn't you force his hand – tell him your company is insisting on a decision immediately?*

gain/get the upper hand win an advantage over something/someone, thus gaining a position of power. *If you once let Henry get the upper hand in an argument you won't have a chance to put forward your point of view.*

give/lend someone a hand help someone physically, e.g. to carry, lift, move something. *You'll have to change the tyre. I'll give you a hand if you like.*

give someone a big/good hand applaud someone, usually after a good performance, speech etc. *The school concert went very smoothly and the headmistress asked the parents to give all the children a really big hand.*

give someone/have (got) a free hand (in something) give someone permission to do as he wishes/be allowed to act as one wants. *I'll give you a free hand in the running of the business, if you are prepared to take on the responsibility.*

hand over fist quickly and uncontrollably. *Share prices were dropping and Scott found himself losing money hand over fist.*

have/take a hand in something be involved actively in something; be responsible for something being done. *The colour scheme is excellent. Didn't Mike have a hand in the redecorating?*

have/take/want no hand in something not be involved in something; have nothing to do with something. *If it's blackmail you're thinking about, I want no hand in it!*

in hand 1 under control, being undertaken. *The work is well in hand and should be finished in a few days.* 2 spare, left over to use or be put to use. *When we've paid all the bills, we shall still have about three hundred pounds in hand.*

keep one's hand in keep in practice. *Joan doesn't teach full time now but she stands in for colleagues sometimes, so that she can keep her hand in.*

live (from) hand to mouth live without saving money, spending it as soon as it is earned. *Ken won't suddenly start saving money when he's been living hand to mouth all his life!*

off hand without much thought or preparation. *'Can you tell me Jeff's new address?' 'Not off hand, but here's my address book.'*

out of hand out of control. Usually **be/get** ~. *If the strike situation down at the shipyard gets out of hand, we shall lose some important orders.*

put one's hand to the plough work hard, with great effort. *When Paul inherited his father's business he did very little work for the first six months. But as soon as he put his hand to the plough, he made a big success of it.*

someone's right hand (man) someone's closest assistant or helper. *Maurice has been the headmaster's right hand man for years.*

show/reveal one's hand let others know one's intentions, plans, position. *If only Richards would show his hand, we would know better how to deal with the situation.*

strengthen one's/someone's hand improve one's/someone's position or power/freedom to act. *It would certainly strengthen Mark's hand, if he knew that he had the entire teaching staff behind him.*

take a hand (in something) intervene, take control. *Jan was asked to take a hand in the arrangements for the Charity Ball, as no one else seemed to have much time.*

take something/someone in hand take control of/deal with something/someone. *Tom's teenage son is causing a lot of trouble in school. It's time his father took him in hand.*

to hand within reach, in one's possession at the moment. *I needed to look up some Spanish words, but unfortunately I didn't have my dictionary to hand.*

wait on someone hand and foot do, fetch, attend to everything for someone who could do it all himself. *I don't mind Aunt Nancy coming to visit, but she always expects us to wait on her hand and foot.*

be (quite) a handful be difficult to manage/control because unruly or strong-willed. *Margaret visited me yesterday with her four-year-old. What a handful he is!*

hands off! don't touch! *Hands off those chocolates! They're mine!*

have one's hands full be extremely busy; have a lot of work, responsibility etc. *I'd love to help you, but I have my hands full with the fashion show at the moment.*

many hands make light work (proverb) a task is easier if many people share the work. *'Do you need any help preparing the vegetables?' 'Oh yes, please. Many hands make light work.'*

play into someone's hands do exactly what someone (e.g. an opponent, a rival) wants you to do, usually involuntarily and without realizing it. *Don't complain to the boss that Henderson has given you too much work to do. Don't you see, that would be playing into his hands? Henderson wants the boss to think that you are not competent enough to handle it all!*

win/beat someone hands down win very easily with a clear lead. *Why don't you challenge Jeff to a game of tennis? He thinks he can beat you hands down, but I think he's wrong.*

head

above/over someone's head too difficult for someone to understand. *I'm sorry but all these technical details are above my head. Can't you simplify them for me?*

be/go off one's head (informal) be/become mad; think unrealistically. *If Mr Green expects the whole department to do overtime on Saturday and Sunday, he must be off his head.*

come to a head reach a crisis (e.g. trouble, a problem, difficulties). *Sue's having a rough time with her boy-friend. If things come to a head, she's going to move back to her parents.*

from head to toe 1 thoroughly. *Mark is a gentleman from head to toe.*
2 all over one's body. *She must have measles. She's covered in spots from head to toe.*

get something into one's head be convinced about something; believe that something is true, likely to happen etc., usually when it is not true or unlikely. *Grandfather has got it into his head that someone's stealing the cabbages out of his garden.*

go to one's/someone's head (e.g. praise, success, money) make someone self-important, arrogant, over-confident. *Lynn has become so arrogant since she was made chief buyer. It's really gone to her head!*

have a (good) head for figures be good at mathematics. *'Can you help me with these accounts?' 'I don't think so. I never had a head for figures.'*

have (got) a head start have an advantage over others (often one's competitors). *Janette has a head start on us all for the job in Paris because she's bilingual.*

have (got) a good head on one's shoulders have a lot of common sense and practical ability. *Phillip has a good head on his shoulders. He should do well in whatever trade he chooses.*

have (got) one's head in the clouds be a dreamer; be out of touch with reality, idealistic, not practical. *Even though Luke is a poet and an idealist, he certainly hasn't got his head in the clouds.*

have (got) one's head screwed on the right way (informal) be sensible, practical and alert. *Debbie is thinking about opening a secretarial agency. I think she will make a success of it because she's certainly got her head screwed on the right way.*

head and shoulders above someone 1 much bigger physically.
2 superior in skill, ability or intelligence. *Catherine is a highly gifted child. She seems to be head and shoulders above most of the others in the class.*

head over heels completely. *Jim met this Swedish girl on a study trip and fell head over heels in love with her.*

keep one's head/a cool head remain calm; not panic. *Just keep a cool head in the examination tomorrow and you should be all right.*

keep one's head above water keep out of debt, out of difficulty. *If we can manage to keep our heads above water in the first year, the boutique should start to make a profit in the second.*

lose one's head panic, lose control, act in a confused way. *When the boy fell into the river, his friend just lost his head and ran away.*

make head or tail of something understand something that is confusing, mixed up etc. Usually used in the negative. *This pupil's essay is so full of mistakes that I can't make head or tail of it!*

put something (e.g. an idea) into someone's head suggest something to someone, start someone thinking about something. *Someone's been putting ideas into Amanda's head about becoming an actress. It's all she talks about.*

put/lay one's head on the block risk failure, defeat, blame, criticism etc.; endanger one's position, good name etc. *I was willing to put my head on the block for you a year ago, but you've been lazy and inefficient, so you can fight your own battles with the management now!*

talk one's/someone's head off talk all the time or for a long time; chatter. *I sometimes pretend not to be at home when the neighbour calls. He talks his head off for hours!*

talk through the back of one's head talk nonsense. *Don't take what Uncle Ben says too seriously. He sometimes talks through the back of his head.*

use one's head use one's intelligence/common sense. *Don't keep asking others how to do things! Use your head!*

put our/your/their heads together consult/work together to solve a problem, work out ideas etc. *This may be a tricky problem to solve. Why don't we put our heads together on it?*

heart

after one's own heart (e.g. a man/woman) of the kind one likes best or approves of most, because he/she is very like oneself in tastes, thinking etc. *Ah, so you enjoy a good drop of claret, too. You're a man after my own heart.*

at heart basically, as one really is by nature. *Tom may put on a tough act, but he's a romantic at heart.*

break someone's heart make someone very unhappy or sad. *If Jimmy has to change schools and leave his best friend, it will break his heart.*

by heart from memory. *We have to learn all these dates by heart for tomorrow!*

have a heart! show some consideration/feeling/pity! *Oh, Miss, have a heart! The school team's playing an important match after school and we all want to watch, so we can't do the essay for tomorrow!*

have a heart of gold be very kind and generous. *Mrs Brown may seem grumpy and bad-tempered sometimes, but deep down she has a heart of gold.*

have one's heart in the right place be a kind person of good intentions. *Herbert has a rough exterior, but he has his heart in the right place.*

have the heart (to do something) be unkind enough to do something. Often used in the negative. *After Benny had tried so hard with his painting, the teacher didn't have the heart to tell him that it just wasn't good enough to be entered for the competition.*

a heart to heart (talk) a frank, personal talk in confidence, usually between two friends, etc. *Sheila's feeling very depressed at the moment. We had a heart to heart talk about her problems yesterday.*

in one's heart of hearts deep inside, in one's innermost thoughts and feelings. *Dick says that he doesn't mind at all if the baby is another boy, but I know that in his heart of hearts he's hoping for a daughter.*

lose heart become discouraged. *Diana has had so many job refusals that she's beginning to lose heart.*

one's heart is not in it one feels little enthusiasm for something one is doing, one lacks motivation. *It's no use expecting Tim to do well at languages when he's much more interested in science subjects. He tries to write good essays, but his heart simply isn't in it.*

one's heart is in one's mouth one suddenly feels very nervous or frightened in case something does or does not happen as one expects. *My heart was in my mouth when Professor Black started to read out the examination results.*

set one's heart on something want something very much. *Jill has set her heart on a holiday in Greece, so she's saving hard at the moment.*

to one's heart's content as much or as long as one wishes. *There will be lots of food and wine, so we'll be able to eat and drink to our hearts' content.*

take heart become confident again; find courage and faith in oneself after a disappointment, failure etc. *Being made redundant has hit Max very hard, but he'll have to take heart and start looking for a new job.*

take something to heart be greatly affected, upset, influenced by something, e.g. a disappointment, a failure, criticism. *Angela's very upset about something her teacher said about her work. It was probably just a casual remark that didn't mean much, but she takes everything to heart.*

heel

a/one's Achilles' heel a particular weakness or fault in a person's character not generally known to others, which could be damaging if discovered; a flaw in a system, organization etc. *Everyone has an Achilles' heel somewhere, and with Roberta it's her jealousy – her sister is head of a highly successful advertising agency.*

down at heel (used to describe a person's clothes or appearance) shabby, poor, worn out. *A man came to the door today looking very down at heel. I gave him some work to do in the garden and paid him generously for it.*

bring someone to heel make someone obey orders; bring someone under control. *Young William is becoming increasingly arrogant and self-assertive. It's time he was brought to heel.*

cool/kick one's heels have to wait, be kept waiting. *The interviewer hadn't arrived, so the secretary kept the four of us cooling our heels in the corridor for two hours!*

take to one's heels run off. *The two suspicious-looking men standing outside the jeweller's shop took to their heels when the police car drew up.*

leg

give someone a leg up help someone towards success etc. *When Martin first joined the company I noticed his talents, and it was me who gave him the leg up he needed.*

not have (got) a leg to 'stand on (e.g. in an argument) have no chance because of one's weak position; be unable to defend oneself or to convince or persuade someone else. *If a defendant changes his mind and pleads innocent after he has already pleaded guilty, he doesn't have a leg to stand on.*

pull someone's leg tease or make light fun of someone by leading him to believe something that is untrue. *Of course Uncle John doesn't want his present back. He was only pulling your leg!*

be on its/one's last legs be in a bad state or condition, close to collapse, breakdown, death. *I don't think there's much we can do about repairing the television. After fifteen years, it's on its last legs.*

stretch one's legs take a walk in order to get some necessary physical exercise. *After such a lengthy discussion, I feel that I need to stretch my legs. Would you like to join me in the garden?*

with one's tail between one's legs in a humble, depressed or sad manner (like a dog after it has been beaten). *Jones was furious when he entered the manager's office, but he left with his tail between his legs. He had been mistaken.*

neck

be neck and neck be equally good; be side by side in a race. *After the latest opinion poll, it would seem that the Labour and the Conservative candidates are neck and neck.*

be up to the/one's neck in something be fully occupied with/ immersed in (work, trouble, problems etc.). *I would come and see you this week, but I'm up to the neck in paperwork, so I'll come next Saturday.*

break one's neck 1 kill/injure oneself badly by doing something risky or dangerous. *Roger goes much too fast on his skate-board. He'll break his neck one of these days!* 2 do something very fast in order to have it finished at a set time. *The taxi-driver almost broke his neck trying to get us to the airport on time!*

breathe down someone's neck watch someone closely; supervise or examine someone's work, behaviour, actions etc., usually in order to criticize. *I shall be so glad to get out of this office and not have Mason breathing down my neck any more.*

get it in the neck (informal) be criticized, reprimanded or punished severely for something one has done. *You'll get it in the neck when the headmaster finds out that it was you who broke the window.*

a pain in the neck an irritating, annoying person; something one dislikes doing. *Rita is such a pain in the neck these days. All she talks about is her trip* *to Australia.* □ *I shall be glad when we've finished checking these figures. They're a pain in the neck.*

stick one's neck out risk saying or doing something that may cause trouble or criticism for oneself. *I don't think that Joan and Kevin are doing the right thing, sending a seven-year-old to boarding school, but it isn't my place to stick my neck out and tell them so.*

nose

have (got) a (good) nose for something be good at detecting or discovering things. *Henry must have a good nose for antiques. When this table's polished up, it will be worth at least five times what he paid for it.*

keep one's nose clean (informal) stay out of trouble, do nothing (criminally) wrong. *He's already served a three-month sentence for house-breaking. If he doesn't keep his nose clean, he'll soon be in prison again!*

keep one's nose to the grindstone work hard without taking any rest. *You'll have to keep your nose to the grindstone if you intend to finish all this paperwork before you go on holiday.*

lead someone by the nose influence someone to do as one wants; control someone's actions. *The workers are determined not to let the management lead them by the nose. They want more than just promises.*

look down one's nose at something/someone show disrespect to someone; consider something/someone inferior. *Simon's a dreadful snob. He looks down his nose at colleagues who don't have an academic background.*

pay through the nose pay more money for something than it is worth. *'This is a lovely apartment.' 'Maybe, but we're paying through the nose for it.'*

turn one's nose up at something reject something because one thinks it is not good enough. *When Sally heard that these children's clothes are second-hand she turned her nose up at them.*

under one's nose very close, easily noticed. *'Where are the scissors? I can't find them anywhere.' 'They're right there under your nose!'*

shoulder

give someone the cold shoulder ignore someone, treat him in a cold, unfriendly manner. *I don't know why Rita's giving me the cold shoulder. Have I offended her?*

put one's shoulder to the wheel work hard and seriously. *You'll never make a success of things if you don't put your shoulder to the wheel.*

rub shoulders with someone come into social contact/associate with someone (often of a different class or life-style). *Since Miriam got the job with the TV company, she often rubs shoulders with famous names.*

a shoulder to cry on someone who listens to one's problems and troubles with sympathy and understanding. *If you need a shoulder to cry on, I'll always have time to listen.*

straight from the shoulder (usually **be/come/talk/tell someone something** ~) directly and honestly, without hiding anything. *'Are you sure that Frank was being honest?' 'Yes. This came straight from the shoulder.'*

skin

be no skin off 'someone's nose (informal) not trouble or concern someone; not adversely affect someone. *Why should you worry if Andrew won't take your advice? It will be no skin off your nose if he doesn't get the job. It's his worry!*

by the skin of one's teeth only just, narrowly, with little time etc. left. *'Did Brian pass his exam?' 'Yes, he passed, but only by the skin of his teeth!'* □ *We arrived late at the airport, but thankfully we caught the flight – if only by the skin of our teeth!*

get under someone's skin irritate someone, cause someone annoyance. *I know that the nasty argument with Jack has upset you, but don't let him get under your skin!*

jump out of one's skin make a sudden uncontrolled movement out of fear or shock. *I suddenly heard a loud bang and nearly jumped out of my skin!*

soaked/drenched to the skin thoroughly wet from heavy rain etc. *They got caught in a thunderstorm and finally arrived home drenched to the skin.*

toe

be/keep on one's toes be/keep alert and attentive, prepared to face a difficult situation. *Vanessa knew that she would have to be on her toes at the interview, as there were another twelve well-qualified applicants for the position.*

toe the line do as someone tells, wishes or expects you to do; obey orders. *The teacher is not usually strict with his pupils, but even the most high-spirited boys know when they have to toe the line.*

toe the party line conform to the general or traditional policies and thinking of one's political party. *Although Sanders did not agree with party policy on the issue of arms trading, he knew that when the vote was taken he would have to toe the party line.*

tread/step on someone's toes offend someone; hurt someone's feelings; interfere with someone's wishes, often unintentionally. *I hope I didn't tread on anyone's toes when I said that solicitors earned far too much money.* □ *If no one else wants to be club treasurer, I'll volunteer. But I don't want to tread on anyone's toes.*

tongue

be/have (got) something on the tip of one's tongue be on the point of remembering or recalling something but not able to do so. *Whatever is that man's name? It's on the tip of my tongue!*

bite one's tongue off regret immediately what one has just said. *I didn't realize that Sandra was listening when I told you I had seen her boy-friend with another girl. I could have bitten my tongue off.*

hold one's tongue say nothing, keep quiet. *I could have told my neighbour whose ball broke his kitchen window, but I thought it best to hold my tongue.*

a slip of the tongue a mistake made when speaking. *I'm so sorry for calling you 'Merry' instead of 'Murray'. It was just a slip of the tongue.*

tongue in cheek not meant to be taken seriously or literally, meant to be ironic. *So many of Peter's remarks are tongue in cheek, that one hardly knows when he's being serious.*

set tongues wagging encourage people to gossip. *Christine's brother from Australia has come to live with her. No one in the village knew that she had a brother, so his arrival with six suitcases certainly set tongues wagging.*

tooth, teeth

fight tooth and nail fight fiercely, with great energy and determination. *Harry is excellent in the court room. He'll fight tooth and nail for a defendant if he believes him to be innocent.*

have (got) a sweet tooth enjoy eating sweet things. *Aunt Martha will love these caramels. She's always had a sweet tooth.*

armed to the teeth fully provided with weapons, tools, any kind of necessary equipment etc. *We left for a weekend's camping armed to the teeth with pots and pans, tins and tents, raincoats and rubber boots!*

cut one's teeth on something make one's first attempts at learning something; gain experience on something easy. *A young barrister has to cut his teeth on straightforward civil law cases. He doesn't deal with criminal law until he has more experience.*

fed up to the (back) teeth (informal) tired of/bored by something unpleasant or tedious. *I'm fed up to the teeth with this routine work. I need a challenge.*

get one's teeth into something (e.g. a job, work, learning) put a lot of effort into it. *'How's the physics revision going?' 'It's too early to say. I haven't really got my teeth into it yet.'*

lie through one's teeth (informal) tell lies openly and without shame. *He was lying through his teeth when he told the police he didn't know Bill Carter. I've seen them talking together.*

Time

day

'any day (of the week) (used for emphasis) at any time. *Ted thinks he's a crack tennis player, but I could beat him any day of the week!*

call it a day choose/decide to stop (doing) something (e.g. a piece of work, a discussion) because one thinks it is a good time to stop. *We've made good progress with painting the kitchen today, so we'll call it a day and continue tomorrow.*

day after day every day, one day after the other. *School's very boring this term. We do the same things day after day.*

day by day as each day passes. *Grandfather's making a wonderful recovery. His cheeks are getting rosier day by day!*

day 'in day 'out every single day without change or exception. *Walter wears those same old trousers day in day out. It's time he bought some new ones.*

for a rainy day for a possible time of financial difficulty in the future. *The older you get, the more you begin to think about saving for a rainy day.*

have a 'field day be extremely pleased by a special occasion, event etc. *The press will have a field day when they get hold of this story.*

have had its/their day be no longer in fashion or in demand. *At the rate that office work is being computerized, typewriters will soon have had their day.*

in 'this day and age in these modern times. *In this day and age, you really don't expect to meet someone who still believes that children should be seen and not heard.*

make a day of something spend the whole day doing one special activity; make something pleasant last the whole day. *After our morning shopping, we decided to stay in town for lunch and make a day of it.*

make someone's day make someone happy with a certain pleasing action or gesture. *Old Mrs Miller got a letter from her niece this morning. She read it over again and again – it really made her day.*

name the day decide on the date when a wedding or other special event shall take place. *Denise and Martin are getting married, but they haven't named the day yet.*

(not) be someone's day be a bad/unlucky or good/lucky day for someone. *I've just found 50 pence, and the boss has given me the afternoon off – it must be my day today! □ It certainly wasn't Ted's day yesterday – he was late to work, lost his glasses and then hit his thumb with a hammer!*

not have (got) all day not have any time to waste. *Come on, children. Off to school! You haven't got all day!*

an 'off day a day when for some reason one does not do one's best work etc. *I did terribly in my driving lesson. It really was one of my off days.*

the order of the day the usual/popular practice; the generally accepted way of doing things. *In many shops and restaurants, payment by credit card is the order of the day.*

the other day recently, a few days ago. *You'll never guess who I bumped into the other day! Barbara Daniels!*

'some day at some time in the future. *I'd like to hitch-hike around Malaysia some day.*

this day week next week on this day, in exactly a week's time. *This day week we shall be relaxing under the Jamaican sun!*

to a/the/this day (a date) exactly. *It's ten years to this day that we met. Remember?*

win/carry the day have a victory or success; win a game. *The game started badly and we were two goals down, but in the end we carried the day with four goals to three.*

have seen better days have been better in the past. Said of things that are old or in bad repair, or about people who were richer, more powerful, happier etc. *Palmer has certainly seen better days. Before he was made redundant he was departmental manager somewhere.*

one's/someone's days are numbered one will soon be no longer needed, i.e. one is no longer useful or desired (e.g. because of a mistake one has made or because it's what a powerful person wants). *Since he voted against the merger with Glaxton and wouldn't support the takeover bid for Dunlow, I suspect that his days on the board are numbered.*

hour

at the eleventh hour at the last possible time before something would be too late. *The management was able to work out a compromise with the union at the eleventh hour, so a strike was averted.*

at an/some unearthly hour at an inconvenient time, either very late or very early. *'When does your flight to Tokyo connect?' 'At some unearthly hour – 5.30 a.m., I think.'*

on the hour every hour at exactly one o'clock, two o'clock etc. *The first bus leaves at six o'clock and then on the hour.*

keep regular/good/bad hours have a normal/bad daily routine; get up, go to bed/work etc. at usual/irregular times. *Mrs Morris will only let rooms to students who keep regular hours.*

the small hours (of the morning) the hours after midnight, usually 1.00 a.m. to 4.00 a.m. *We had a good night out and didn't get home until the small hours.*

minute

(do something) at the (very) last minute at the latest possible time or opportunity, even though it could have been done earlier. *Michael knew that he had a dental appointment this afternoon, but he left the house at the very last minute.*

have (got) a minute have time/be available to do something. *I'll get you the information as soon as I've got a minute.*

(not) have (got) a minute to call one's own be very busy doing things, often for other people; have no time for oneself. *I've been busy all day. I haven't had a minute to call my own.*

in (half) a minute very soon. *Hold on and I'll be with you in half a minute.*

the minute (that)... as soon as, immediately when... *I'll ring you the minute that he arrives.*

to the minute exact(ly), punctual(ly). *Jack arrives every morning at the same time – 8.20, to the minute.*

up-to-the-minute (adjective) the most modern or most recent. *And now over to our reporter Jim Dale in Paris for up-to-the-minute news on the Prime Minister's visit.*

moment

at a moment's notice without much warning, very quickly. *You can't expect me to pack my bags and jump on a flight to New York at a moment's notice!*

at any moment very soon, within the next few seconds/minutes. *The guest speaker hasn't arrived yet, but we're expecting him at any moment. Ah! Here he is now!*

at the moment at the present time; now. *The secretary's on holiday, so we've got a temporary one at the moment.*

for the moment for the present; temporarily. *That will do for the moment. If I need any more information I'll let you know.*

on the spur of the moment on impulse, without hesitating to think; spontaneously. *The trip to Poole wasn't planned. I went there on the spur of the moment when I heard that my brother was there.*

have one's moments have moments/times (of success, happiness etc.) that are better than usual. *Barry isn't usually very good around the house, but he does have his moments. Yesterday he repaired a leak!* □ *The course on management skills was rather boring but it had its moments, I admit.*

night

call it a night stop some activity, work etc. to go to bed. Used only late in the evening or at night. *Well, I haven't finished filling in these tax forms, but I'm tired, so I'm going to call it a night and continue with them tomorrow.* (See also **call it a day**.)

have a night 'out go out for an evening of entertainment. *I feel like a change. We haven't had a night out for months.*

have a good/bad night sleep well/badly. *Did the patient have a good night, nurse?*

a 'night cap a drink (often alcoholic) taken before going to bed. *How about a night cap, Paul? Whisky and soda?*

a night on the town an evening of fun and entertainment with other people in one or more restaurants, public houses etc. *After winning the match, a few of the team decided to have a night on the town.*

a 'night owl a person who likes to stay out/up late at night because he feels more alert than during the day. *When he was at university Andy was a night owl, but that all changed with his first job.*

time

at the time then; at that particular time in the past. *Looking back, I'm glad I didn't get the job in Algeria, but at the time I was disappointed of course.*

be in time (for something) come at the right time to do something; be early enough for something. *I've made some tea. You're just in time for a cup.*

be on time be punctual. *Don't be late. Make sure you're on time.*

be pressed for time be in a hurry, have little time. *Sorry I can't stop for a chat. I'm extremely pressed for time at the moment.*

bide one's time wait patiently for a favourable opportunity. *Jeff's job doesn't offer any prospects of promotion, so he's just biding his time there until he finds something better.*

born before one's time said of persons of genius whose thinking or ability is more advanced than that of the society in which they live. *People like Columbus, Galileo and Einstein were all born before their time.*

buy time try to get more time than is available/allowed before something has to be done. *Tell the bank we have got some new orders and that we shall soon be able to pay off the loan. Anything to buy time and stop them foreclosing!*

do/serve time be in prison; serve a prison sentence. *He's had a difficult life. He even did time once for fiddling the company's books.*

a 'fine time (to do something) (ironic) a bad time because it is unsuitable, inconvenient, too late etc. *'Oh, before I forget, I've found you a customer for your old car. He'll pay you £750.' 'Now's a fine time to tell me. I sold it yesterday for £600!'*

for the time being for the present time, until something else happens/is arranged etc. *We haven't hired any permanent staff yet. For the time being, we have a few part-time secretaries.*

from time to time not often, occasionally. *Pat and Ray visit us from time to time, but we don't get to Yarmouth very often.*

have an easy time of it (informal) lead a comfortable life without worry or hard work. *Mark married into a very rich family, so he doesn't need to work and generally has a very easy time of it.*

have the time of one's life have a lot of fun, a very pleasant and enjoyable experience. *We took the children to Disneyland and they had the time of their lives!*

in the nick of time only just; just before it would have been too late. *We got on to the platform in the nick of time, just as the guard was blowing his whistle!*

in no time (at all) very quickly/soon. *'The heel's come off my shoe' 'No problem. This glue will stick it back on in no time at all.'*

in someone's own (good) time without hurry, when someone is ready to do something. *There's no rush for the translation. Just do it in your own good time.*

in time (referring to the future) after a certain length of time has passed. *Marion's fiancé has broken off their engagement. She's very upset at the moment, but she'll feel better in time.*

(it's) about time! said about something that should have happened or been done earlier but which was delayed. *'Here's the bus.' 'About time, too! It's ten minutes late and my feet are freezing!'*

keep good/perfect/bad time (a watch/clock) show the time correctly/incorrectly. *This clock was given to us as a wedding present twenty years ago, and it still keeps perfect time.*

kill time do something often useless or boring in order to pass a time of waiting more quickly. *The only time I read magazines is in doctors' waiting rooms to kill time.*

now's the/your time! now is the right/best opportunity for you to do something. *If you need some new skis, now's your time. Look, they're all reduced.*

play for time use delaying tactics, try to win/gain time before being forced to do something. *Don't believe Marsden's story of having to consult his partner before guaranteeing a delivery date – he's only playing for time.*

sing/play in time sing/play with the correct musical rhythm. *Don't ask Ed to join the group – he can't play in time!*

take one's time (over/about something) not hurry, do something as slowly as necessary. *Just calm down, take your time and tell me exactly what happened.*

there's no time like the present (saying) it is best to do something that has to be done now, not later. *'I ought to apologize to Barry for being rude to him.' 'Yes, you should. And there's no time like the present.'*

time after time/time and (time) again repeatedly, many times. *I've told Ben time and time again not to stick his chewing gum under the table.*

time flies! (saying) time passes very/too quickly. *Goodness, it's six o'clock! Time flies! We've been chatting all afternoon!*

time is money (saying) time, like money, is valuable, so one should not waste it. *Get on with your work! Remember, time is money!*

time (alone) will tell (saying) the future will show whether decisions, actions etc. in the present were right or not. *Jane has decided to give up journalism and go into politics. She isn't sure that it's the right decision – time alone will tell.*

time's up! there is no time left, no more time is allowed. *Time's up now, so put down your pens and pass your papers to the front.*

at the 'best of times when conditions are most favourable. *My French isn't very good at the best of times, but it's hopeless when I have to speak it unexpectedly on the telephone.*

at times occasionally; sometimes. *I enjoy life as a bachelor, but I suppose I do get a bit lonely at times.*

behind the times old-fashioned in one's thinking, ideas, dress etc. *Aunt Maggie dresses a bit behind the times. She won't wear modern fabrics and fashions.*

keep up/move with the times adapt one's thinking, way of life etc. to modern and contemporary standards. *Mother doesn't think that people should live together if they're not married. She just hasn't moved with the times.*

10 Idioms with comparisons

Comparisons with **as … as**

as bald as a coot completely bald.

as black as coal/soot dirty, e.g. a child's hands, face or clothes.

as black as pitch very dark, e.g. a room, cellar, street without lights.

as blind as a bat having bad eyesight. Used humorously.

as bold as brass impudent, shameless, defiant.

as brown as a berry having brown skin from being in the sun.

as busy as a bee busily occupied with many (usually enjoyable) activities, tasks etc.

as clean as a new pin very clean and tidy, with no dust or dirt, e.g. a room, house.

as clear as crystal/day(light) obvious, easy to realize/understand, e.g. a situation, problem, someone's intentions.

as clear as mud (informal) not at all clear or easy to understand, e.g. an explanation, someone's instructions. Used ironically when something is not clear.

as cold as ice very cold. Used of things, substances, people's hands and fingers, the temperature of a room etc.

as cool as a cucumber calm and controlled at a time of upset, difficulty or danger.

as cunning as a fox sly, scheming, planning secretly to one's own advantage.

as deaf as a post extremely deaf. Used humorously.

as different as chalk and/from cheese very different in appearance, character, temperament etc.

as drunk as a lord/newt very drunk.

as dry as a bone very dry, containing no moisture.

as easy as ABC/pie/anything easy to do/solve, e.g. a task, small problem.

as fit as a fiddle in good physical condition, active.

as flat as a pancake 1 very flat or flattened, e.g. countryside, a flat surface, a car tyre. 2 something that does not arouse the expected interest, e.g. a poor joke, a dull social event, a disappointing surprise etc.

as fresh as a daisy lively, wide awake and alert, looking and feeling fresh.

as gentle as a lamb very gentle. Used of a person or larger animal.

as greedy as a pig very greedy. Used of a person who eats more than he needs.

as happy as a king/a lark/the day is long in a carefree, contented mood or state, having no worries.

as hard as nails physically tough, able to endure much; without feeling, ruthless in dealing with others.

as large as life in person, in the flesh.

as light as a feather having little weight, not heavy.

as like as two peas (in a pod) very much alike in appearance.

as mad as a hatter/a March hare eccentric, peculiar, abnormal in one's behaviour, even insane.

as miserable as sin unhappy; in a dull mood.

as near as dammit (informal) very close, very nearly but not quite.

as old as the hills very old. Used to describe a story or tale which everybody already knows; also used of a person or a thing.

as plain as the nose on your face obvious, not to be overlooked, easy to guess.

as pleased as Punch delighted, very happy about something.

as quick as lightning/a flash very quick in physical actions or in one's thinking.

as quiet as a mouse reserved and shy by nature; making no noise.

as regular as clockwork said of persons who do things at set times or who are totally reliable and of things/events that always happen at the expected or planned time.

as right as rain as healthy as one usually is; in one's best emotional and physical condition.

as safe as houses 1 secure and stable, not likely to collapse, e.g. any kind of construction. 2 not likely to go wrong or cause loss, e.g. a business risk, an investment.

as sharp as a needle/razor intelligent and quick-witted, perceptive.

as steady as a rock reliable (e.g. in an emergency); firm and standing safely on the ground (e.g. a ladder).

as sure/true as I'm sitting/standing here used to emphasize that something is certain or true without any doubt.

as tough as leather/old boots (of meat) hard to cut and chew; (of persons) 1 physically strong. 2 insensitive to criticism and abuse, not easily hurt.

as true as steel totally loyal, reliable and dependable.

as warm as toast pleasantly warm and cosy, e.g. fingers or toes when well clothed in winter, a pleasantly warm room.

as weak as a baby/kitten physically very weak, e.g. after illness.

as white as a sheet/chalk used of someone's face turned pale after a shock or fright; pale due to illness.

Comparisons with **like**

(be) like a bear with a sore head in an angry, irritable, bad-tempered manner. *What's wrong with David? He's like a bear with a sore head!*

(be) like a bull in a 'china shop in a clumsy, rough manner; without the necessary fine feeling for the delicacy of a particular situation. *Keep out of Jeff's way. He's been like a bull in a china shop since he arrived!* □ *Don't tell Uncle John about Sally's misfortune, or he'll mention it when he sees her. You know he's completely tactless – like a bull in a china shop.*

(be) like a cat on hot bricks restless and nervous, unable to sit still or keep calm. *There he was, waiting at the hospital, jumping up and down like a cat on hot bricks. At last the nurse came with the news 'It's a boy!'*

(be) like the cat that stole the cream look very pleased with or proud of oneself. *Look at Linda, she's like the cat that stole the cream. I bet she's passed her driving test after all.*

(be off) like the clappers with great speed and energy. *She realized that the bank would be closing soon, and was off down the street like the clappers!*

be out like a light fall quickly into a deep sleep. *Billy was so tired after the birthday party. When I put him to bed he was out like a light in no time.*

be like looking for a needle in a haystack said when looking for something small or difficult to see in an untidy heap or large number of other things. *John has got toys all over the floor of his room. So looking for the missing piece of jigsaw puzzle is like looking for a needle in a haystack.*

be like a red rag to a bull provoke anger, violent argument or dispute, e.g. a certain topic. *When you mention the word 'unions' to Jack, it's like a red rag to a bull! He thinks they are ruining the country's economy.*

(be off/back/in etc.) like a shot immediately, with great speed and energy. *When the boy saw the policeman coming, he was off like a shot!*

(be) like water off a duck's 'back making no impression on someone. Used when giving advice which is not followed. *We've told Peter to spend less time playing football and more doing his homework, but it's like water off a duck's back.*

come 'down on someone like a ton of bricks reprimand or criticize someone severely and sharply. *If Father knew that you had had this information over a week, he would come down on you like a ton of bricks for not telling him about it.*

drink like a fish drink large quantities of alcohol, especially beer. *If you've ever been in a pub with Harry, you'll know that he drinks like a fish.*

eat like a horse have a healthy appetite and eat large quantities. *Fred's trying to lose a few pounds. He goes jogging for an hour every evening but when he comes home he eats like a horse.*

fight like cat and dog disagree or argue violently, often repeatedly. *Viv and Oliver have a very emotional relationship. They sometimes fight like cat and dog, but they're really very close.*

fit like a glove (clothing) fit very well. *It's a classic style, Madam, and I must add that it fits you like a glove.*

get on like a 'house on fire 1 (two people) be friendly and compatible, enjoy each other's company. *Bob and Paul are good friends. They've always got on like a house on fire.* 2 make fast progress with a task or piece of work. *'How are you progressing with the invitations?' 'We've written over fifty already. We're getting on like a house on fire!'*

go like a bomb (a car) drive and accelerate fast. *Have you been for a drive in Ian's new car? It goes like a bomb!*

go like the wind move very fast and smoothly, e.g. a car, a fast runner. *Richard is sure to win the 800 metres. When he's on form, he can go like the wind.*

grin like a Cheshire 'cat smile with a broad, contented grin as if highly amused or knowing a secret. *Tom watched me trying to use the computer for the first time, pressing all the wrong keys. He just sat next to me grinning like a Cheshire cat.*

have (got) a hide like a rhinoceros said of an insensitive person who is not affected by criticism, insult etc. *Ken didn't answer when Brian insulted him. He must have a hide like a rhinoceros.*

have (got) a memory like an elephant have an excellent memory, especially for things that happened long ago. *Father can tell you the time and place of every holiday he's ever had. He's got a memory like an elephant.*

have (got) a memory like a sieve have a bad memory, often and easily forgetting things. *I'm so sorry. I've forgotten to bring you my dictionary again. I've got a memory like a sieve these days!*

know something like the back of one's hand be thoroughly familiar with something, e.g. a place, a subject. *Bill spent years in Argentina working as an engineer. He knows the country like the back of his hand.*

look like a drowned 'rat be very wet from rain etc, especially one's hair. *Cathy got caught in a thunderstorm without an umbrella and came in looking like a drowned rat.*

look like something the 'cat dragged/brought in (informal) look very untidy, be of dirty or scruffy appearance. *Nicky had been fighting at school. He came home looking like something the cat dragged in!*

run like a hare/deer run very fast. *Mike should win the race easily. He can run like a hare when he's in training.*

sing like a bird/lark/nightingale (a woman's voice) sing with high, clear tones. *She was up at six making breakfast, singing like a lark, too.*

shake/tremble like a leaf shake/tremble with cold or fear. *It's a dreadful feeling waiting for one's final exam results. I remember that I was shaking like a leaf.*

sleep like a log sleep very deeply and soundly. *'Did you sleep well?' 'Oh, yes thanks. Like a log.'*

smoke like a chimney smoke large quantities of cigarettes. *There's no wonder that Charlie has a bad cough. He smokes like a chimney – at least forty a day.*

spend money like water be extravagant; spend money often, quickly or in large amounts, usually on luxuries. *Joe says his wife earns a lot of money but she also spends it like water.*

spread like wildfire (said of news, a rumour etc.) spread quickly and to all parts. *Once the word gets out that there is to be a company takeover, it will spread like wildfire in the financial world.*

swear like a trooper use swear-words frequently. *Uncle Bert swears like a trooper, even when the children are present.*

swim like a fish swim fast and easily. *She said her daughter could swim like a fish at the age of four.*

'**take to something like a duck to water** get used to something new quickly and easily; enjoy something new immediately, e.g. a new job or task, a new skill which has to be learnt. *Mary's learning how to sail. She's taken to it like a duck to water.*

treat someone like dirt treat someone badly, without consideration of his feelings. *Robert treats Ted like dirt. You wouldn't believe they were cousins.*

turn up/keep turning up like a bad penny appear at frequent intervals, again and again. Said humorously or of someone not welcome who repeatedly arrives unexpectedly or uninvited. *Pete lost his job here three years ago, but he keeps turning up like a bad penny, hoping we'll ask him to come back.*

watch someone like a hawk watch what someone does very carefully and critically. *I'm sure Sylvia thinks that someone is stealing from the petty cash box. She watches you like a hawk if you go anywhere near it!*

work like a Trojan work very hard, with great perseverance and energy. *I've been working like a Trojan all day, trying to finish the roof repairs.*

Index